# Early Christian Dress

# Routledge Studies in Ancient History

1 Cicero and the Catilinarian
Conspiracy
*Charles Matson Odahl*

2 Ancient Graffiti in Context
*Edited by Jennifer Baird and
Claire Taylor*

3 Early Christian Dress
Gender, Virtue, and Authority
*Kristi Upson-Saia*

# Early Christian Dress
## Gender, Virtue, and Authority

# Kristi Upson-Saia

Routledge
Taylor & Francis Group
NEW YORK   LONDON

First published 2011
by Routledge
711 Third Avenue, New York, NY 10017

Simultaneously published in the UK
by Routledge
2 Park Square, Milton Park, Abingdon, Oxon OX14 4RN

*Routledge is an imprint of the Taylor & Francis Group,
an informa business*

© 2011 Taylor & Francis

The right of Kristi Upson-Saia to be identified as author of this work has
been asserted by her in accordance with sections 77 and 78 of the Copy-
right, Designs and Patents Act 1988.

Typeset in Sabon by IBT Global.
Printed and bound in the United States of America on acid-free paper by
IBT Global.

*Library of Congress Cataloging-in-Publication Data*
Upson-Saia, Kristi, 1974–
    Early Christian dress : gender, virtue, and authority / by Kristi
Upson-Saia.
        p. cm. — (Routledge studies in ancient history ; 3)
    Includes bibliographical references and index.
    1. Sex role—Religious aspects—Christianity.  2. Clothing and
dress—Religious aspects—Christianity.  3. Women in Christianity—
History—Early church, ca. 30–600.  I. Title.  II. Title: Gender, virtue,
and authority.
    BT708.U67 2011
    391.0088'2701—dc22
    2011005280

ISBN13: 978-0-415-89001-4 (hbk)
ISBN13: 978-0-203-80645-6 (ebk)

**To Steve**

*Est enim amicitia nihil aliud nisi omnium divinarum humanarumque rerum cum benevolentia et caritate consensio, qua quidem haud scio an excepta sapientia nil quicquam melius homini sit a dis immortalibus datum.*

**Cicero,** *De amicitia* **6.20**

# Contents

| | | |
|---|---|---|
| *List of Figures* | | ix |
| *List of Abbreviations* | | xi |
| *Acknowledgments* | | xiii |
| | Introduction | 1 |
| 1 | Elite Roman Women's Dress in the Early Imperial Period | 15 |
| 2 | Scripting Christians' Clothing and Grooming | 33 |
| 3 | Performance Anxiety: Dress and Gender Crises in Early Christian Asceticism | 59 |
| 4 | Narrating Cross-Dressing in Female Saints' *Lives* | 84 |
| | Conclusion | 104 |
| | *Notes* | 109 |
| | *Bibliography* | 155 |
| | *Index* | 167 |

# Figures

1.1  Funerary relief of servants beautifying their mistress, second
     to third century CE.                                            28
1.2  Funerary relief of servants beautifying their mistress.         28

# Abbreviations

Throughout this book, I use existing translations of ancient sources or I offer my own translations. I cite the editions and translations I use in notes. Where no reference is listed, the translation is my own.

Abbreviations of ancient authors and their works are taken from G.W.H. Lampe (ed.), *A Patristic Greek Lexicon* (Oxford: Clarendon Press, 1961); Albert Blaise and Henri Chirat (eds.), *Dictionnaire Latin-Français des auteurs chrétiens* (Turnout: Brepols, 1954); and Simon Hornblower and Antony Spawforth (eds.), *Oxford Classical Dictionary*, 3rd ed. (Oxford: Oxford University Press, 1996). Abbreviations of journal titles are taken from *L'Année Philologique* and Patrick H. Alexander, John F. Kutsko, James D. Ernest, Shirley A. Decker-Lucke, and David L. Petersen (eds.), *The SBL Handbook of Style for Ancient Near Eastern, Biblical, and Early Christian Studies* (Peabody, MA.: Hendrickson, 1999). Supplemental abbreviations are as follows:

| | |
|---|---|
| *Act. Eugen.* | *Acta S. Eugeniae* |
| *AJS* | *American Journal of Sociology* |
| *AugSt* | *Augustinian Studies* |
| *BSNAF* | *Bulletin de la Société Nationale des Antiquaires de France* |
| *B&CT* | *Bible & Critical Theory* |
| *BTB* | *Biblical Theology Bulletin* |
| *FemStud* | *Feminist Studies* |
| *G&H* | *Gender & History* |
| *IQ* | *International Quarterly* |
| *JHC* | *Journal of the History of Collections* |
| *JMEMS* | *Journal of Medieval and Early Modern Studies* |
| *RecAug* | *Recherches Augustiniennes* |
| *ROC* | *Revue de l'orient chrétien* |
| *SP* | *Studia Patristica* |
| *Vit. Apoll.* | *Vita S. Apollinariae Syncleticae* |
| *Vit. Dan.* | *Vita Abba Daniel* |
| *Vit. Euphr.* | *Vita S. Euphrosynae, virginis* |
| *Vit. Hil.* | *Vita S. Hilariae* |

| | |
|---|---|
| *Vit. Mar.* | *Vita S. Marinae dicta Marinus* |
| *Vit. Matron.* | *Vita S. Matronae* |
| *Vit. Pelag.* | *Vita S. Pelagiae* |
| *Vit. Sus.* | *Vita S. Susannae* |

# Acknowledgments

This project began as a dissertation written at Duke University under the direction of Elizabeth A. Clark and Lucas Van Rompay. I am indebted to Liz and Luk for their guidance, their exacting feedback, and, most of all, their kindness and encouragement throughout. I feel incredibly fortunate to have been trained under their tutelage and to be a part of the Duke family. Liz has continued to offer feedback as the project progressed beyond a dissertation. Her generosity of time and spirit is matched only by her keen comments and suggestions.

I wish to thank the many other readers who have provided helpful suggestions at various stages of writing and revision and who offered much needed friendship and support: Bart D. Ehrman, Zlatko Pleše, Julie Byrne, David Hunter, Susanna Drake, Kate Blanchard, Christine Luckritz Marquis, Kyle Smith, Tina Shepardson, Jeremy Schott, Andrew Jacobs, Catherine Chin, Pam Mullins Reaves, Eric Scherbenske, Stephanie Cobb, Jennifer Graber, Lori Baron, Bart Scott, Wendy Kim, and Steven Upson-Saia. I am exceedingly grateful for the thoughtful and detailed comments I received from the anonymous reviewers, who gave me excellent advice on how to layer my analysis and who saved me from several errors.

Over the last four years, my colleagues at Occidental College have provided me with an intellectually vibrant environment in which to complete this project. I would like to thank in particular my colleagues in the Department of Religious Studies, especially Dale Wright and D. Keith Naylor, the lively community of junior faculty, and participants of the Faculty Research Working Group. I am grateful for Occidental's generous pre-tenure leave, which enabled me the time to polish the manuscript, and for funding provided by a Faculty Enrichment grant from the dean's office.

I would like to thank the editorial staff at Routledge, especially Laura Stearns and Stacy Noto, and Michael Watters at Integrated Book Technology, for ushering me through the review and publication process with ease. A shortened version of Chapter 4 was originally published as "Gender and Narrative Performance in Early Christian Cross-Dressing Saints' *Lives*" in *Studia Patristica* 45 (2010): 43–48, and appears here by permission of Peeters Press (Leuven).

I owe the most to my friends and family without whose support this book, let alone a career in academia, would not be possible. First and foremost, I wish to thank my parents, Bob and Barb Upson, who never questioned the horizons open to me and who provided me with unparalleled encouragement. I owe many thanks to Gus and Mary Blanchard, who hospitably allowed me to finish revisions at their quiet and inspiring home at Torch Lake, and to Kate Blanchard, Chris Moody, and Gus Moody for a year we will never forget. Finally, I wish to thank my dear friends, especially Steve, for filling this journey with laughter and love.

# Introduction

[Marcella] took her gold necklace . . . and sold it without her parents' knowledge. Then putting on a dark tunic, the kind her mother would not allow her to acquire, piously clothing herself, she consecrated herself to God. Looking at her tiny body, those around her perceived her resolve . . . always in the same dress, she condemned the world.

Jerome, *ep.* 24.3 (CSEL 54.215–16)

[Demetrias] resolved to cast aside, as hindrances, all of her adornments and worldly attire. She returned to their cases her valuable necklaces, costly pearls, and sparkling gems. She assumed a cheap tunic, which she covered over with an even cheaper cloak . . . putting on display who she really was (*quae esset ostendens*).

Jerome, *ep.* 130.5 (CSEL 56/1.180)

It is commonplace in the *encomia* of early Christian ascetic women to find stories of dramatic vows that involved radical changes of attire. Any scholar of early Christian asceticism can easily recall stories of the young girls—often aristocrats—who cast aside the opulent garb befitting their status to don the humble and modest clothing appropriate to their newly vowed life of renunciation.[1] Although such stories litter the pages of early Christian literature, we regularly skim over them. Perhaps we understand them to be rhetorical flourishes that simply add color to the dramatization of an ascetics' vow. Or perhaps we have underestimated the significance of dress in early Christian contexts, considering the careful construction on one's physical appearance to be evidence of frivolity, sexuality, and *luxuria*, characteristics that ought not define the good Christian, especially the good ascetic.

Yet on closer inspection, we find dozens of early Christian texts that stress the consequence of Christians' dress and grooming. We find that Christian ascetics in particular were required to meticulously and thoughtfully craft their new ascetic look so as to project an accurate representation of their piety. Clothing was a crucial mode through which early Christian ascetics publicized their identity. For this reason, Christian bishops, councils, and ascetic leaders devoted a great deal of energy exhorting ascetics to adopt particular forms of dress, while also censuring garments and accessories they found troublesome. Moreover, Christian leaders carefully interpreted the theological and social significance of ascetics' garb, offering their audiences—Christian or non-Christian, lay or ascetic—the proper lens through which to understand and interpret ascetics' looks. Finally, they narrated descriptions of famed ascetics' dress in order to naturalize and historicize their sartorial preferences. As it turns out, dress mattered quite a bit.

Throughout late antiquity choices in ascetic attire were left largely to community leaders and followed regional customs. Although particular communities prescribed certain styles of dress (see, for example, the *Rules* of Pachomius, Basil, and Cassian), there was no overarching consensus across the Mediterranean about what ascetics were to wear. In fact, even by Benedict's sixth-century *Rule*, Benedict assumed that monks' clothing would vary according to the local conditions and climate in which the monks lived. Thus he leaves it to individual abbots' discretion to dole out clothing that was appropriate for the particular monks in their charge.[2] Ascetics who practiced house asceticism or participated in "spiritual marriages," who were removed from the oversight of a monastic rule or director, had even fewer constraints on what they wore. Although they received suggestions from clergy and ascetic mentors, it is clear that they did not always heed this advice.

Although, or perhaps because, a monastic habit had yet to be standardized through late antiquity, much advice was given on how ascetics—particularly female ascetics—ought to dress. Church and ascetic leaders (mostly male) counseled female ascetics on the proper look of a Christian woman, especially one who had made a vow to God. She was to forsake cosmetics, elaborate hair styles, and adornments, and conversely, to don plain clothes that were deemed better suited to their new mode of life. Whether she adopted mourning garments or clothing of the poor, an ascetic's dress ought to communicate simplicity and humility. The fabric should be coarse, made of materials such as goat or camel hair. Likewise, the material should remain unbleached and undyed,[3] and should never be embellished with colored thread, gems, or other ornaments. Finally, the female ascetic should wear a head covering—again undyed and unadorned—to obscure her simply styled hair.

As we see from the passages that open the chapter, this was a dramatic departure from women's customary attire, a departure that clearly and visibly signaled ascetics' newly adopted lifestyle and identity. As Gillian Clark writes, " 'changing one's clothes' became an immediately recognizable metaphor for 'adopting the ascetic life' or for 'entering a community.' "[4] Whether an ascetic's appearance was understood to be an outward expression of her inner character and resolve—in the words of Jerome, manifesting "who she really was"—or whether it served as an ever-present reminder of the virtue and discipline toward which she strove, her distinctive dress was to be an outward sign of her ascetic pledge. Namely, she was to *appear* disinterested in the worldly trappings of status, wealth, and sexuality.

Ascetics' distinctive garb and grooming set them apart from lay Christians as well as from their pagan neighbors.[5] It marked their exceptional piety in a visible way, according them distinction and honor.[6] Additionally, ascetics' clothing worked on a communal level. While exhibiting something of her individual character, an ascetic's distinctive style of dress also announced the superior virtue of Christianity in general, contributing to Christianity's communal endeavor for respect, prestige, and authority.

In either case, the virtue conveyed through an ascetic's dress was intimately linked to late ancient gender ideals. Female ascetics demonstrated their appropriation of masculine virtues of rationality, discipline, and moderation by renouncing feminine vices of vanity, greed, indulgence, and hyper-sexuality. Because such feminine vices had been thoroughly mapped onto Roman women's conventional dress and adornment (e.g., in their cosmetics, ornaments, and lavish clothing), ascetics were urged to abandon feminine styling in order to exhibit their progress in piety. Thus we find that Christian leaders' dress prescriptions were driven by their concern to promote Christianity's status in an empire that prized notions of virtue defined in masculine terms and exhibited through masculinized images.

In this book, therefore, I argue that the construction of early Christian ascetic identities must be understood in part through the fused virtue, authority, and gender signified in ascetics' dress and physical appearance. I investigate how ascetics' looks were imbued with meaning and then put on public display in order to construct an image of Christian ascetics that served to elevate the standing of Christianity throughout the Mediterranean world. Specifically, I ask: How were the contours of Christian identity interpreted from one's dress and physical appearance? How were Christian ascetics' dress performances deployed in social rivalries? Finally, how did ascetic attire draw from and reshape notions of gender?

It is this last question on which I linger. While the simple and humble attire of female ascetics signaled their manly spiritual and moral progress, it concurrently disrupted a coherent performance of their femininity. What difference did this make? Students of early Christian asceticism who know that it was standard fare to deem ascetic women "virile" or genderless "like the angels" might not expect that transgressively gendered dress would be alarming. On the contrary, vigorous debates arose over the ways in which female ascetics' dress properly and improperly blurred the signs of their gender. Even those Christian leaders who championed ascetic women's ability to achieve a degree of virility were troubled by ascetics' dress practices that threatened to materially dissolve gender categories, difference, and hierarchy. Why? Whereas a female ascetic's performance of manly virtue and piety might advance the standing of Christianity in the eyes of outsiders, when taken too far it threatened the stability of gender categories on which communal and ecclesial hierarchies were based. In the chapters that follow, I analyze how Christian leaders, councils, and storytellers attempted to manage the ways in which ascetics' dress and physical appearance communicated their ascetic identity, authority, and gender. Overall, I conclude that dress functioned as a contested symbol in the negotiation of power and identity between pagans and Christians, ascetics and laypeople, and women and men.

ANALYTICAL FRAMES

My approach to the study of early Christian dress was inspired by historians and theoreticians in the fields of dress and performativity studies. Although most of these scholars work outside the world of late antiquity, they prompted questions and modes of analysis that led me to read late ancient texts in new ways. They helped me to understand that dress is a "jumbled code" that constructs a range of individual and group identities (including nationality, wealth, status, virtue, and sexuality) at once. As John Carl Flügel writes: "In the case of an individual whom we have not previously met, the clothes he is wearing tell us at once something of his sex, occupation, nationality, and social standing, and thus enable us to make a preliminary adjustment of our behaviour towards him."[7] Most importantly, these theorists taught me to see how gender was implicated in the performance of *each* of these identities, at times leading to complex and even competing expressions of gender.

## Distinction

Two recurrent themes in this scholarship structure my analysis. First is the distinctive function of dress: the use of dress to differentiate and rank social groups. Historians of dress have long demonstrated how clothing and accessories have been used to measure cultural sophistication. From the sixteenth century, Europeans and Americans displayed the dress of "primitive" or "foreign" populations as a way to advertise a cultural hierarchy, one that implicitly assumed their own superior standing. *Wunderkammern* (Cabinets of Curiosity), for instance, displayed the clothing and artifacts of the "uncivilized" with the intent of astonishing viewers with spectacles of cultural difference.[8] Dutch physician Bernardus Paludanus (1550–1633) was proud to assert that each visitor who laid eyes on his collection "is smitten and forgets to shut [his] mouth."[9] Western missionaries also exhibited the clothing and accessories of "uncivilized" populations at fund-raising events, using the dress of the "unchristianized" as a symbol of their depravity and as material evidence of their need to be evangelized.[10] Even displays that wished to idealize and protect indigenous communities—such as George Catlin's exhibition of Native American clothing that hoped to inspire Congress to set aside land for Native Americans—used dress to symbolize cultural distinction.[11] Whether the displays of "native" clothing and memorabilia were meant to shock or cultivate esteem, both types of collections emphasized the difference between the viewer and the viewed. By the time national European museums began displaying clothing exhibitions in the late eighteenth and early nineteenth centuries, dress had become such a recognizable symbol of cultural difference and hierarchy that curators arranged the structural flow of the exhibitions so as to guide the visitor through a route that tracked the progress of civilization, with "native" dress on one end and European high fashion on the other.[12]

Just as clothing has been used historically to distinguish insiders from outsiders, it has also been used to register differences of status within a society. As economist Thorstein Veblen explains, dress manifests certain individuals' wealth and class through displays of conspicuous leisure and consumption that are out of reach for the lower classes.[13] By wearing extravagant clothing made from costly materials and embellished with expensive adornments,[14] by discarding clothing before it is fully worn out and donning the latest trend, and by wearing garments that "hamper the wearer at every turn and incapacitate her for all useful exertion,"[15] the wealthy demonstrate a "pecuniary superiority" over other members of the community, a superiority that is visibly evident on first sight. Wealth is not the only measure of social ranking made evident in dress. As sociologist Pierre Bourdieu has shown, certain forms of dressing and grooming can also conspicuously convey class-specific "tastes," building cultural as well as economic capital.[16]

In late antiquity, dress and adornments similarly proved to be useful signs of moral, cultural, and economic status that could be used to rank social groups and classes. To Romans, some styles of dress represented the highly civilized nature of Roman society (*Romanitas*) whereas other forms of dressing represented the uncivilized, "barbarian" societies of the rest of the world. Moreover, within Roman society certain styles of dress distinguished notable individuals, families, and religious groups from purportedly subordinate groups. Finally, dress served to differentiate the supposedly inherent virtue of Roman men from the depraved inclinations of Roman women.

Throughout we find an interesting mixture of arguments that understood dress to be either a product of nature or culture. At times, dress was assumed to be an extension of the wearer's soul, whether one's clothing exhibited his inherent self-mastery or self-indulgence. At other times, culture was presumed to either rein in or exacerbate the wearer's natural inclinations toward virtue or vice. The same authors appealed selectively to both sorts of arguments. Whereas Roman men might point to the difference between their dress and that of foreigners in order to prove Roman *cultural* superiority, they also argued that the different dress of Roman men and women exhibited their *natural* characterological difference. So too, Christians argued that Christian forms of dressing and grooming were evidence of Christianity's ability to galvanize piety and virtue, while they also argued that Christian women were naturally inclined to dress impiously if left unchecked.

We also find that different features of dress were read as measurements of individual or group superiority. At times, luxe garments and adornments could signal one's cultural sophistication and domination, such as when elite Roman's dress was juxtaposed with the humble dress of foreigners or the impoverished within the empire. But the distinguishing function of dress was not always based on a model such as Veblen's that privileged displays of opulent wealth or leisure. At other times, one's superiority was signaled by a *moderate* appearance, which communicated advanced self-control and reason. Elite Roman men, for instance, offered their restrained manner of dressing as evidence that they were more virtuous than barbarians and Roman women. So too, early Christians claimed that the simple and humble dress of their members—especially their women—proved that they possessed greater virtue than their pagan neighbors. In the first two chapters, I trace how and why different values—extravagance or moderation—could be prized even while the intent to assert cultural or natural superiority remained constant.

No matter what measure was used, the dress of the individual or group deemed superior was always coded masculine so that the Roman man sporting luxury goods as a sign of his military, political, or economic prowess could claim to project a manly look as much as the Roman man who donned less elaborate garments to communicate his self-mastery and control. By the early Imperial period, Roman men even interpreted the dress of their women in ways that would reinforce their own manly dominance, wealth, and power. As Thorstein Veblen explains, women's dress does not always signal their own status, but is regularly interpreted as a sign of the status they derive from men. Veblen argues that women dress

> in behalf of some one else to whom she stands in a relation of economic dependence; a relation which in the last analysis must, in economic theory, reduce itself to a relation of servitude . . . The only reason for all this conspicuous leisure and attire on the part of women lies in the fact that they are servants to whom, in the differentiation of economic functions, has been delegated the office of *putting in evidence their master's ability to pay.*[17]

So too, Roman women's dressing was regularly made to reflect honor to her male kin and city; as such they became another layer of men's dressing. Roman women's decadent dress gestured to the general opulence and power of the Empire resulting from Roman conquest and trade. It also communicated the prosperity and status of her particular family. In fact, even when her devotion to luxury and consumption was criticized (for violating Roman ideals of temperance), she still rendered the pecuniary strength of her husband potent because he proved himself able to withstand her wasteful expenditures and to tolerate her nonproductive participation in the household economy.[18]

Just as Roman men claimed that their dress exhibited their natural superiority, so too they argued that elite women's extravagant dress and adornments exhibited their natural female character and impulses—namely, their vanity, greed, predilection for decadence, and hyper-sexual impulse to seduce—that stood in direct opposition to men's inherent virtue. The adorned Roman woman was made out to possess interests foreign to Roman men (and alien to *Romanitas* in general), a foreignness underscored by her affinity for foreign goods imported from abroad—jewelry, unguents, clothing, and cosmetics—which were depleting Roman men's wealth, health, and security in the Empire. Through the symbol of dress, therefore, Roman men were able to distinguish themselves from inferior populations: foreigners and women. Moreover, by linking "feminine" dress with foreign goods—and by extension feminine and foreign vice—elite Roman men justified their need to dominate both populations as a moral prerogative. In the end, I argue, interpretations of Roman women's dress were used to highlight the distinctively noble character of Roman men, the only individuals in the empire who possessed the self-mastery necessary to rule.

I conclude that the elite Roman woman's dress, therefore, served as a flexible symbol that could be interpreted to signify multiple referents simultaneously. Women's decadent and expensive clothing and adornments gestured to the wealth and status of her male kin, a prosperity derived from Rome's successful campaigns abroad. At the same time, the vice associated with such decadence was deemed inherently feminine, deriving from the woman's own predilection for vice, and thus safely distanced from the men of the household.

Within early Christian communities, women again served a distinguishing function, although they were called to be "dressing" not only for the men to whom they were most closely related, but for the Church as a whole. Simply dressed and unadorned Christian women were presented as spectacles of Christians' extraordinary virtue and piety. They were offered as proof that Christianity was able to overcome even its weakest members' natural vice. Christian women's dress became a chief symbol of the virtue shared by *all* Christians—women and men—enabling Christians to argue that their community's morality trumped that of neighboring pagans.

Whereas pagans' interpretations of dress distinguished insiders from outsiders and men from women, reinforcing cultural and gender hierarchies simultaneously, Christians' dress innovations were more socially problematic. When Christian women, especially female ascetics, altered their dress in order to moderate the appearance of feminine vice, they constructed a productive difference between Christians and pagans. At the same time, however, their new mode of dressing problematized a conventional measure of the difference between men and women, troubling the stability of gender categories as a result. Moreover, they threw into disarray the social roles and order previously based on gender difference.

## Discourse and Performativity

The second theme running throughout this book is the relationship between discourse and dress. As contemporary scholars have argued, particular forms of dress are not intrinsically tied to particular meanings. Rather, clothing and accessories convey certain meanings only when spectators are guided to interpret dress signs in certain directions (and not others) and when individuals consistently dress their part, making such interpretations appear stable and natural. Roland Barthes and Judith Butler have persuasively explicated the tandem processes by which discursive signification and performativity imbue meaning to certain features of dress.

In *Système de la mode*, Roland Barthes contends that in fashion magazines it is the combination of images and captions that creates meaning. Readers and spectators have an interpretive freedom as they scan an object of clothing, but,

> Language [the caption] eliminates [readers'] freedom . . . it conveys a choice and imposes it, it requires the perception of this dress to stop here (i.e., neither before nor beyond) . . . Thus, every written word has a function of authority insofar as it chooses—by proxy, so to speak—instead of the eye . . . words determine a single certainty.[19]

Discourse focuses attention and imbues a particular significance to clothing. Moreover, Barthes continues, discourse that directs meaning also always participates in broader, ideological projects by forcing images into their service. Discourse provides the "supercode" that dictates not only how to read particular styles of dress, but also how to understand the world.[20]

More recently Judith Butler has noted the importance of discourse and performance in regulating notions of gender.[21] Butler contends that the material bodily differences used to construct a sex binary are indissociable from the classificatory program that names certain bodily features as criteria of difference and from the discursive system that structures an understanding of them.[22] Working with human subjects rather than images, Butler moves one step beyond Barthes in arguing that discourse not only names, labels, and categorizes materiality but actually forces material difference: once a schema of gender difference is in place, individuals draw from the set of acceptably gendered appearances (i.e., from a set of "intelligible bodies") as they decide how to dress.[23] That is, individuals continually engage in performing their sex as they

> compel the body to conform to an historical idea of "woman" . . . [to] induce the body to become a cultural sign . . . [to] materialize oneself in obedience to an historically delimited possibility, and do this as a sustained and repeated corporeal project.[24]

These repeated citations of conventional gendered appearances reinforce the bounded categories of male and female as natural until the role of discourse in defining and provoking distinctive gendered appearances becomes transparent and material bodies take on the appearance of being *inherently* distinguishable. Thus, it is through the combination of discourse and reiterative bodily practices that categories of male and female gain the impression of uniformity and stability.[25]

I too analyze interactions between discourse and performativity throughout this book.[26] I find that late ancient writers—pagans and Christians—expended a great deal of energy attempting to coach their audiences to interpret dress signs according to their perspectives and agendas. Elite Roman men constructed a sartorial system—that focused attention on luxury goods and that paired the attire of women and foreigners—in a way that undergirded their supremacy over both groups. Christian leaders also imbued Christians' clothing with theological and moral significance. Their interpretations of Christian dress trained spectators to see Christians' extraordinary virtue every time they laid eyes on them. Furthermore, they hoped their significations would impel Christians to dress within a set of acceptable styles, which would in turn reinforce the naturalness of Christian virtue. Throughout we find discourse constraining the meanings that could be derived from dress—meanings that ultimately participated in broader ideological projects—as well as pressuring individuals' dress practices.

Yet, with Butler, I wish to stress the *mutual interaction* of discourse and performativity. When we focus only on the ways in which discourse shapes material experiences and subjectivities, we miss the ways in which bodily performances buttress or contest discursive work.[27] It is important to recognize that many Christians dressed in ways that bolstered Christians' claims to be morally superior. It is equally important to understand how certain Christians' dress practices disrupted a unified (and thus natural) presentation of Christian ideals and that these bodily practices were compelling and forceful enough to require formal written responses from nearby Christian leaders.

In order to evaluate the interactions between discourse and dress performances, I examine three types of texts. First, in Chapters 1 and 2, I analyze how texts direct readers to fashion their appearance in ways that support and sustain the worldview and agenda of the author. Here, we see discourse attempting to constrain the signification of dress, as well as dress practices themselves. Second, in Chapter 3, I examine how texts attempt to corral and negate dress performances that challenge the authors' views. In these instances, we understand the power of dress performances to resist and challenge the meanings that Christian leaders wish for them to portray. We also find authors struggling with ascetic practitioners to control the signification of their dress. Third, in Chapter 4, I analyze narratives of cross-dressing saints in order to demonstrate how the authors limit the interpretation of cross-dressing ascetic women through their description of ideal ascetic heroines.

Because this project focuses on ascetics' dress and physical appearance, one might assume that I would pay attention to late ancient art, presuming that artistic renderings might provide a closer connection to late ancient dress performances than do textual remains. While I agree that a study of artistic depictions of dress could surely yield important results, I have chosen not to pursue these sources in detail because I do not believe that visual representations give us a closer connection to actual dress practices than texts. Both artwork and texts are inherently representative, imbued with the sociopolitical aims and ideologies of the artist or writer and conveyed through rhetorical or symbiological tropes. Whereas both visual and textual representations can certainly help us understand how ancients interpreted and deployed dress signs, the logic and patterns of representation need to be carefully analyzed on their own terms.[28] Because I am primarily interested in the ways in which discourse and dress performances interacted, textual representations were the most appropriate sources for me to consult.

## CONTRIBUTIONS

The primary aim of this book is to contribute to the scholarly understanding of gender in antiquity. In recent years, scholars have argued that gender difference in antiquity was not primarily defined according to anatomical features of the body. Rather, the view predominantly held by ancient philosophers and physicians, such as Aristotle, Galen, and Soranus, was a one-sex model that plotted all humans on the same anatomical spectrum of maleness, with individuals achieving more or less perfection of the ideal. As Thomas Laqueur writes: "Instead of being divided by their reproductive anatomies, the sexes are linked by a common one" that takes different forms in the bodies of men and women so that the "boundaries between male and female are of degree and not of kind."[29] We now know that ancient theorists understood bodily variation to be merely an expression of extracorporeal differences wherein the most virile would develop into a fully formed man and the least virile into an underformed woman. Thus, as Laqueur concludes, there was "no goal to ground social roles in nature [i.e., biology]; social categories themselves are natural . . . biology only records a higher truth."[30]

Although individuals' natural gender was not measured primarily from genitalia, it was nonetheless exhibited and interpreted through the body. Gender was a performed and embodied identity. Men consistently demonstrated reason (*logismos*), discipline over the passions (*apatheia*), and domination, whereas women fell short of these ideals. Scholars, therefore, have begun to study how individuals in antiquity constructed their public personae to exhibit the above traits, in turn positioning themselves on the gender gradient.[31] Several recent studies have examined how Romans' gender identity—especially masculine identity—was established and maintained through military and athletic feats, rhetorical performances, and even sermons and theological debates.[32] My study builds on this recent scholarship that analyzes the performative maintenance of gender, though my focus is squarely on dress and physical appearance.

Although several monographs on dress and gender have been published recently in the field of classical studies, my research addresses several gaps in these studies.[33] First, they address only a handful of Christian sources, which are collapsed together with non-Christian treatments of dress. I agree that pagans and Christians both employed interpretations of dress in similar ways, but such minimal treatment and conflation neglect the innovations to sartorial discourse and practice introduced by Christians and overlook certain issues regarding dress that uniquely troubled Christian communities. Second, nearly all of the past research has concentrated on performances of masculinity in dress, neglecting the far more complicated construction and evaluation of women's physical appearance.[34] For men, the goal was clear: they were to consistently and competently perform masculinity in order to forestall charges of effeminacy. Women, however, were censured for performing too much femininity *or* too much masculinity. They were criticized for donning conventional female garb that expressed aspects of womanly vice and for overstepping their place in the order of society (and the order of creation) when they dressed too much like men. The ideal dress performance for the virtuous woman seems to have been largely contradictory: she should strive to exhibit a masculine manner of dress that never troubled her firm identification with femininity.

Finally, this book contributes to scholarship on gender in early Christian asceticism. In the past few decades scholars have attempted to make sense of how and why female ascetics were deemed virile, manly, or genderless.[35] From this research, we understand that early Christians conceptualized the gender transformations that accompanied an ascetic life in a variety of theological, moral, and social ways. For several first- and second-century Christians, gender came into being with the creation of material bodies; it did not exist in the spiritual, incorporeal realm.[36] Some thought, however, that gender difference could dissolve at certain moments, even while in the body, when Christians experienced their true spiritual nature, such as during the temporary ecstasy of baptism (which makes sense of the Gal. 3:28 baptismal formula, "there is no longer male and female")[37] and the permanent state of celibacy.[38] Unlike pagan and Christian matrons who were viewed in terms of their earthly sexual relationships with men—and especially the "fleshly" activities of intercourse and childbearing—ascetic women were "representations in the appearance of flesh of the purely spiritual, nongendered, presocial essence of human beings."[39]

Other Christian writers privileged the Fall—as opposed to Creation—as the decisive moment of gender differentiation. For them, God, armed with the foreknowledge of humanity's impending Fall, created bodily difference to make procreation possible after humans were expelled from the garden. Variations in genitalia, however, proved insignificant in a prelapsarian Garden free of sexual activity. Only after the first sin and the punishment of death did procreation become necessary, activating bodily differences already present.[40] The goal of the Christian ascetic was to reverse the trajectory of history and return to the original paradisiacal condition through the renunciation of sexual activity and procreation. Returning to her prelapsarian state, the ascetic could recapture her nongendered spiritual essence even while existing in a corporeal body.[41]

From still other early Christian sources we find that ascetics who renounced sexual activity were understood to have acquired the genderless, heavenly state of the angels.[42] For these thinkers, the angelic condition of the future life lacked sexual activity—if not also bodily genitalia—and thus ascetics' gender was somehow neutralized (even if they still possessed bodily genitalia).[43]

Yet early Christians need not choose between these conceptual models. They regularly conflated the genderless paradisiacal body with the genderless eschatological body.[44] Although they linked the beginning of gender difference to various moments in Christian history—Creation, Fall, or the heavenly future—they agreed that gender difference was primarily defined by the corporeal difference required for heterosexual union and reproduction. Thus, by rejecting marriage and heterosexual activity, ascetics were thought to trigger a corollary dissolution of gender identity. As Daniel Boyarin summarizes: "By escaping from sexuality entirely, virgins thus participate in the 'destruction of [gender],' and attain the status of the spiritual human who was neither male nor female."[45]

In addition to the theological logic that shaped conceptions of ascetics' gender—or genderlessness—ascetics' social roles also prompted a rethinking of their gender identity. As Elizabeth Clark has shown, the monastic styles of elite men and women were quite similar, flattening the distinction between men and women.[46] Female ascetics were also afforded social opportunities that were previously unavailable to women. Some were permitted to travel on Christian pilgrimage, allowed to engage in theological study (and possibly public debate), and overall accorded more public honor and attention than Christian matrons.[47] For these reasons, attributions of masculinity seem appropriate, "based on an accurate representation of the concrete conditions of their lives, conditions that resembled the men's."[48]

Finally, a gendered scale was also used to describe Christians' virtue and spiritual progress.[49] Women who strove to achieve a state of *apatheia* by mastering and conquering feminine vices were depicted as "advancing along the manly way."[50] Furthermore, spiritual progress was gauged by a "masculinist ideologies of transcendence" beyond the body, appealing to the highly gendered association of mind with male and body with female, which clearly betrayed distaste toward all things feminine.[51] Paradoxically, then, when Christian writers asserted that an early Christian woman progressed to a higher spiritual or moral state, they simultaneously claimed that she transcended her gender and that she become male. Clement of Alexandria, for example, inquires: "Is not the woman translated into a man when she becomes equally unfeminine, and manly, and perfect?"[52] Jerome similarly writes:

> Inasmuch as a woman is devoted to birth and children, she is different from a man, as the body is different with respect to the soul. If, however, she should wish to be devoted to Christ more than to the world, she will cease to be a woman and be said to be a man.[53]

As Elizabeth Castelli correctly observes: " 'Becoming male' marks for these thinkers the transcendence of gendered differences, but it does so only by reinscribing the traditional gender hierarchies of male over female, masculine over feminine."[54]

Thus, we find that in pro-ascetic Christian literature, gender worked on multiple levels: it could be understood as betokening spiritual, social, and moral identities. Because the ascetic ultimately strove to achieve a genderless spiritual state and because notions of virtue and spiritual progress were conceptually linked to masculinity, writers praised a female ascetic by claiming that she had surpassed and overcome her femininity and that she had "become male." In this sense, gender categories were used to rank the continuums of virtue, piety, and spirituality. But Christians also highlighted corporeal aspects of gender, such as the use of bodily genitalia in sex acts and childbirth, precisely because it was these aspects of heterosexual marriage that ascetics renounced. The gender of female ascetics, therefore, was also defined against the femininity of matrons who made use of their gendered bodies. At the same time, however, the female ascetic was often still identified with the feminine according to her bodily form. Regardless of her refusal to *use* certain body parts or of her ability to demonstrate manly virtue or spiritual progress, a female ascetic's bodily *form* was frequently culled as a limit to her complete gender transformation. In this context, Christian writers regularly split ascetic women's gender identities, praising their progress in virtue or piety through attributions of masculinity or genderlessness, while at the same time reminding readers of ascetics' still feminine bodies. John of Ephesus, for example, describes Mary the Anchorite as "a woman who by nature only bore the form of females, but in herself also bore the character and soul and will not only of ordinary men, but of mighty and valiant men."[55]

The primary aim of this book is to draw attention to the manner in which female ascetics' dress performances contributed to the layered understanding of their gender. Whereas it might have been relatively easy to *speak* or *write* about an ascetics' split gender identity—gesturing simultaneously to her manly virtue and spiritual state, as well as to her womanly body—how was a female ascetic to *perform* a split gendered identity in her dress and physical appearance? How was she to communicate multiple registers of gender from the same dress signs? If an ascetic exhibited her advanced virtue and spiritual condition through a manly or genderless appearance, she complicated a proper reading of the female body beneath her clothing that likewise called for expression. I have found that when female ascetics manipulated their dress in order to exhibit their piety, they regularly upset conventional ways of registering gender difference. This study analyzes deliberations between ascetics and Christian leaders over how ascetics were to properly perform their piety and gender through their physical appearance. In so doing, we gain a broader view of how female ascetics' gender was constructed, perceived, and contested in the world of early Christian asceticism.

We also become aware of the energy expended by male Christian leaders to manage ascetics' looks so that they might appear appropriately virtuous *and* appropriately gendered. Although scholars regularly assume that it was common for early Christians to attribute some sort of gender transformation to ascetics, we find that gender was not quite as flexible as we might have thought. We will see that the same Christian leaders who eulogized female ascetics' manly moral and spiritual progress also imposed a material limit to their total gender transformation. They argued that ascetics ought to exhibit their progress in piety by renouncing physical markers of feminine vice (e.g., cosmetics, jewelry, and ornamentation that communicated feminine vanity, decadence, and hyper-sexuality), but they ought not complicate gender too much, especially by obscuring the most salient markers of bodily femininity (e.g., long hair) or adopting too masculine of an appearance by cross-dressing. Christian leaders and counsels were far more conservative than their rhetoric initially suggests. In fact, my study shows that many Christian leaders aimed to make gender categories more rigid. When Christian ascetics relinquished the sartorial signs of femininity, Christian leaders quickly constructed new gender models based on the order of Creation and hunted down new bodily criteria, such as hair and breasts, by which to distinguish women from men. Thus, I argue that the radical innovation to gender introduced by early Christians was not a dissolution of gender categories but rather a move toward a bodily basis of gender more closely akin to modern sex categories. This move to stabilize gender difference, I conclude, was based on a desire to maintain order in Christian communities, an order firmly based on gendered difference and hierarchy.

Overall, this study reveals the amount of discursive and sartorial work necessary to secure stable gender categories within the world of early Christian asceticism. Female ascetics had to comply with the dress prescriptions of their mentors, as well as submit to orthodox interpretations of their looks. By so doing, female ascetics might be held up as extraordinary paragons of Christian virtue while the social hierarchies based on gender difference likewise might be preserved. Unfortunately for early Christian leaders, not all ascetic women complied, and for this reason certain ascetics' clothed bodies became flashpoints for debates over early Christian definitions of gender.

# 1 Elite Roman Women's Dress in the Early Imperial Period

When I tell people that I study dress and adornments in late antiquity, they often look at me quizzically and ask, "What is there of scholarly value in dress?" From the ensuing conversations it becomes clear that the realm of fashion has been so firmly associated with frivolity and even wastefulness that, to many, it seems misguided to devote a serious work of scholarship to the topic.[1] It is my contention, though, that such a disposition toward dress is the product of an effective rhetorical campaign of the early Imperial period that aligned elaborate displays of dress with notions of triviality, leisure, decadence, and impiety and that linked all of the above to femininity. It is precisely because these significations—and the trivialization of those realms presumed to relate to the feminine—remain in force still today that we ought to study late ancient dress.

I wish not to say that these connotations were entirely new in the early Imperial period. Dress, vice, and femininity had been aligned throughout Greco-Roman history.[2] There was, however, a sudden increase in discussions of women's dress in this moment when new, more luxurious and ornate forms of dressing and grooming became available through trade and conquest. As a result of these innovations, Romans' manner of dressing was more closely scrutinized. In this chapter, I investigate how particular forms of dressing and grooming were connoted, uncover the social goals these connotations served, and evaluate the effects these connotations had on notions of masculinity and femininity.[3] By parsing the sartorial system that developed in the early Imperial period, we are better able to understand how Christians' dress practices deviated from the norm and how Christians adopted and revised the rhetoric of dress used by their pagan neighbors.

## INTERPRETING LUXURY

From the second century BCE, Rome's military achieved victories throughout the Mediterranean, rapidly expanding Rome's territories and opening new routes for trade. In the process, Romans acquired many previously unknown or rare products from their provinces and beyond, including new aromatics, jewels, metals, and textiles. According to historians of the period, at first these products were highly esteemed: these products, along with newly captive peoples, were paraded into the city in triumphal processions as symbols of Rome's military and cultural victories.[4] When these products were incorporated into the sartorial displays of Rome's leading citizens, they symbolized Rome's growing prosperity and her cultivation of a truly global empire.[5] As demand grew, foreign products were imported so widely that, in his oration to the city, Aelius Aristides could boast:

> Here is brought from every land and sea all the crops of the seasons and the produce of each land, river, lake, as well as the arts of the Greeks and barbarians, so that if someone should wish to view all these things, he must either see them by traveling over the whole world or come to Rome . . . there can be seen clothing from Babylon and ornaments from the barbarian world beyond, which arrive in much larger quantity and more easily than if merchantmen bringing goods from Naxus or Cythnus had only to put into Athens . . . everything comes together here, trade, seafaring, farming, the scourings of the mines, all the crafts that exist or have existed, all that is produced and grown. Whatever one does not see here is not a thing which has existed or exists.[6]

Yet soon thereafter, many Roman moralists would view the impact of conquest, expansion, and trade quite differently. They complained that Romans had come to lust for foreign luxury items, making themselves vulnerable to the vices of *incontinentia* and *luxuria* that characterized non-Roman peoples.[7] Whether Rome's moral decline began with the conquest of Asia Minor or the destruction of Carthage, Roman moralists were convinced that when Rome came into contact with foreign products and ways, they were forever tainted with immorality that was likewise foreign to the superior character of Rome. Pliny sums up the prevailing concerns:

> It was this triumph of Pompeius Magnus that first introduced a general taste for pearls and precious stones, just as the victories gained by L. Scipio and Cneius Manlius had first turned the public attention to engraved silver and Attalic clothing . . . the austerity of our ancient manners was defeated in what was not a triumph of conquest, but rather a triumph of luxury.[8]

Catharine Edwards has argued convincingly that allegations of declining morality stemmed largely from a growing crisis of Roman identity.[9] With the incorporation of new provinces throughout the Mediterranean, Rome could no longer be defined by the borders of the city, and thus needed other measures to emphasize her distinctiveness.[10] Quickly assimilating foreigners' customs, philosophy, literature, and goods, yet not wishing to feel inferior as a result of this vast cultural borrowing, the Roman elite—from historians to politicians to poets—Edwards argues, attempted to define *Romanitas* in terms of Rome's superior morality.[11]

Whereas assertions of Rome's exceptional character and piety marked a difference between Romans and their neighbors, it also justified Rome's colonial pursuits. According to Roman moralizing discourse, foreigners' propensity for depraved excess demonstrated their inability to control themselves. Romans, on the contrary, who enjoyed a history of moral fortitude, were thus obliged to govern the weak.[12] Edwards, and more recently Jennifer Knust, thus warn historians not to take accusations of immorality at face value because they had less to do with the *real* behavior of Romans and non-Romans than with the desired *perception* of the complainant as morally superior. In other words, these moral judgments should be understood in terms of the juxtaposition of the accuser and the accused and of the power dynamic resulting therein.[13]

At this time, it was not only foreigners who were the target of moral critiques. Just as non-Romans were understood to be prone to indulgence and excess, so too immoderate Romans were thought to be particularly susceptible to the contagion of foreign vice. The *nouveaux riches* and women in particular exhibited an inordinate desire of for luxe garments and adornments imported from abroad, eagerly purchasing whatever goods they could get their hands on. Those who considered themselves to be the true elite—those men connected to the *mores maiorum* because they understood how to use their wealth prudently—critiqued especially women for misusing their money in such immoderate fits of profligacy.[14]

Thus we see that, in this expansionist period in Rome's history, accusations of immorality were increasingly articulated in terms of foreignness and femininity. Roman moralists linked female vice to foreign vice through the luxury products they shared. Foreign and feminine identity and vice, I argue, were not abstract concepts. Both could be deciphered—once spectators were trained to "see" according to the Roman moralists' gaze—from elite Roman women's lavish attire. Because such moralizing discourse was primarily interested in demarcating boundaries—between Romans and foreigners, among the classes, and between men and women—it was advantageous for such divisions to be made *visibly* perceptible in this way.

Through these new significations of women's dress, I argue that the concepts and especially the measurement of Roman gender shifted. Whereas women continued to be cast as the "weaker sex," characterized by immoderation, greed, vanity, and hyper-sexuality, in this moment women's allegedly natural vice came to be read primarily from their appearance. In fact, so thoroughly could one gauge the nature and realm of women from luxurious garments and adornments that women's beautification products and regimens were referred to simply as *mundus muliebris*, playing on the double meaning of *mundus* as either "adornment" or "world."[15] Moreover, as women's nature came to be read from their looks, the notion of femininity became more deeply conceptualized as foreign to Roman masculinity due to the material link made with foreigners.

As Maria Wyke astutely notes, late ancient interpretations of Roman women's dress and appearance tell us no more than how men "made up" the image of the adorned woman: that is, how they directed attention to certain features of elite women's dress and then interpreted their significance in ways that best served their political agendas, bolstered their social status, and enhanced their personal reputations.[16] In this chapter, I argue that men's interpretations and critiques of women's dress stemmed from their anxiety over their waning consolidation of power and wealth. The Roman prosperity that accompanied the acquisition of foreign lands had a direct impact on Roman women's independent wealth. Because elite women retained more control of their property from the first century BCE, as Rome's wealth grew in general, so too did the wealth of elite women.[17] Roman men, unable to garner women's legally protected assets, aimed rather to undermine elite women's power and influence by critiquing their naturally immoderate use of their wealth. Roman men fixed their attention on dress and physical appearance as the chief indicator of characterological difference between men and women. Then they attempted to persuade their audiences to "see" what they saw in order to ultimately prove the naturalness of power hierarchies that placed Roman men above women.

In the rest of this chapter, I describe and analyze Roman men's attempts to persuade spectators to read women's dress as evidence of women's weak and wanton character and nature. No matter how diligently or persuasively they might have attempted to train Romans' ways of seeing, we should not assume that all Romans shared their "views."[18] That dress terms such as *stolata femina* or *matrona stolata* came to be used from the later second century AD onwards as a term of social rank for those of equestrian status or above, the equivalent of *honesta femina*" indicates that many were reading women's dress and adornments as indicators of their individual status, rank, and prestige.[19] In fact, as Kelly Olson and others have recently speculated, it is very likely that aristocratic women declared their personal wealth through their choices of dress and ornamentation.[20] Whereas women could certainly fashion their appearance so as to be perceived in this way, it is my contention that elite Roman men aimed to take control of the sartorial significance of women's dress. Indeed, the vehemence with which Roman men interpreted women's dress and grooming may reflect their exasperation with women's own alternate interpretations. The point of this chapter, therefore, is not to foreclose other interpretations of women's dress that surely existed alongside the extant arguments of Roman men, but rather to highlight the extreme efforts made by elite men to circumscribe alternate interpretations, especially those that might undermine elite men's authority.

## SIGNIFYING ELITE ROMAN WOMEN'S DRESS

As noted above, in the early Imperial period there was a sudden swell of interest in Roman women's dress. Most writers of the period argued that elite Roman women's clothing was a symbol of either Rome's weakness or greatness. On the one hand, elite women's indulgent dress was read as a sign of unleashed feminine excess that was leading Rome into a state of moral decline, as well as eroding Rome's new prosperity. On the other hand, elite women's ornate and costly manner of dress was used to broadcast the wealth and prestige of Rome's leading families, according honor especially to their male relatives.

Classicists who have studied these discussions regularly argue that these distinct evaluations represented discrete camps in Roman society. They pit the poets who encouraged women's immoderate displays of decadence (which consequently fed illicit sexual affairs) against the moralists who urged Romans to dress and act according to the rational and restrained character appropriate to Roman morality. Moreover, scholars juxtapose writers who attempted to use luxurious dress to communicate the prestige of Rome with writers who regarded decadence and luxury to be hopelessly irredeemable.[21] It seems to me that historians who persist in presenting two distinct opinions on women's dress are merely replicating the picture offered by the Roman historian Livy, who casts the two sides against one another in his depiction of the Oppian law debates in 195 BCE.[22] Livy reconstructs the dispute between consuls Marcus Porcius Cato, who spoke for the conservative party, and Lucius Valerius Flaccus, who spoke for those seeking to repeal the laws. In his reconstruction, Livy maps the discussions of morality and dress of his own period onto these past events, creating the impression of two divergent views on adorned women in both periods.[23] In my reading, however, both sides share a common depiction of women's natural vice and, when read together, both combined to secure men's positions of power.

At the end of the third century BCE, the Roman Senate passed the Oppian laws, which limited women's use of luxury items, restricting the amount of gold and dyed clothing an elite woman could wear. Twenty years later, the Senate contemplated repealing the laws. According to Livy's account, Cato the Elder opened the debate by decrying women's luxurious, vain, and avaricious nature. Roman matrons, he argued, expressed a longing to "glitter with gold and purple . . . so that there might be no limit to our spending nor to our luxury."[24] If one excess was allowed, Cato reasoned, how many other excesses would follow? In fact, in their desire to overturn this law, Roman women were already overstepping conventions of modesty and decency. Just look, Cato contends, at the throngs of women in the Forum rallying against the law. These matrons feel no shame at being seen in public, much less for speaking with other women's husbands (in an attempt to win them over to their side), and they might even be using the legal battle as an excuse to comingle publicly with these men.[25] Thus to legally sanction decadent dress, Cato concludes, would permit even greater indulgence of women's natural "female extravagance (*luxuriam muliebrem*)" of the kind witnessed at that very moment.[26]

Livy's Cato argues that the infusion of foreign goods activated Roman women's vice. In Rome's past, when Roman women lacked the goods and leisure time to indulge their base appetites, they were properly subdued, submissive, and virtuous. Cato blames Rome's prosperity, and especially the imported goods tainted with foreign vice, for triggering women's vicious nature. For instance, the richest women now wonder, "Why do I not stand out conspicuously with distinctive markers such as gold and purple? Why does the poverty of other women lay hidden under the looks required by law, so that it may seem that, had it been legal, they might possess and wear [wealth]?"[27] To repeal the law and allow women more elaborate modes of dress and ornamentation would be to unleash their naturally depraved vanity and lust for attention.

Moreover, if women were allowed free exercise to dress as extravagantly as they pleased, they would surely use their newly embellished looks to seduce and prevail over men. For Cato, "it is [men's] liberty, that is conquered at home by womanly vice and even in the Forum is crushed and trampled. Because [husbands] have not kept their own wives under control, we dread them all universally."[28] Cato asks his audience: "Do you imagine that you will be able to refuse them? The moment they begin to be your equals, they will be your superiors."[29] In this way, women's adornments are doubly foreign in that they are imported from non-Roman territories and they underscore women's opposition to Roman men.[30] The Oppian legislation, Cato concludes, aids men in resisting and restraining their wives' natural lasciviousness and thwarts their dangerous threats to men's self-control and rule. Thus the restraint imposed by the legislation is imperative because the inferior feminine nature requires safeguarding for the sake of both women and men.

According to Livy, Consul Lucius Valerius objected to Cato's presentation of adornments as extensions and tools of women's vanity, greed, lasciviousness, and dominance. The Oppian law, he argues, was not passed to "contain female luxury" or to "bound feminine lasciviousness."[31] Rather, the law was enacted as an emergency measure meant to increase the public treasury in support of the war effort. The law, Valerius concludes, should be repealed in the present time of Roman peace and prosperity.

Lavish adornments, Valerius continues, should not be considered threatening tools of women's seduction because they function more importantly as signs of status. Because Roman women could not hold civic or religious office, nor revel in the spoils of war, Valerius continues, extravagant dress and adornments were their only recourse for esteem. He writes: "Elegance (*munditiae*), adornment (*ornatus*), and a cultivated look (*cultus*)—these are women's badges of honor (*feminarum insignia*); in which they delight

and are glorified."[32] How malicious it is, Valerius argues, for "your horse
to be dressed in more splendor than your wife."[33] Moreover, if even aristocratic men would bristle at any restriction to their liberties, how much
more do these regulations affect "weak women, who are upset by even little
things?"[34] In the end, both speakers presume women's weak nature. Cato
wishes to curb women's depravity by restricting their use of adornments,
while Valerius argues that women's weakness requires concessions and a
repeal of the restrictive legislation.

Valerius's appeal, though, hints that women's sartorial displays did more
than confer honor to individual women. Their looks additionally commend
the city of Rome as a whole. When the highly ornamented women of other
Latin cities, decked out in fine clothing and jewels, parade through the
city, Valerius grumbles, spectators are left to wonder "if their cities are
sovereign, not Rome."[35] Thus Valerius's support of elite women's adornment clearly indicates his concern to visibly broadcast the prosperity and
prestige of the city of Rome.[36] Moreover, Valerius's support of the repeal
also intended to enhance men's authority within the household. He argues
that if the law were repealed, women would be required to follow their
husbands'—not the state's—instructions about how they might dress.[37]

Again, the Oppian Law debate has been used by historians to argue that
there were two prevalent views on how Roman women ought to dress and
adorn themselves. Whereas certainly there were different views on these
matters, I wish to argue that the two evaluations of elite Roman women's
attire illustrated by Livy were not completely at odds. Both painted similar
pictures of women's weak nature; they advocated either restraint or latitude in women's dress in order to accommodate their presumed weakness.
Moreover, as I will demonstrate in detail below, both strands of the debate
together enhanced the reputations and authority of Roman men on either
side of the divide. By positioning a city's or household's wealth in the attire
of its women, the male elite could claim the honor associated with that conspicuous display of domination and prosperity, while they were themselves
shielded from being personally charged with the vices of *luxuria* or *incontinentia*.[38] In the following sections, I detail the typical ways in which early
Imperial Roman writers, like Livy, construed women's nature from their
attire before I demonstrate how men turned interpretations of women's
dress to their advantage.

## Roman Women's Luxurious Attire and Adornments as Signs of Women's Vice

In the early Imperial period, Roman moralists carefully interpreted features of elite women's dress in order to assert women's inferior nature. In so
doing, they offered their readers an interpretive framework for reading the
appearances of the women they daily encountered. Whereas Roman moralists' interpretations of woman's vice followed and developed tropes from

earlier Greek and Roman diatribe,[39] what is new in the literature of this period were the assertions that this particular moment of increased prosperity, and especially the infusion of foreign luxury goods, had activated and exacerbated women's vice and that women's vice was most clearly evident in their physical appearance.

"The cause of [our] ruin is certain and obvious," Propertius writes; "the path of high living has become too free. The Indian ant sends gold from the caves of her mines, and from the Red Sea comes the shell of Venus; Cadmean Tyre purveys her crimson tints and the Arabian distiller [sends] rich scents and cinnamon."[40] Women in particular, moralists alleged, had quickly succumbed to the immoral influences of outsiders because of their naturally immoderate disposition.[41] Their unrestrained *luxuria* and *incontinentia* were clearly evident on first glance as they bedecked themselves with ivory hairpieces imported from India, donned garments dyed with new hues from Tyre, wore imported gems, earrings, and necklaces, and claimed to be clothed when wearing silk garments from China and Cos that reduced them to nakedness.[42] Richly dressed and adorned women were criticized for "taking pains to please" spectators, exhibiting their seductive impulses.[43] Yet, moralists added, women also wished to satisfy their own vanity. Captivated by their own appearance, women found "pleasure too in self-satisfaction; pleasing to the heart of girls is their own appearance."[44] Finally, moralists claimed that women's wanton greed impelled them to possess novel goods, such as pearls and gemstones from Greece and bronze and silver from Africa.[45]

Another aspect of women's natural vice was their propensity for deception and for deceptive seduction.[46] Moralists alleged that most women were not naturally beautiful, so they needed the help of cosmetics, jewelry, and fine clothing to supplement their natural deficiencies. In his *Epigram* to Galla, Martial, for example, describes every aspect of her appearance as artificial, illusory, and false: she wears a wig ("your hair is manufactured in your absence"), dentures ("you lay your teeth aside at night"), cosmetics ("your face does not sleep with you"), and false lashes (which are "brought to you every morning").[47] Horace agrees that some women use gems and pearls to enhance their beauty. Other women, he adds, cover over their bodily flaws with ornate, flowing garments that leave the woman's body to men's imaginations and fantasies, which will inevitably be more generous than reality. So adept were women at distorting their natural looks (and so prone were men to be utterly taken by women's illusions of beauty), Lucretius adds, that "women who are in many ways crooked and unsightly we see to be charming and they are held in the highest honor . . . the sinewy and wooden is [seen to be] a gazelle, the squat little dwarf is [seen to be] one of the Graces."[48] Although Horace criticizes Roman men for secretly courting other men's wives, he finds women's enticing displays to be the true root of the problem because even rational and disciplined men are unable to resist women's wiles.[49]

Although Ovid's discussions of female beautification are somewhat unique in this period—in that he reveled in the decadences and indiscretions of his time, instructing men and women in the art of seducing a (usually illicit) lover[50]—he agreed with his contemporaries that women were only able to seduce men once they had constructed an artifice of beauty. Very few women, he contends, can boast natural beauty and even the natural beauty of woman will inevitably fade with age.[51] The cultivation of beauty, therefore, is extremely important. "Care will give good looks"; a woman's *ornatus* will construct beauty "better than the real."[52] Ovid, therefore, recommends a broad beautification regimen to create the impression of beauty where nature is lacking. He writes:

> You know how to gain a bright hue by applying powder: she who does not blush with blood, nevertheless, will blush by art. By art you will fill in your bare eyebrows, you will make smooth your cheeks with little patches . . . those who are slender should wear a full garment . . . a pale girl should scatter purple on her body [to brighten her complexion] . . . Let her with a narrow chest build it up with breastbands. Let her who has fat fingers and rough nails mark her speech with small gestures . . . If you have teeth that are black or large or out of place, laughing will cause you great injury.[53]

The images women constructed through beauty regimens were construed to be so thoroughly artificial that Ovid concludes: "We [men] are carried away by adornments. All is concealed by gold and gems. The least part [of the attraction] is the girl herself (*pars minima est ipsa puella sui*)."[54]

Through arguments such as these, Roman men constructed women's looks to be both natural and artificial. On the one hand, the woman's seductive appearance was made out to be an extension of her naturally lascivious and devious disposition. On the other hand, she was thought to achieve her good looks and allure only through artificial enhancements. Thus, the adorned woman could be charged with possessing innate vices of pride, vanity, and passion, while she might also be criticized for constructing a deceptive, artificial beauty.[55]

Women's false beauty was understood to pose a threat to the traditional modes of coupling. Some writers argued that all women delighted in being the center of attention, so that even after they had procured husbands they retained an insatiable need to attract suitors. Others claimed that formerly modest women had became tainted by the introduction of novel adornments imported from abroad, which renewed their interest in attracting attention. Either way, women were accused of seeking not the notice of their husbands, but rather men outside of the household. They satiated their desires by manufacturing alluring displays of beauty. Juvenal writes:

She encircles her neck with green emeralds and fastens massive earrings to her [now] stretched out ears . . . Meanwhile she ridiculously inflates and disfigures her face with dough or Poppaean fat, which stick to the lips of her unfortunate husband. For her lover, she will wash her skin, but when does she ever wish to be seen this way at home? It is for her lovers that she wears fragrances, for them that she purchases whatever the slender Indians sell us.[56]

Trimalchio, of Petronius's *Satyricon*, recites a similar reproach: "Why seek precious pearls or Indian 'berries' in order that your wife, ornamented with the spoils of the sea, might lift her feet on a stranger's bed?"[57]

In a cyclical way, women were accused of beautifying themselves with adornments in order to impel their lovers to give them additional gifts of clothing, jewelry, and gems that would further enable women to keep their men under their control.[58] The exchange of sex for luxury gifts was such a prevalent charge that even the *possession* of such gifts could be used as legal evidence of adultery. Porcius Latro, for instance, accused his wife of adultery because she accepted presents from a man while he was abroad (though she and the suitor insisted that she did not succumb to his advances).[59] He writes: "I am accusing her of adultery only now that she has become rich . . . she has acquired more in a single neighborhood than I did on all the seas there are."[60] Even if she remained chaste, he concludes, it was not because she was morally innocent, but rather because she was merely holding out for "a fatter price."[61]

Many writers complained that when men fell victim to women's deceptive beauty, they were unwittingly forced to surrender control to their lovers. Propertius, for example, bemoans the fact that many men of his time were enslaved to richly adorned women (just as he was to his lover, Cynthia). Utterly consumed by their beauty and retaining their lovers' affections, men submitted to women's every whim.[62] Women, conversely, became fiercely independent and influential, inverting the traditional gender order in which Roman men dominated women.[63]

Richly adorned women's dressing was criticized not only for imperiling Roman men's self-mastery—and thus also the stability of a properly ordered city—but also for threatening the stability of Roman households. Women's beautification regimes were condemned for detracting substantially from the productivity of the household. Juvenal alleges that women were so consumed with their personal appearance that they neglected their household duties. In fact, they even distracted their servants from attending to the work of the household, because matrons kept them busy with dressing them, constructing intricate hairstyles, and applying cosmetics.[64] Moreover, the expense of luxury goods—whether for wives or lovers—was draining Roman households of their accumulated wealth. Juvenal complains that women's uncontrolled spending on foreign extravagance would "torment and plunder" their husbands and eventually exhaust the household treasury.[65] Lucretius concurs,

Wealth vanishes and turns into Babylonian coverlets . . . For her, soft and beautiful Sicyonian shoes laugh on her feet, great emeralds set in gold shine their green light, the sea-purple dress is well-worn and, in constant use, absorbs the sweat of Venus. The well-won wealth of his fathers turns into a headband that binds her hair or a *palla* made of silks from Alinda and Cos.[66]

Horace and Propertius likewise claim that men squander their "fathers' estates" in order to afford the expensive gifts required by the women in their lives,[67] and Lucretius complains that men "kill themselves with labor" to afford expensive gifts—especially expensive foreign goods—for women, endangering men's health as well as their wealth.[68] Women's excessive consumption was depleting Rome's wealth and making foreigners rich: "For the sake of jewels, our wealth is transferred to alien or enemy peoples."[69] Imported clothing and adornments, thus, were figured as a threat on multiple levels: they functioned to undermine the proper order of society as defined by men's dominance and sovereignty over Roman women and over the peoples of the provinces.

Through interpretations such as these, blame for the downfall of Rome rested squarely on the shoulders of women and foreigners. This is not to say that Roman men accepted no responsibility for Rome's weakening morality and waning prosperity. Tacitus's Tiberius, for instance, castigates the men of the Roman army who became used to "wast[ing] the substance of others" while they plundered and looted the territories of foreigners.[70] Similarly, Sallust notes that Roman soldiers too quickly adopted the "luxury and license" of the foreigners they conquered.[71] When the soldiers returned to Rome, they spread these vices to their women, whose natural inclination toward immoderation, wastefulness, and consumption was immediately unleashed. Such acceptances of blame, however, cast Roman men's vice as merely a bad habit of war, cultivated in foreign cultures teeming with vice. Unlike a woman who exhibited deep-seated natural vice, men's innate fortitude and self-mastery enabled him to correct such bad habits once he returned home.

But the boundaries of nature and culture are often difficult to disentangle in these discussions. Whereas Roman men claimed that women were naturally inclined toward vice, they also did not wish to undermine their assertions that Romans were morally superior to foreign peoples. In other words, they wished to criticize Roman women as less virtuous than the Roman man *because they were women*, but they were still more virtuous than the peoples of the rest of the world *because they were Roman*. Thus Roman writers regularly argued that their women indulged their natural vice only *after* they came into contact with foreigners. Until that point, Roman culture was able to curb women's natural excesses and vice. In fact, Roman moralists proved that Roman women were capable of far more restraint than women from other parts of the world by culling examples of women from Rome's past who acted and dressed moderately, demonstrating the sheer power of *Romanitas*.[72] From the beginning of Roman society, the moralists alleged, Rome's women were so busy building up a great city and so thoroughly constrained by its great culture that they had no occasion or desire to indulge their natural vices.[73] Although the women of Rome's past had beautification routines, their adornments were cast as far better than those in use in the early Imperial period in that they were easily accessible, *natural* ornamentations that were found *at home*. Propertius, for instance, praises Roman women of the past for wearing only flowers and covering themselves in animal skins.[74] Only greedy women of the present, Pliny and Seneca add, "torture" Mother earth, "wounding" her by digging deep into her "entrails"; they "quarry the mountains for their marble . . . explore the depths of the Red Sea seeking the pearl and the very bowels of the earth for the emerald."[75] By enumerating examples of women from Rome's past who were able to discipline their natural inclinations toward vice, moralists could criticize richly adorned Roman women for being naturally less virtuous than Roman men, without undermining completely their claims of Roman cultural superiority.

Throughout these discussions that linked feminine vice and dress, male Roman writers attempted to articulate a difference between Roman and foreign, past and present, and especially masculine and feminine, by visualizing such differences in the dress and physical appearance of elite Roman women. As suggested at the outset of the chapter, I argue that this discourse was caught up in elite men's anxiety over their waning power in relation to foreigners and women. As the examples above have illustrated, the concerns men had with women's dress commonly crystallized around issues of women's newfound wealth and status. They do not dispute the fact that women were wresting more control of money and power from men; this they readily admit. But, I argue, they could interpret women's newly acquired wealth and influence to be a result of women seductively and deceptively pilfering money, goods, and power from their rightful owners, men, eliding the perfectly lawful ways in which women inherited and cultivated their property and wealth. Roman men's accusations seem perfectly reasonable once they have successfully trained the gaze of spectators to read women's decadent attire no longer as a sign of her individual status, but now as evidence of her vice and of her violation of the proper distribution of wealth and power. Here, I argue, Roman men turned the signs of women's prosperity and status against them to defend their own place in society.

## Roman Women's Luxurious Attire and Adornments as Signs of Men's Status

This was not the only way in which Roman men interpreted women's looks so as to highlight men's self-worth. Roman men also turned the image of the richly adorned Roman woman into a potent symbol for the status and power of her household and of the city at large, further securing the ruling power of elite men. Although Roman writers frequently criticized their women for using particular types of foreign imports, such as "foreign dyes" and "Belgian paints" (i.e., cosmetics),[76] they looked favorably upon imported adornments that proved to be useful—because more easily perceptible—symbols of Roman authority and power. For instance, when Roman women donned the blonde hair of the Germans or the jet black hair of the Indians, Rome's dominant place in the Mediterranean was made immediately and visibly evident. This explains Ovid and Martial's preference for Roman women to don wigs made of "captured hair" rather than to dye their own locks.[77]

At the level of the household, *every* lavish sartorial display could boast a family's wealth by publicizing the household's ability to absorb its women's wastefulness and idleness. A woman who donned clothing made from expensive fabrics, adorned herself with gold, silver, and jewels, and smelled of costly unguents clearly belonged to a prominent family who could afford to waste money on materials of extravagance. Moreover, her look demonstrated the family's ability to waste labor—whether the wife's or servants'—on the preparation of such extravagant displays.[78] For instance, the towering and intricate hairstyles characteristic of this period could not be achieved on one's own, but required the assistance of servants, evidencing the household's surplus labor.[79] Additionally, women's luxe apparel was often so cumbersome that spectators could clearly see that its wearer would be unable to engage in productive labor.[80] Women would wear rings on their knuckles, for instance, hampering the functional use of their hands.[81] In this way, a matron's vice of wastefulness—on superfluous and expensive luxury goods and of time and labor—could be viewed as positive cultural capital for her *familia*.[82] In fact, so effectively did elite women's beautification communicate their families' status that it became concretized as the lasting image depicted on many funeral *stelae* from the late first century BCE (Figures 1.1–1.2), cementing in stone the family's prestige.[83]

Finally, we should also read the countless complaints of men who grumbled about their wives' or mistress' careless expenditures or wasted time on beauty regimens, as other ways in which elite men drew attention to their own pecuniary strength. When they calculated the "idle hours" their wives spent on their personal appearance,[84] itemized the number of *ancillae* necessary to make these elite women beautiful, and tallied the total labor lost by their beauty regimens, they publicized their ability to absorb their wives' wastefulness and lack of productivity.[85] Moreover, their complaints revealed the costs of their women's expenditures. They complained that a cluster of pearl earrings cost "two or three patrimonies,"[86] that a man's full annual income was needed to finance the items in his wife's closet,[87] and that Romans as a whole spend 100 million sesterces a year on pearls and perfumes from India, China, and the Arabian peninsula: "So dearly do

*Figure 1.1*   Funerary relief of servants beautifying their mistress, second to third century CE. Permission and photo: Rheinisches Landesmuseum, Trier, Germany.

*Figure 1.2*   Funerary relief of servants beautifying their mistress. Permission and photo: Musée national d'histoire et d'art, Luxembourg.

we pay for our luxury and our women."[88] We must be careful, therefore, not to read the critiques leveled against adorned women as *only* attesting concerns about women's vice and Rome's lapsed morality. They also publicized Roman men's pecuniary strength in a way that simultaneously distanced men from accusations of *luxuria* and *incontinentia*. As men criticized the garb of their women, greed, vanity, luxury, immoderation, and lust were made out to be thoroughly feminine vices and men were made out to be paragons of manly restraint, discipline, and moderation.[89] Moreover, Roman men imbued these feminine vices—and the attire that communicated such vices—with layers of foreignness to further divorce them from the realms of manliness and *Romanitas*.[90] By feminizing these vices and siphoning them away from themselves, elite Roman men could use the image of a richly adorned wife, daughter, or servant to garner prestige while preserving their place of moral supremacy.

Casting luxury and immoderation as the natural vices of women, men were able not only to distance themselves from the vice associated with their female kin's lavish attire but they were also afforded a justification for reasserting control over their women.[91] The feminine excess and unrestrained sexuality interpreted from elite women's dress and adornments served as proof that women lacked the requisite discipline necessary to manage their wealth responsibly. Elite men, on the other hand, possessed a naturally moderate disposition, as evidenced by their moderate appearance and by their criticisms of women's decadent dress. At a time when Roman women's independent wealth and influence were growing ever larger, men argued that they were required—by necessity and by nature—to control these lesser members of society.

## FEMININITY AND MASCULINITY RECONCEIVED

From before the early Imperial period Roman gender identity was already read from one's physical appearance. Even as elite women altered their dress to signal periodic changes in status—from virgin to matron to widow—they were always visibly marked as women, distinct from their male counterparts.[92] The bride, for instance, wore a special hairstyle (*seni crines, hasta caelibaris*) and hairnet (*reticulum luteum*), a flame-colored veil (*flammeum*), and a crown.[93] Once married, the woman assumed woolen hair bands (*vittae*), a *stola*, and often a mantle to cover her head (in public).[94] A woman in mourning wore a dark woolen mantle (*ricinium*) over her head.[95] Elite Roman women were differentiated from men and were further differentiated from each other at various stages in life; their clothing firmly identified them as women throughout.

As we have just seen, however, by the early Imperial period women's dress and adornments began to signal much more than just their marital or social status. At this time, certain forms of dressing and grooming were deemed typically feminine and came to symbolize female nature more broadly. I believe that the introduction of physiognomy to the Roman west at this time helped to prompt this interpretive impulse. Physiognomy was a Greek science that aimed to interpret the disposition of individuals' souls or nature through physical signs of the body.[96] As we might expect, physiognomic interpretations were highly gendered. According to handbook author Pseudo-Aristotle, well trained physiognomists could clearly discern the different dispositions of men and women. Basing their analyses on comparisons with the animal kingdom, they argued that women's builds, which tend to be diminutive (e.g., narrow face, slender neck, small and weak chest), most closely resemble the panther, whereas a man's body was larger, stronger, with a broad chest and shoulders, and overall better proportioned, like the lion. The female disposition, therefore, must likewise resemble the panther: tamer, less powerful, and less courageous than lion-like males, whose souls are "generous and free, magnanimous and ambitious, yet gentle and just and affectionate towards his associates."[97] Gendered physiognomic discourse such as this coupled with interpretations of women's dress until many believed that humans' nature—especially their gender—was materially recognizable in their body, physical appearance, and dress.[98] We see, though, that notions of gender read from women's attire were neither necessary nor inherent, but rather constructed. Roman historians, poets, and moralists signified women's dress with consistent tropes, training spectators to reach certain conclusions about a woman, her family, and her city as soon as they laid eyes upon her. In this regard, they acted similarly to physiognomists, who legitimated the gender hierarchy by creating a physiognomic taxonomy that authenticated preexisting gender stereotypes. In Maud Gleason's words: "What purports to be an inductive science, built up from myriad specific observations becomes a deductive science based on generalized impressions and preexisting prejudices that are confirmed by observed details."[99]

In this chapter, I have aimed to show that the Roman concept of femininity was now more than ever focused squarely on and assessed from the attire and adornments of elite women. Of course, most women in Rome could not afford the clothing and adornments donned by the elite, nor could they spare the time to fashion such elaborate looks. Nonetheless, these select women's attire and adornments were read as ciphers for the vicious nature of *all* women, because it was presumed that, if all women were granted the same opportunities, they would surely indulge in similar fashions. In fact, even these women who could not afford to dress like stereotypical women served as negative objects of comparison that reinforced the boundaries of the feminine. As Judith Butler notes, to be "not quite feminine is still to be understood exclusively in terms of one's relationship to . . . the 'quite feminine.' "[100]

The concept and look of Roman masculinity was also defined against this version of femininity.[101] Once Roman moralists had proficiently associated *ornatus* with the feminine and the foreign, it became dangerous for men—even emperors—to demarcate their status and power through lavish sartorial displays.[102] Any man who paid *too much* attention to his appearance could be ridiculed for being "effeminate (*mollitia*)" and thus also un-Roman, putting him at a marked disadvantage in aristocratic competition and undermining his standing in social hierarchies.[103] For instance, Suetonius castigates Caligula for his choices in dress, especially his silken and richly jeweled cloaks: "In his attire, he neither followed the custom of his city, his fellow citizens, nor even that of other men."[104] Even more pronounced is the censure of Elagabalus, who originally hailed from Syria. His practice of wearing jewelry and silk clothing evoked obvious associations with both foreign and effeminate decadence.[105] Although we might expect emperors to be allowed to don ornate attire given their need to communicate their political status and authority, here we see that lavish and expensive garb had been so thoroughly imbued with notions of femininity and foreignness that even they had to be careful about how richly they dressed.

Of course, interpretations of a man's dress were driven by the observer's stance toward him. If one was inclined to undermine another's authority, he might argue that any embellishments in a man's dress exhibited an excessive—and effeminate—attention to his appearance (*ornatus*).[106] If one was inclined to praise his subject, however, he might interpret a man's careful grooming (and maybe even his adornments) as manifesting the care (*cultus*) proper for a man of standing. In fact, one could cite Quintilian, who argued that any man of position ought to pay ample attention to his appearance so as to be deemed "distinguished and manly."[107]

Because there was this interpretive flexibility, the appearance of Roman masculinity needed to be policed in order to appear natural. A number of sartorial prescriptions were issued by emperors who insisted that Roman men dress "as men."[108] Augustus and Hadrian urged Roman men—especially senators and equites—to wear a white toga in public rather than the dark colored *pullati*.[109] Most notably, Tacitus and Dio report that Tiberius prohibited Roman citizen men from wearing silk clothes.

> At the next session [of the Senate], the ex-consul, Quintus Haterius, and a former praetor, Octavius Fronto, spoke at length against the city's extravagance; and it was resolved that neither should tableware be made out of solid gold, nor that men should be degraded by dressing in silk.[110]

These regulations addressed the concern that both social rank and gender be immediately clear in Roman men's physical appearance. They hindered elite Roman men from dressing down—like women who expended too much care on their looks or like men from the lower classes who did not expend enough care on their looks. At the same time when women's ornate dress was being imbued with notions of feminine and foreign vice, men's dress was equally regulated so as not to undermine the naturalness of these sartorial taxonomies.[111]

Although the image and notion of femininity manufactured in the early Imperial period proved to be a useful means by which to bolster elite male power and prestige, it would later cause problems in the context of early Christian asceticism. In the next chapter, we turn to early Christian sources. Like their pagan predecessors, Christians also used physical appearances as a measure of morality and identity, hoping that the looks of certain Christians might secure honor for their Christian community. In some ways, their interpretations of Christian women's dress followed Roman stereotypes about gender, while in other ways their sartorial prescriptions and interpretations rendered certain women's gender status ambiguous. Thus male Christian leaders, who still desired to maintain a gender hierarchy, would be required to naturalize and materialize gender in new ways.

# 2 Scripting Christians' Clothing and Grooming

> It is necessary, then, that when [the virgin] makes her regal entrance into the marketplace that she appear as the very image of all philosophy and astound everyone (ὥσπερ ἄγαλμα φιλοσοφίας ἁπάσης φαίνεσθαι, καὶ πάντας ἐκπλήττειν), as if she were an angel just now descended from heaven. If one of the cherubim themselves appeared on earth it would attract all men towards itself; so the virgin too ought to throw everyone who sees her into wonder and terror at her holiness (οὕτω καὶ τὴν παρθένον τοὺς ὁρῶντας ἅπαντας εἰς θαῦμα καὶ ἔκπληξιν τῆς ἁγιωσύνης αὐτῆς ἐμβάλλειν δεῖ).
>
> John Chrysostom, *On the Necessity of Guarding Virginity* 7[1]

Although writing decades—sometimes centuries—after the authors discussed in the previous chapter, Christian writers from the second through the fifth centuries adopted the rhetorical stance of their predecessors: they too aimed to demonstrate their superiority in terms of morality. But ascetically inclined Christian moralists raised the bar set by early Imperial writers, competing in the "economy of *sophrosyne*" in innovative ways.[2] They expanded the traditional paradigm of evaluating sexual virtue on a spectrum from moderation to excess. Christian writers extended one end of the spectrum to include higher degrees of restraint and discipline, up to full abstinence. Thus, Christian virginity was framed as a degree of self-mastery beyond pagan *sophrosyne* (*pudicitia*).[3] According to this newly revised model of sexual virtue, they could then impute sexual immorality to their pagan (and sometimes fellow Christian) opponents for activities that in the past would have escaped critique, and indeed might even have been deemed modest.[4]

This move may very well have been a defensive maneuver. The need to rethink the spectrum of sexual virtue was especially urgent as pro-ascetic Christians had come under attack for their ascetic tendencies that were regarded as antisocial and antifamilial. Too stringent a sexual ethic unsettled elite family lines, and thus also the preservation of family names and inheritances that kept a family's wealth intact.[5] Ascetically minded Christians, therefore, needed to find a way to spin the critiques of asceticism to their benefit. By redefining the taxonomy of virtue and by employing the standard language of Roman moral discourse, Christian writers used a culturally conventional rhetoric to legitimate and even extol ascetic behaviors that were viewed by many as countercultural.[6]

In addition to the moralizing rhetoric, Christians also employed the familiar images of early Imperial moralists, now turning them back on the aristocratic Romans who earlier wielded them with such success.[7] Just as Roman writers created notions of difference between Romans and barbarians, as well as between men and women, by pointing to the morality communicated through clothing, so too early Christians argued that their piety was distinctive and visibly perceptible in Christians' dress and physical appearance (especially when juxtaposed with the dress of pagans).[8] Because their success lay in their capacity to create a convincing image of Christianity, Christian writers labored to imbue the dress of Christians with moral and theological significance so that their claims appeared— even on the surface—to be completely natural.[9] There would be no need to discursively assert or defend the group's morality once it became clearly evident—to properly trained viewers—every time they looked upon the dress and physical appearance of Christians. Through strategic semiology, they, in Averil Cameron's words, worked to constitute the "framework within which most people looked at the world and the words that they used to describe it."[10]

But it was not only outsiders whom Christian leaders hoped to persuade. They also needed to convince Christians to present themselves to the public in particular ways.[11] And it seems clear from the extant discussions of Christian dress that this was not an easy task: Christians were not always dressing, and interpreting the significance of their dress, as Christian leaders wished.[12] As we will see below, many Christians were not willing to dress simply as an expression of their Christian identity for fear that other aspects of their identity—namely their social and marital status—might be obscured. Given the resistance they met, Christian leaders employed a range of scriptural, ethical, and theological arguments to convince their audiences of the orthodoxy of their dress prescriptions.

While the dress and grooming of all Christians was carefully scrutinized, we find that the looks of Christian women, and particularly female ascetics, mattered most. These women were made the chief spectacles of Christian ideals. Christian leaders fervently urged Christian women to cast aside ostentatious and expensive garments, accessories, hairdressings, and cosmetics in order to prove—through a humble and modest appearance—that even the lowliest members of the Christian community possessed extraordinary discipline and virtue. This sartorial counsel was ubiquitous in early Christian literature, appearing in the letters, sermons, catechetical lectures, and theological treatises from throughout the Mediterranean world and addressed to Christian women in all stages of life: unmarried, married, widows, and dedicated virgins. Christian matrons, on the one hand, were allowed some latitude to adorn themselves in particular situations (e.g., to attract a husband or to exhibit a family's status at a public event). Female Christian ascetics, on the other hand, were urged to renounce entirely lavish dress, adornments, and cosmetics. The ascetic woman's stark appearance— either a simple, colorless garment or dark mourning clothes—was to be a material demonstration of her religious vow, expressing her commitment to a humble lifestyle, as well as her renunciation of sexual intercourse and her turn from womanly sexual enticement.

Because humility and sexual incorruptibility were visibly imperceptible—the true marks of which lay tucked away in the soul or hidden under clothing—female ascetics were expected to publicize their virtue through their garments and grooming. As ascetics materialized their virtue, they made evident their distinction from other women. As Teresa Shaw observes, "each feature of her image crystallizes the virgin's distinction from 'them': the worldly, the married, the pagan, the heretical."[13] When female ascetics fashioned their dress and physical appearance in a way that corresponded with Christian leaders' significations of them, they served as potent showpieces of Christianity and secured social capital for their Christian communities.[14]

Even while female ascetics were the hallmark of Christian virtue, Christian writers (following their Roman predecessors) aligned immorality with femininity and mapped both onto women's conventional dress. In fact, Christian writers now added biblical and theological rationale to bolster the—now Christianized—association of luxurious apparel and adornments with femininity and vice. Christians intent on demonstrating their women's piety urged their female audiences to forsake forms and accessories of dress that had previously marked them as women. When Christian women, especially ascetics, heeded the advice of their mentors and dressed in ways that properly communicated their Christian humility, modesty, and virtue, they demonstrated their repudiation of feminine vice by renouncing garb typically associated with women and sometimes even adopted the dress of men. In so doing, they destabilized one of the primary ways to read gender identities in antiquity. These new forms of dressing opened the door for crises of gender that will be explored in the next chapter. Yet, I will argue, in most cases such troubles were not as pronounced as they might have been because Christian women's public performance of piety was still feminized in that it was still tied to feminine models of display and feminine strategies of seduction. In fact, it was precisely this hyper-feminized—and hyper-sexualized—performance that helped to garner attention for Christian asceticism, and paradoxically to communicate a message of superior moral discipline. By the end of this chapter, we will see how the female Christian ascetic accorded prestige to her community (in a manner similar to the non-Christian woman who was "dressing" for the men of her household and her city) and how notions of Christian ascetics' gender were reworked and deployed in the process.

## SCRIPTING CHRISTIAN DRESS

Christian writers found frequent occasion to comment on Christians' dress and adornments. In this section, I survey their sartorial prescriptions and interpretations in order to demonstrate the manner and degree to which Christian leaders wished Christians' dress—especially Christian women's dress—to be visible, material expressions of Christian identity. Again, I suggest that through these arguments Christian leaders were attempting to consolidate certain perceptions of Christians' physical appearance in order to achieve two objectives: first, to persuade and motivate Christians to dress in particular ways by convincing them of the orthodoxy of their interpretations of dress and, second, to infuse such appearances with scriptural, ethical, and theological meaning until Christians' physical appearance could ultimately signify the group's superior morality on its own.

First, a caveat: although I am using multiple Christian sources collectively, I do not wish to imply that all of these sources can or should be read in the same way. The authors wrote to different communities across the Mediterranean world (including Asia Minor, North Africa, Rome, Alexandria, and Palestine), addressed different audiences (e.g., men and women, widows, a group of monks, or individual ascetics), spanned different time periods (from the second to fifth centuries), and addressed their specific, local circumstances and issues. We know, for instance, that John Chrysostom's discussions of dress were driven largely by his concerns about the hoarded wealth in his congregations, whereas Clement and Tertullian were interested in shaping a range of public behaviors among the members of his congregation (from dressing, to eating, to engaging in public spectacles) in order to craft a holistic vision of the proper Christian lifestyle. Additionally, I do not wish to imply that there were not differences of opinion among the writers I survey. As I discuss below, for instance, they allowed different degrees of latitude in Christian women's—especially matrons'—use of adornments. Simply put, I do not presume that all Christian writers addressed, prescribed, and interpreted Christian dress in precisely the same way.

In the end, what does unite these authors is the unequivocal agreement that early Christian female ascetics—whether they practice house asceticism or reside in a monastic community—should dress in *distinctively* modest attire, renouncing *all* superfluous ornaments and beautification, as a measure of their religious identity. Moreover, Christian writers regularly employed similar logic and rhetorical strategies. By collecting the sources together, therefore, I hope to demonstrate just how prevalent certain significations of Christian dress were across geographic region and time in order to better understand why the female ascetic was such a ripe symbol for Christian distinction.

In the following sections, I have categorized the types of biblical, ethical, and theological arguments early Christians used to interpret and prescribe Christian dress. Although these classifications are artificial (and Christian writers regularly paired them in order to lend strength to their advice), they helpfully delineate the range of appeals Christian writers used to circumscribe their particular views of Christian identity made manifest through dress.[15]

## Scriptural Precedents and Answering Scripture

From the early years of Christianity, church leaders criticized adornments and embellishments of dress for violating biblical principles. Whereas some biblical passages were easily employed to bolster their sartorial prescriptions, Christian leaders also had to deal with passages that seemed to allow for immoderate displays of dress. Their aim was to interpret all of the passages so that they spoke with a single voice against lavish dress. Only then might they ask their audiences to prove their faithfulness to scriptural reasoning and precedents through a particular manner of dressing and grooming.

Christian leaders found a clear scriptural basis for their sartorial recommendations in the letters of 1 Tim. 2:9–10 (" . . . women should dress themselves modestly and decently in suitable clothing, not with their hair braided, or with gold, pearls, or expensive clothes, but with good works, as is proper for women who profess reverence for God") and 1 Pet. 3:3–4 ("Do not adorn yourselves outwardly by braiding your hair, and by wearing gold ornaments or fine clothing; rather let your adornment be the inner self with the lasting beauty of a gentle and quiet spirit, which is very precious in God's sight"). Considering both letters to be authored by prominent apostles, Clement, Tertullian, and Chrysostom merely appealed to the authors' apostolic authority.[16] Chrysostom, for example, cites the 1 Timothy passage and simply adds: "The words are not mine, but they were spoken by the blessed Paul."[17] In an attempt to endow their counsel with even more influence, Tertullian paired the prescriptions of both Paul and Peter to accumulate a ballast of authoritative support[18] and Clement argued that these were not only the teachings of the apostles, but they originated from their teacher, Christ.[19]

The original scriptural instructions, though, were directed presumably at Christian *wives*. Although the γυνή in both passages could be read either as "woman" or "wife," in 1 Peter the γυνή is opposed to ἀνήρ, making "wife" the most plausible interpretation.[20] While the passages could be applied seamlessly to contemporary Christian matrons, how might they also address female ascetics? Cyprian employed an *argumentum a fortiori*, asking, if married Christian women, who have a legitimate excuse for dressing to attract their husbands, must heed this scriptural advice to renounce adornments, *how much more* should virgins who have no need to attract a spouse dress modestly?[21]

Although we might expect Christian writers to rely chiefly on the above scriptural precedents as they counseled Christian women to fashion appropriate looks, they appealed to other biblical characters and narratives as well, employing inventive exegesis.[22] Cyprian, for instance, argues for ascetics' complete renunciation of alluring adornments from his reading of Gal. 1:10: "If I were still *pleasing men* (ἀνθρώπους πείθω), I would not be a servant of Christ." Cyprian reads ἄνθρωπος not in the general sense of "humanity," but in exclusively masculine terms. He furthermore introduces a sexual edge to the interpretation of πείθω. Thus, the passage is no longer about Paul's reluctance to seek the approval of other humans, but is now read as a model directive for female ascetics: they ought to refuse to appear *sexually appealing* to the *"male sex"* in order to be a servant of Christ.[23]

When counseling Christian men and women, Clement looks to scripture to distinguish between essential and inessential aspects of dress. According to Clement's reading of Luke 12:22 ("He said to his disciples, 'Therefore I tell you, do not worry about your life, what you will eat, or about your body, what you will wear' "), Jesus directed Christians to be inattentive to the very necessities of life. How much more, he asks, should they be unmindful of superfluous adornments?

> Now, if Christ forbids solicitude once and for all about clothing and food and luxuries, as things that are unnecessary, do we need to ask him about finery and dyed wools and multicolored robes, about exotic ornaments of jewels and artistic handiwork of gold, about wigs and artificial locks of hair and of curls, and about eye-shadows and hair-plucking and rouges and powders and hair-dyes and all the other disreputable trades that practice these deceptions? Are we not reasonable in concluding that what he says about the grass is to be applied also to this disgraceful ostentation?[24]

Clement then pairs this Lukan passage with Paul's aphorism, "All things are lawful, but not all things are expedient," to lend even more scriptural resistance to overly showy forms of dress.[25]

Speaking specifically to women (although we might assume, given the gender of his examples, that Christian men were meant to heed this warning as well) who were caught up in appearances "like silly children," Clement reminds his readers of several biblical protagonists who ought to serve as models of unattractiveness. Clement prompts his readers to recall that the prophet Samuel did not choose Jesse's oldest and most handsome son to be king of Israel, but selected rather the youngest and least attractive child in the family.[26] According to Clement, this clearly proves that neither Samuel nor God placed value in good looks and that God even *opted* for the ugly.[27] Clement finds an even more influential model of unattractiveness in Jesus. He notes that, according to Isaiah's prophecy, Jesus was supremely unattractive. "The Spirit gives witness through Isaiah that even the Lord became an unsightly spectacle: 'And we saw him, and there was no beauty or comeliness in him, but his form was despised, and abject among men.' "[28] Jesus's beauty, rather, laid exclusively in his good deeds and the splendor of his body in its immortality. Clement, therefore, advises his readers to follow the lead of these exemplars of unattractiveness in abandoning beauty products, ornate dress, and adornments.

Other Christians bent biblical passages to fit their anti-adornment agenda through the translation of nebulous phrases. For example, readers could choose between two credible translations of the Sermon on the Mount teaching recorded in Matt. 6:27 (Τίς δὲ ἐξ ὑμῶν μεριμνῶν δύναται προσθεῖαι ἐπὶ τὴν ἡλικίαν αὐτοῦ πῆχυν ἕνα): "And can any of you by worrying add a single *hour to the span of your life?*" or "And can any of you by worrying add a single *cubit to your height?*" When discussing which sorts of hairdressings are suitable for Christian women, Tertullian employs the latter translation.[29]

> Some women prefer to tie up [their hair] in little curls . . . some of you affix to your heads I know not what monstrosities of sewn and women wigs . . . [in] open defiance of the Lord's precepts, one of which declares that no one can add anything to his/her stature (*ad mensuram neminem sibi adicere posse pronuntiatum est*). Yet you do add something to your weight by piling some kind of rolls or shield-bosses upon your necks![30]

This translation choice allows Tertullian to warn his readers not to be overly desirous for (i.e., "worried" about) hairstyles that heap masses of hair atop their heads (thus adding height) because such hair dressings were clearly forbidden by Jesus himself.

Christian writers also recontextualized scripture by citing only a portion of a text to lend support to their sartorial prescription. Tertullian and Cyprian, for instance, decontextualized Matt. 5:36's statement about oaths ("And do not swear by your head, for you cannot make one hair white or black") by citing only the second half of the verse, asking: "Which of you can make a white hair black, or a black hair white?"[31] This selective citation allowed them to use the verse as a condemnation of hair dying. If humans should not turn their hair white or black, Tertullian asks, how much more insubordinate are the women who dye their hair *blonde*?[32]

Just as Christian writers found support in biblical passages, they also had to deal with troublesome passages that might undercut their dress prescriptions. Christian exegetes found ingenious ways to turn challenging texts—texts that could be used by Christians who wished to justify their lavish garments and adornments—into warnings against such dress practices. Clement, for instance, found it necessary to address Jesus's approval of the woman who anointed him with a costly ointment (Luke 7:36–50), fearing that Christian readers—male and female alike—might conflate Jesus's endorsement of the woman with an endorsement of perfumes or crowns. Clement points to the chronology of the event as described in Luke's gospel and argues that the "sinful woman" made the offering at Jesus's feet while "she was still a sinner"; *as a sinner*, "she paid the Master honor with what she considered the most precious thing she had, her perfume."[33] Clement concludes that this is an example of inappropriate gift-giving and, thus, that her use of perfume should not be a model for Christian men and women who wish to wear fragrant perfumes and wreathes.

How were Christians to read the story of Esther, in which the Queen's beautification saved the defenseless Israelites from King Ahasuerus (Esth. 1:1–2:17)? When interpreting this narrative, Clement spotlights Esther's godly objectives: throughout the story, Esther is intent on safeguarding her people from mortal danger. She is willing to do anything necessary in order to ensure their security. For Clement, Esther's transgression—her immoderate use of cosmetics and adornments, as well as the strategic use of her sexual allure[34]—was not an example to be followed by all women at all times, but rather was a permissible concession given her extraordinary circumstances. Clement then contrasts Esther's virtuous objectives with the less-virtuous beautification of another royal lady: Helen. Helen's beautification, which aimed only at self-gratification, led not to the deliverance of a people, but rather to disorder, divisions, and death. From a close reading and intertextual appeal, Clement thus precludes his readers from following Esther's example because they are not in a position to adorn themselves for virtuous spiritual purposes, like Esther; they, like Helen, aim only to indulge their vanity, greed, and desire.[35]

Christian writers also had to address the biblical vision of heaven, resplendent in rich ornamentation. How were they to dissuade their followers from wearing jewels and gold when they read in the Apocalypse of John that the walls of heavenly Jerusalem would be decorated with such items (Rev. 21:18–21)? They used figurative exegesis to soften scriptural passages that, in their opinion, placed too much value on ornamental luxury goods. For example, Clement argues that the gold, gems, and jewels of heaven are merely metaphors: "[b]y the incomparable brilliance of gems is understood the spotless and holy brilliance of the substance of the spirit."[36] Only "ignorant" Christians would interpret such descriptions *literally*.[37]

Finally, Christians had to respond to loose interpretations of even the more straightforward proscriptions found in 1 Tim. 2:9–10 and 1 Pet. 3:3–4. For instance, some members of Chrysostom's congregation, after reading Paul's ban against gold, pearls, and costly apparel, wondered *which* materials should count as "costly apparel." Might they continue to wear silk because this fabric is not *as* expensive as gold? Here, Chrysostom attempts to force a very literal interpretation of these passages by pairing them with an intertext, 1 Tim. 6:8 ("having food and clothing, let us be content") in order to argue that Paul permitted *only* simple clothing.[38] When dealing with these troubling passages, Christian leaders utilized close reading techniques, intertexts that constrained the reading of difficult texts, and either figurative or literal interpretations as their argument required to accumulate scriptural support for their sartorial prescriptions.

# Dressing Ethically

In addition to the above arguments from scripture, Christian writers also employed ethical arguments to discipline and signify Christians' dress and grooming. The piety required of a Christian, they argued, should be manifested in and shaped by Christians' simple and modest dress. Conversely, overly fastidious beautification was linked to a range of commonly accepted sins, such as contempt for creation, lying, pride, idolatry, improper use of wealth, and sexual depravity, more characteristic of pagans' indulgence and immorality than of Christians' unique character and virtue. By linking particular forms of dressing to preconceived notions of virtue and vice, and by juxtaposing the ways in which virtue and vice were embodied in the dress of Christians and pagans, Christians writers further motivated their audiences to obey their counsel, and signified the pious Christian look.

## *Lying, Pride, and Sins Against Creation*

Christians, like their pagan neighbors, similarly objected to the foreignness of adornments, though not only because ornamental goods were imported from abroad, but also because they were alien to God's created order. Christian writers who considered human bodies to be the created work of God argued that God's creation did not need additional accessories to be beautiful. In fact, those who modified the handiwork and artistry of God were charged with lying.[39] Tertullian, for example, claimed that "to wear a fictitious face" covered in cosmetics and jewelry was "to lie in your appearance."[40] Cyprian too rebukes women who changed the hair color God gave them, corrupting what was natural and true "into a lie by deceitful dyes."[41] Clement adds: "What must [God] think of artificial beautification when he abhors so thoroughly every sort of lie?"[42] Women who re-created their own images were also liable to the charge of arrogance or pride. By redoing the work of the Creator, Christian writers argued, these women considered their own artistic ability to surpass even God's[43] or implied that they blamed God for not "giv[ing] them the beauty they deserve."[44]

The distortion of creation need not be linked to the sins of lying and pride to carry weight. Adorned Christian women were criticized simply for interfering with the natural order when they concealed, enhanced, or altered creation. Whether adorned Christian women used dress, gems, and cosmetics to cover over a naturally attractive or unattractive form, they could be charged with obscuring God's intended creation. Clement writes:

> Either a woman is already beautiful, and then nature is sufficient (and let art not contend with nature, that is, let deception not vie with the truth), or else she is naturally ugly, and then she proves what she does not have [according to nature] by attiring herself with all these things.[45]

Christian women should neither "overshadow" God's attractive handiwork with gold[46] nor paint over it with cosmetics,[47] nor should they deceive their viewers by concealing "natural" deformities with "artificial" beauty aids. Any such addition shrouds the "image and likeness" of God instilled at the time of creation.[48]

Adornments and beautification were criticized not only for concealing God's creation, but also for distorting the proper order and use of creation. Clement and John Chrysostom disparage women who pierce their ears and create a hole that nature (i.e., God) had not intended.[49] Additionally, women who dyed wool so that their garments might be colorful skewed God's original color palette. Had God intended sheep to be blue or purple, Tertullian contends, God would have made them so at the time of creation. In fact, if these vibrant colors were not the intention of God, they must be the work of God's opponent and adorned women might rightly be called Satan's accomplices.[50] Clement additionally claims that humans' use of plants and flowers for dyes and crowns distorts the enjoyment of these items as originally intended by God: when Christians pluck flowers from the ground and place them in crowns atop their heads, they "destroy the pleasure" of God's creation because the flowers will immediately begin to wither and because humans can no longer admire the flowers that are out of their sight, nor smell the fragrances that are above their noses.[51]

Christians were criticized for further transgressing the natural limits set by creation when they cultivated and imported materials used for ornamentation. Tertullian, for instance, argues that at the moment of creation God intentionally distributed gold, silver, and gems throughout the earth so that they might be abundant in some regions—where God foreknew the community would rightly use them without becoming overly attached— and scarce in others. Tertullian concludes that Christians who seek to possess foreign objects not found in their own region are therefore guilty of overstepping God's deliberately imposed boundaries.[52] Clement similarly claimed that God organized creation so that all humans might have ready access to the items they most needed for sustenance, while God removed superfluous goods to the remotest reaches of the earth. For this reason, water, air, and food are readily available, whereas gold, pearls, and gems are hidden in the depths of the earth and sea. Christians who trouble themselves with recovering items they do not need, Clement argues, are thus "completely ignorant of the will of God."[53]

Finally, Tertullian and Jerome claim that older Christian women who adorn themselves act counter to God's deliberate ordering of the human life span. Although God planned for human creatures to be physically attractive at the beginning of their lives, at the time when they are ripe for procreation and thus need to attract a suitor, God intended for human beauty to decline naturally at the end of one's life, when beauty no longer provides a necessary reproductive function. Women who adorn themselves into old age, refurbishing the natural beauty that had long since faded, are charged with disrupting God's purposeful plan of human aging.[54]

## Idolatry

Christians argued that those who adorned and beautified themselves, thus creating an "image" of themselves, participated in a form of image worship.[55] They picked up pagan critiques of women's artificial beauty to serve their comparison of adornment with idolatry. For instance, adorned Christian women and men, Clement alleges, participate in image worship "in the true sense of the word" because they turn "to *imitation* beauty, *artificial* ornamentation, [rather] than to Beauty itself."[56] After Clement deems the adorned woman an image worshipper, he also vividly likens her to the pagan temple itself. Just as pagan temples are luxuriously ornamented on the exterior, with lavish gardens and sacred groves, vestibules surrounded by huge columns, and filled with gems, paintings, and richly embroidered veils that cover the inner sanctuary, so too adorned women lavishly cultivate their exterior appearance. But when one peeks past the veil into the interior of the temple, one is shocked to find not the magnanimous God one might expect, but rather a cat, crocodile, or snake that is "suited for life in a cave or den or in the mud, but certainly not in a temple."[57] Likewise with the adorned woman,

> If anyone draw back the veil of this temple—I mean the hairnet and the dye and the garments and gold and rouge and cosmetics or the cloth woven of all these things, which is a veil—if he draws back this veil to discover the true beauty that is within, I am sure he will be disgusted. He will not find dwelling within any worthy image of God, but, instead, a harlot and adulteress who has usurped the inner sanctuary of the soul. The beauty within will turn out to be nothing more than a beast . . . a deceitful serpent, it will devour [the wo]man's intellect with love of ornaments and make the soul its den. Filling the whole soul with its deadly drug and vomiting out the poison of its deception, this serpent-seducer has transformed women into harlots.[58]

To further reinforce this point, Christian writers regularly noted that the materials used for women's adornments doubled as the supplies of idolatry. Clement and Tertullian, for instance, reminded their readers that the golden calf was constructed from women's gold jewelry, "provid[ing] our women a striking lesson on the advantage of laying ornaments aside."[59] Clement further warns Christians not to wear crowns of flowers on their heads, not only because they disrupt the proper enjoyment of God's creation, but also because of their close association with idol sacrifice and worship.[60] Tertullian concludes that because women feel particularly compelled to dress up when attending temples or public shows and because Christian women never need to attend these spectacles because of the idolatry complicit with them, they are never required to dress and adorn themselves like their pagan neighbors.[61]

## Undermining Sacraments, Blessings, and Salvation

John Chrysostom, Clement, Jerome, and Cyprian additionally expressed concern that adornments hindered the efficacy of certain Christian sacraments or blessings. For instance, Chrysostom protests that lipsticked mouths partaking of the Eucharist threaten to defile the sacrament (as much as vile, gossiping, and perjuring mouths).[62] Clement warns that women wearing wigs or hair extensions might not receive a priest's or bishop's blessing (i.e., the laying on of hands); rather, his blessing might consecrate the woman whose hair she wears.[63] Finally, Jerome and Cyprian argue, God might not be able to recognize a Christian woman "masked" with cosmetics.[64] In fact, her disguise will be ruinous on the day of judgment when God will pass by the adorned woman, saying,

'This work is not mine nor is this our image.' You have defiled your skin with lying cosmetics; you have changed your hair with an adulterous (*adultero*[65]) color; your face is overcome by falsehoods; your appearance is corrupted; your countenance is that of another. You cannot see God since your eyes are not those which God has made, but which the devil has infected. Him you have followed; the red and painted eyes of the serpent have you imitated; adorned like your enemy, with him you shall likewise burn.[66]

## Improper Use of Wealth and Almsgiving

Certain Christian leaders were concerned with the fact that immense expenditures on adornments detracted from Christians' ability to care for the poor. The problem of luxurious dress and ornamentation was singled out as a particularly critical issue for Christian leaders of urban areas, where plentiful wealth existed alongside crippling poverty. John Chrysostom was one of the most vocal opponents of excessive expenditures on dress and adornments. He addressed the topic in many of his sermons and writings in both Antioch and Constantinople.[67] At times he juxtaposes the good Christian's dress with that of immoderate pagans. More frequently, though, Chrysostom compares the dress of the rustics with that of his congregation in order to shame the latter into submission. For instance, on one occasion in 387 when his Antiochene church hosted rural visitors, Chrysostom argued that although these visitors might not possess a sophisticated understanding of Christian doctrine (like the Antiochene philosophers), their simple mode of life proved that they had a firm grasp on the essence of Christianity: the rustics lived lives of labor and simplicity, knowing nothing of Antioch's decadence or idleness, and "amongst them, there is not one woman who wears showy dress; there are no ornaments of dress, nor who colors or paints (herself) . . . there are no fragrant perfumes to stimulate the senses."[68]

Many of these church leaders who decried the amount of money wasted on ornamentation endorsed some vision of communal living. While they were aware that most laypeople were unwilling to pool their resources, they nonetheless appealed to their sense of responsibility for their Christian neighbors' fiscal well-being. Clement, for example, insisted that in earthly Christian communities (modeled on the heavenly community) "everything is common, and the rich should not grasp a greater share."[69] Women who hoarded their wealth, spending it on expensive adornments, therefore, prevented the even distribution of God's goods to all of humanity.[70] John Chrysostom goes even further, accusing the wealthy who spend lavishly on dress and ornamentation of stealing the poor's proper share, and of "squeez[ing] the bellies of the poor."[71] He holds spendthrifts wholly responsible for the lowly state of the poor because their spending on "cosmetic items" curtails their "giving of charity" and the proper redistribution of wealth among the members of the Christian community. Chrysostom further scolds the wealthy of his congregation who "encircle their slaves and mules and horses with gold necklaces, and disregard the Lord was he goes about naked" in the form of the poor and needy (following Matt. 25:35–36).[72]

These Christians, Chrysostom urges, must heed the warning of the prophet Isaiah, who demonstrated that "captivity, slavery, and terrible troubles awaited the Jews because of their [spending on] ornamentation," blaming the Babylonian captivity on Jews' inability to properly manage their wealth and tend to the poor in their communities.[73] The same punishment awaits Christians who continue to spend money on luxurious clothing and ornaments rather than giving charitable alms.[74] To avoid such retribution, Chrysostom, Ambrose, and Clement urge their readers to sell superfluous adornments and give the proceeds to the poor, heeding Jesus's numerous exhortations to care for the poor, as well as the general rubric to "love one's neighbor."[75]

Sizable expenditures on adornments were also criticized on the grounds of poor household management (based on recycled charges from the early Imperial period). Wives especially were reprimanded for spending the household's money unwisely. Not only do adorned women squander their husbands' money, but they also neglect their household duties, avoiding chores that might dishevel the appearances they worked so hard to cultivate. Moreover, they were charged with wasting the time of household servants, who were constantly engaged in arranging and maintaining their beauty.[76]

A final economic argument comes from Clement, who acerbically declares that many women wear adornments that hold more value than the woman herself. If the adorned woman, he argues, were to "sell her body" she would receive far less than she paid for her clothing and ornaments. Decadent dress and grooming, Clement concludes, do not elevate a woman's status, but rather proves "that [women] are less valuable and profitable than their clothes." [77] Clement thus advises women to renounce clothing and ornaments that highlight their insignificance and rather dress in ways that demonstrates their worth (i.e., their virtue and piety).[78]

## Sexual Sins

Christian writers seemed most concerned about ornate dress and adornments because of their association with indecent sexual desires and behaviors. Christian leaders regularly attempted to curb Christian women's use of adornments by charging adorned women with a range of sexual transgressions. In fact, the adorned Christian woman need only *appear* to be sexually promiscuous to be held responsible for sexual impropriety. Christian writers argued that a woman's garb alone could indicate her sexual inclinations if not also her sexual conduct. Clement writes, "Just as smoke indicates fire, [and] a good complexion and pulse [indicate] good health, so also, with us, such garments makes evident the bent of our character."[79] Tertullian further reminds his readers that it was by appearance alone that Judah deemed Tamar to be a prostitute.[80] If one's garb "preannounces" one's character, Tertullian concludes, adorned Christian women are broadcasting themselves as harlots and could rightly be charged with sexual sin.[81]

Christian women's sexual propensities—as expressed in their choice of dress—were frequently interpreted relative to the dress and sexual sins of other women. As part of a shaming strategy, Christian writers likened adorned Christian women to their allegedly immoral non-Christian neighbors who paraded about at the theater, games, and other places of spectacle.[82] Clement criticized the adorned Christian women who likewise displayed themselves in public—even in the sacred places—so that "they might give everyone ample opportunity to look at them."[83] If adorned Christian women fashioned their appearance to attract attention like pagan women and especially like prostitutes, then they also could be accused of sharing these women's propensity for licentious sexual behavior.[84]

Although adorned Christian women might not have committed acts of fornication, they were not, however, excused from culpability for leading their "brothers" into temptation and sin. Through skillful intertextual exegesis, Christian writers accused adorned Christian women of violating the tenets of scripture that warned against being a "stumbling block."[85] Although the scriptural "stumbling block" lessons specifically addressed dietary regulations (claiming that although Christians are free to eat meat sacrificed to idols, they should abstain from this dietary practice so as not to confuse new converts or weak members of the community), Christian opponents of lavish dress found the general principle against tempting the weak useful.

In fact, they paired the "stumbling block" passages with Jesus's stringent interpretation of adultery (Matt. 5:27–28), which deemed guilty even those who experienced lust in the mind, in order to implicate adorned women in the mental, sexual transgressions of their viewers. Tertullian, for instance, accuses the adorned woman of seducing the man who sees her: he "perishes as soon as he looks upon your beauty with desire, and he has already committed in his soul what he desires."[86] Chrysostom describes the seemingly irresistible lure of adorned women's visual seduction as highly intentional. With gazes, gaits, and perfumed bodies, he argues, adorned women "launch their engines of war from all sides against the onlookers, exerting force to thrust themselves into the indecorum of prostitutes."[87] Even if she never engaged in a physical act of intercourse, Chrysostom argues that she will be punished for the lust that she incited in her onlooker: "That man's madness is your work. It is plain to anyone anywhere that the woman who *makes* a man an adulterer can never escape the punishment for adultery."[88]

Tertullian does not stop at blaming adorned women for arousing lust in spectators, but actually accuses adorned women of participating in a sort of visual copulation. Tertullian describes the adorned woman being "tickled" by pointing fingers and "penetrated" by her onlookers' eyes, while a "warmth creeps over her amid [the visual] embraces and kisses" until finally her "forehead hardens" in orgasmic pleasure.[89] Clement also concluded that individuals could commit "adultery with the eyes, since lust operates at a distance through [the eyes]."[90] Because ancient notions of vision understood the eyes to emanate particles that bounced off seen objects, the acts of seeing and being seen were perceived to involve a high degree of physical contact.[91] Thus, Tertullian's and Clement's depiction of lustful seeing and being seen as physical acts is perfectly comprehensible.

The adorned Christian woman is charged not only with stimulating lust, but also with experiencing lust in such situations. Tertullian eroticizes the process of crafting and donning adornments as he describes women "slowly rubbing" stones and gems so that they might shine and "carefully piercing" their ears in order to affix jewels.[92] Both Clement and Tertullian further characterize feminine lust as the woman's desire to "be seen." In other words, female lust is not only defined in terms of a woman's own stimulation, but also that a woman is herself stimulated by her ability to stimulate her spectators. Accessories such as jewelry, gold, and cosmetics, then, are regarded as "supplies of women's lusts" because they aid her in "being seen."[93]

So closely connected were adornments to the arousal of lust that Jerome concludes that an unadorned or poorly dressed woman has the power to quash lust.[94] The biblical story of Judith and Holofernes provides proof of this claim (Jdt. 12–13). Jerome interprets Judith's mean dress (sackcloth and widow's garments) as a symbol of chastity: her "outward squalor indicated not so much the regret which she felt for her dead husband as the temper in which she looked forward to the coming of the Bridegroom."[95] As Judith (through her clothing) stands for chastity, Holofernes stands for lust. Thus Jerome interprets Judith's slaying of Holofernes as the vanquishing of lust by chastity: "Here a woman conquers men, and chastity beheads lust."[96]

With arguments such as these, Christian leaders hoped to align their prescriptions for humble and simple dress with an orthodox reading of scripture and the virtue expected of a Christian lifestyle. They constructed an image of the Christian piety that could only be made manifest in Christians' simple and humble attire. Those who wore lavish clothing and adornments were compared with debaucherous and licentious pagans and they were warned that they would lose out on the blessings of Christian sacraments and salvation.

## RESISTANCE AND ALLOWANCES

As Christian leaders strenuously advocated simple and modest dress, we sense that they encountered resistance from their audiences. The most resistance seems to have come from wealthy, aristocratic Christians who wished to demonstrate their standing in the social hierarchy through conventional displays of social status in their dressing and grooming. As Chrysostom's need to continually repeat his exhortations makes clear, there were Christians who saw no inconsistency between lavish dress and Christian identity. In fact, Clement addressed just such a group who expressed concern that if they abandoned their extravagant attire, they would become indistinguishable from their servants. Clement urges these wealthy Christians to declare their elite status through their composure, carriage, and refined gait rather than through decadent apparel.[97] Clement wished to convince them that this was the only way for a noble Christian to display his or her familial status and Christian identity in the same look.

We see that Christian leaders did not wish to dismiss the distinctive function of dress altogether. In fact, they appealed to aristocratic Christians' desire to exhibit their distinction by asking them to demonstrate degrees of self-mastery and decorum that went beyond the mere moderation expected of other aristocrats, noble pagans. Furthermore, as I will describe in detail below, they rewarded Christians who heeded their advice with public rites and acclaims of praise, which drew attention and notoriety to those who now renounced decadent aspects of dress. In these ways, Christians aimed to reorient Christians' (and non-Christian spectators') appraisal of status markers, elevating displays of virtue over displays of wealth, and to distinguish social standing through other modes of discursive and ritualized displays.

Allowances, though, were sometimes made for Christians who showed some need to don more ornate garb than the ordinary Christian. In order to determine who might require concessions, Christian leaders devised a utility principle meant to guide Christians' clothing choices. They plotted the functions of clothing on a continuum, prioritizing some (e.g., protection) over others (e.g., sexual attraction, desire for novel goods).[98] Christian writers often argued that clothing was principally designed for covering or protective purposes.[99] For Clement, clothing was intended to defend against the elements (e.g., heat and cold, wind and rain),[100] while Chrysostom, recalling God's act of clothing Adam and Eve in the garden, found clothing to be most useful for protecting against the immodest exposure of nakedness.[101]

Although protection of some sort was the chief godly use of clothing, some writers thought that there were other justifiable uses for more elaborate clothing and accessories. For instance, Tertullian allows that there were legitimate times when men of status needed to dress up to communicate their occupation.[102] Perfumes and unguents, Clement adds, could sometimes be used for medical purposes[103] and rings could be worn (by women as well as men) to seal documents.[104] Using clothing and adornments for the purpose of attracting attention and stimulating spectators' desire, however, was a far more contentious matter. Some Christian writers allowed matrons a modicum of adornments in order to secure and maintain the affection of their husbands *in private*.[105] With 1 Cor. 7:33–34 in mind ("the married man is anxious about the affairs of the world, how to please his wife . . . the married woman is anxious about the affairs of the world, how to please her husband"), Augustine grants that scripture provides a concession for Christian couples to appear visually pleasing to their partners. Augustine is quick to make two qualifications: first, scripture does not encourage the use of adornments, but merely tolerates the practice within the bond of marriage; and second, adornments are to be used for attracting only one's spouse.[106] In fact, although at times the use of adornments could be a "distraction" within marriage, Augustine characterizes the concern to remain attractive to one's spouse as the very essence of "conjugal conduct."[107] In the case of mixed marriages, Augustine permits even more freedom. Following Paul's instructions, again in 1 Cor. 7, Augustine urges the Christian spouse not only to remain married, but even to consider how best to be "pleasing" to his or her partner for the sake of Christian conversion.[108] Even when Christian leaders permitted the use of adornments for marital love, however, they required matrons to keep these dress practices private. If the Christian matron dressed up outside of the household, she would prove her ill intention to please others besides her husband.

Other Christian leaders were less enthusiastic about recommending adornments to Christian matrons. Attracting attention, they argued, was completely useless for Christian women, who were barred from becoming spectacles of desire. Only harlots and actresses, they argued, had any need for alluring garb.[109] When certain Christian matrons expressed fear that their husbands might revile them if they remained unadorned, Tertullian,

Ambrose, and Chrysostom maintained that adornments would only work against their desire to secure their husbands' affection and these writers suggested alternate ways to appear "pleasing" to their men.[110] They argued that adornments do not make Christian matrons more attractive, but conversely produce anxiety in husbands. They ask: How can a husband find pleasure in ornaments that deplete his wealth? Instead, decadent dress and adornments are constant reminders of his wife's wasteful expenditures and make him anxious for the fiscal well-being of the household.[111] Moreover, they stir up his envy and jealousy as he wonders if her good looks are meant for him or for another man. In Chrysostom's words, a wife's use of adornments and cosmetics will only "plunge [your husband] into jealousy, hatefulness, contentiousness, and strife, for nothing is more odious than a suspicious face."[112]

Moreover, if the Christian matron chooses to adorn herself with elaborate hairdressings, gold, gems, and cosmetics, Chrysostom, Ambrose, and Clement warn, she will have to compete with other adorned women who would surely outrival her: harlots and prostitutes. Because the Christian matrons will never be able to win in the sport of seduction against a professional seductress, they are better off changing the rules of the game. They ought rather to teach their husband to be attracted to virtuous behavior, such as good manners and modesty, which they possess in greater measure than harlots.[113] Rather than wearing precious jewels, they should put on "that holy stone, the Word of God (called somewhere in Scripture, 'a pearl')."[114] And rather than donning ostentatious clothing, they should adopt only modesty[115] and adorn their mind and body with "the holy garment of self-control."[116] The wife adorned in Christian virtue will draw her husband to her "more strongly than any bond,"[117] Chrysostom adds, because the beauty of virtue is far more enduring that good looks that fade with sickness and age.[118] In fact, Chrysostom claims, a wife who shows no need or regard for her husband is most desirous. Thus, by ceasing to request costly adornments and even spurning her husband's voluntary gifts, his interest in her will be piqued.[119]

At times Christian leaders allowed their audiences to don extravagant garments and adornments as expressions of their social or marital status, but they did so in ways that would not ultimately undermine the public performance of their Christian identity. When they allowed Christian matrons the use of adornments for the purposes of securing their husbands' affections, they exhorted them to don such items only in private. Although they admitted that there might be appropriate times for upper-class Christians to adopt more lavish forms of dress and adornment in public, they urged them to consider displays of virtue to be more valuable indicators of status than displays of wealth. If their audiences heeded their advice, the result would be that Christians would present a somewhat uniform—simple and discreet—style of dressing in public that would confirm claims of Christians' extraordinary virtue and piety.

## THE FEMALE CHRISTIAN ASCETIC

### Performing Status

Even though all Christians were meant to display Christianity's status through their physical appearance, the female Christian ascetic was upheld as the paradigmatic emblem of Christian morality. Why? Whereas allowances might be made for other lay Christians, female ascetics alone had no plausible reason for requiring any superfluous garments or adornments. They could be held to a higher standard and they could be set apart, Christian leaders argued, by remaining wholly unadorned, dirty, and clad in humble, modest garb. Thus, their distinctive looks alone could materialize the *full range* of Christian virtues and piety.

In accordance with ancient notions of vision, Christian writers hoped that the image of female ascetics would *project* and *impress* the extraordinary virtue of Christianity into the minds of spectators. Tertullian, for instance, writes that an ascetic's chastity ought to "flow out from [her] mind to the garb, and burst out from [her] conscience to [her] outward appearance, so that from the outside" it may be examined.[120] Indeed, Christian leaders demanded that ascetics' virtue be made visible in order that "no one on seeing a virgin should doubt as to whether she is one."[121] Tertullian concurs: "It is not enough for Christian modesty merely to be so, but [it must] *seem* so, too."[122] Gregory of Nyssa calls for a "holy appearance of virginity"[123] and Jerome extols the "conspicuous chastity" of Christian ascetics.[124] Ascetics' appearance should not only be distinct, but it also ought to shock and startle spectators as illustrated by the passage that opened this chapter and in Cyprian's description of virgins: "They are the flower of the tree that is the Church, the beauty and adornment of spiritual grace, the image of God reflecting the holiness of the Lord, the more illustrious part of Christ's flock."[125]

Because Christian leaders wished to use female ascetics as symbols of Christian piety, it was imperative to carefully monitor and constrain their dress and physical appearance. Ascetics were continually urged to exert fastidious care to their appearance, an appearance that paradoxically was to communicate neglect and disinterest.[126] They were to express their disinterest in feminine trappings, by extension proving their renunciation of feminine vice. Those who chose to adorn and beautify themselves were regularly construed to be lacking the virtue and fortitude required of their vow. Christian writers, like Tertullian, argued that virginal status is not merely about the "integrity of the flesh and the avoidance of actual fornication."[127] True virginity is defined both by its "essence," physical intactness, as well as by its "accessories," the appearance of modesty.[128] Virgins who adorned themselves with cosmetics, therefore, failed to achieve virginity in its fullness and thus violated their vows. The Christian ascetic ought to guard against incomplete modesty and strive toward "perfect modesty" following

Matthew's exhortation: "Be perfect as your heavenly father is perfect."[129] Writing to his sister, Pelagius too argued for a definition of virginity that took into account appearance.[130] Because the body is the union of all its members, he claimed, when one part transgresses, the entirety is made impure. Thus, although a woman might be physically pure in her "lower parts," if her head becomes impure with the pollution of cosmetics, her neck with the adornment of gold or gems, or her shoulders by the decoration of her hair, she did not live up to the wholly pure state of a virgin.[131] By linking the definition of virginity to certain looks, these Christian leaders limited an acceptable set of ascetic appearances, creating the impression that such appearances arose naturally from the Christian discipline of asceticism.

Such appearances, though, were noticeable and noteworthy only when an ascetic's renunciation of adornments, status, wealth, and feminine vice was clear. In other words, she must appear to be not simply a poor or mourning woman, but a woman who *voluntarily chose to appear* this way. Chrysostom, for instance, argues that the elite Christian woman who dons simple garb can be a far greater spectacle than her richly adorned neighbors. If she followed the traditional dress habits of women of her status, she would blend into the crowd, but when she strays from the traditionally elite look, all eyes are drawn to her. He writes,

> Even if you wish to receive glory from men, you will not obtain it [by wearing gold, pearls, and costly adornments]. We do not marvel as much at the wife of a rich man who wears gold and silk (for this is the common practice of them all) as when she is dressed in a plain and simple garment made merely of wool. This all will admire. This they will applaud. For, indeed, by adorning herself in ornaments of gold and in costly apparel, she has many to share with her. And if she surpasses one, she is surpassed by another. Yet even if she surpasses all, she must yield to the Empress herself. But in the case of the unadorned and simply attired woman, she outdoes them all, even the Emperor's wife herself. *For she alone in wealth, has chosen the [dress] of the poor. So even if we love glory, in this one the glory is greater.*[132]

For Chrysostom, the woman who has access to luxury goods and yet voluntarily chooses to dress in humble garb will be remembered more often and with more honor than a richly adorned empress, becoming a powerful spectacle for the virtue of the church.[133] It is her deviation from custom that garners attention and enables Christian writers to profitably use her differently dressed bodies as a symbol of Christian distinction.

To simultaneously perform elite status and voluntary renunciation in one's appearance, however, was tricky, as illustrated by an anecdote from Palladius's *Lausiac History*. When Melania was harassed by the consul of Palestine, who did not know her familial pedigree, she sharply replied:

I am so-and-so's daughter and so-and-so's wife. I am Christ's slave. Pray do not look down upon my shabby clothes, *for I could make more of myself if I would.* I have made [my status] clear to you so that you may not fall under legal charges without knowing the reason.[134]

Although she competently performed her identity as "Christ's slave" through her "shabby clothes," Melania had to declare her elite status in words because it was not as easily discernable from her appearance.[135] As we might expect, it was far easier to describe voluntary renunciations of elite status in written works on female ascetics. See, for example, the *Life of Macrina*, in which Gregory clearly sets apart Macrina and Emmelia as noble ladies despite the fact that they abolished all visible distinctions of status between themselves and the household servants.[136]

Perhaps because of the difficulty of reading renounced status from one's appearance, Jerome, Augustine, and Tertullian urged female ascetics not to appear too dirty. Jerome advised young Eustochium, "Let your dress be neither too neat nor too slovenly,"[137] and Augustine urges the ascetics in his late sister's monastery, do not "go out of the monastery with your hair either too carelessly neglected or too meticulously arranged."[138] Although ostensibly the issue at hand in these texts is to keep ascetics from taking too much pride in their appearance, it is clear that an overly unkempt appearance would have made it difficult to recognize the ascetic as one who renounced adornments that were properly available to her because of her Christian discipline and virtue.

I suggest that the veiling ceremonies (*velatio*) that became formalized by the end of the fourth century were developed, in part, to publicly advertise ascetics' disavowal of status and renunciation of lavish garments. Throughout the West, as Ambrose, Siricius, Jerome, and Basil of Ancyra testify, dedicated virgins participated in a ritual veiling ceremony that imitated the conventional wedding rites, thus symbolizing the virgins' commitment and allegiance to her new husband, Christ.[139] After the girl processed from her father's house, the bishop delivered a sermon especially for the occasion, offered a prayer of consecration, and veiled the newly dedicated virgin. There is some indication that the virgin then recited or sung the Song of Songs antiphonally with the other consecrated virgins who were present. According to Ambrose, these veiling ceremonies were momentous affairs that drew immense crowds.[140] Additionally, we know that, at least in some places, ascetics were separated from the congregation and granted reserved seating in houses of worship.[141] So, despite the moral imperative to keep ascetics out of view—in order to properly restrain their desire for attention and to avoid their becoming stumbling blocks to their "brothers"—these rites put female ascetics on display in order to enable their dressing and grooming to be perceived as renunciatory acts of devotion.

## Performing Gender

Whereas Christian ascetics' simplified, humble, and modest dress proved productive for Christian communities competing in the "economy of *sophrosyne*," it threatened to complicate a coherent understanding and performance of ascetics' femininity. Female Christian ascetics were considered to be virtuous only insofar as they demonstrated a *lack* of feminine vice. In other words, female virtue was understood to be a deviation from woman's naturally vicious state. Moreover, Christians followed the lead of their pagan neighbors, linking gender to particular forms of dress and adornment (calling them "womanly attire [*muliebri cultu*],"[142] "girlish scents [κορασιώδεις ὀδμὰς],"[143] and "womanly paraphernalia [σκεύη γυναικεῖα]"[144]). Thus, virtue could only be communicated through a departure from woman's presumably natural mode of dressing and grooming, unsettling ascetic women's conventional gender identification. By adopting a simple, unadorned appearance, the Christian ascetic communicated her eradication of feminine vice, but in so doing what was left of her femininity?

As noted in the Introduction, female ascetics were often praised for their manly virtue and spiritual progress and thus their renunciation of feminine vice and dress need not have been terribly alarming. Yet it seems that many Christian writers were careful to argue that female ascetics retained aspects of their female nature and vice even while they extolled female ascetics as paragons of Christian morality to outsiders. In the next chapter, in which I address crises of ascetics' gender and dress, the motivations behind this move will become more clear, but here let me demonstrate the ways in which female ascetics continued to be cast as women through their physical appearance even as they stopped acting and dressing as such.

First, Christian writers claimed that women's weak nature and innate vice limited their ability to be considered completely defeminized. Even though ascetic women could prove their moral and spiritual progress through their simple, unadorned dress, they purportedly still retained some degree of their feminine desires and motivations. Ambrose argues that it is not only the woman in the theater or in a parade who "sets out to be pleasing, going about like a float at a parade, making herself the object of everyone's glance and talk," but all women in one form or another seek the notice of men.[145] Even ascetics, Clement adds, prance about like peacocks showing off their tail feathers so that their piety may "be seen conspicuously."[146] Such tendencies were presumed to be so strongly situated in the nature of woman that Tertullian doubts whether there are any women who do "not earnestly desire to look pleasing even to strangers," no matter what form of dress is considered to please.[147] Even if disinterested in the attention of men, Jerome insists that ascetics retain their vanity: "Many whose chastity is beyond question dress not for men but for themselves."[148] Vanity is such a strong impulse in all women that Chrysostom warns against spiritual marriage, in part, because male monks were sure to be emasculated when surrounded by female ascetics' concerns and goods.[149]

Christian writers believed these gender-specific inclinations and motivations to be so firmly rooted in even ascetics that they appealed to them even as they counseled ascetics to fashion moderate looks. Jerome, for instance, hoped to secure Demetrias's ascetic discipline by appealing to her presumed vanity and desire for attention: "Had you become a man's wife only one province would have known of you; while as a Christian virgin you are known to the whole world."[150] Rather than quashing Demetrias's desire for attention, Jerome presumes to put it to good use. Female ascetics also were urged to turn their natural desire to please men to a Christian end: they were now to stimulate God's desire through their virtuous and modest dress.[151] According to Pelagius, just as an engaged woman inquires about her fiancé's desires before marriage, so too an ascetic who hopes to please God, her spiritual fiancé, needs to seek advice from his servants, his apostles. If they consulted the apostles' directives in scripture, they would understand that they could best "please" God through an unadorned appearance.[152] Similarly, Jerome points ascetics who wish to appear pleasing to God to the wishes he expressed in 1 Sam. 16:7: "The Lord does not see as mortals see; they look on the outward appearance, but the Lord looks on the heart."[153] Chrysostom concurs, writing, the "woman who adorns her soul has God as the lover of her beauty," because the woman with "inner beauty leads God to desire."[154] Here Pelagius, Jerome, and John Chrysostom appeal to women's alleged desire to be desirous in order to prompt them to simplify their dress. In so doing, they reinvigorate associations between femininity and vanity, pride, and seduction, so that these vices continue to be cast as wholly feminine. Moreover, even though ascetics' appearance might exhibit an erasure of their femininity, Christian writers imagined the *motivations* that guided their dress choices still to be thoroughly feminine, instilling the perception that female ascetics are never able to break entirely from their female nature. These Christians wished to extol the moderating influence of Christian *culture*, which was able to largely curb ascetics' indulgences, while simultaneously asserting that all women, even ascetics, remained distinct from men by *nature* (even if the latter was no longer visibly perceptible in their dress).

Additionally, female ascetics continued to be feminized through their public performance of chastity in that they were put on display as objects of desire. In an effort to demonstrate Christianity's superior morality, the ascetic needed to appear in public in order for her appearance to communicate her renunciation of status and wealth, her lack of concern to attract attention, and her sexual inaccessibility. Her public performance of sexual chastity, though, served to heighten her onlookers' attention and increase their desire for her.[155] Ambrose, for instance, declares that no man is attracted to a woman who displays herself boldly and unashamedly, but all men find the virgin who cares not about attracting attention far "more becoming."[156] Tertullian agrees, noting the "bloom" of virgins that was irresistible to the fallen angels (i.e., the "sons of God" who bedded the "daughters of men" in Gen. 6) was equally irresistible to human men.[157] Tertullian concludes: it is the spectator's awareness that his lust for an ascetic would never be consummated that amplifies his desire for her.[158] In much the same way, Chrysostom claims that the desire of monks cohabiting with virgins in a "spiritual marriage" is similarly kindled by the proximity of an unavailable woman, calling the lust that is simultaneously enflamed and restricted by these living arrangements a "double desire" and a "bleak and wretched pleasure."[159] In the end, female ascetics' performance of sexual innocence was never entirely disentangled from the trope that women possess a power to seduce, although the traditional tools of seduction—jewelry, cosmetics, and other adornments—were now replaced by the alluringly stark appearance that communicated ascetics' sexual renunciation.[160]

In addition to stimulating desire, ascetics were furthermore feminized as they were charged with *attempting* to seduce spectators. Some female virgins, Jerome claims, must purposefully tear their garments (under the pretense of being poor, we presume) with the intention of exposing the fairer parts of their bodies to spectators. Moreover, knowing that desire is heightened by a play between revealing and concealing, Jerome continues, "occasionally you allow your *pallium* to fall," ostensibly from weakness, "so that you might expose your white shoulders and, as if unwilling to be seen, you quickly cover what you have purposefully disclosed."[161] Jerome also argues that some ascetics cover their faces in public not for the sake of modesty, but rather because they know that men's curiosity will be triggered by the face that is (partially) obscured.[162] Chrysostom too complained that some virgins intensified the desire of their viewers by ensuring that their lowly garments hug more closely her curves (in contradistinction to the many folds of matron's garb) so that onlookers could see every heave of her breath. How seductive is the ascetic who beguilingly concealed and revealed her white forehead behind her veil or who sometimes cinched her belt tightly and other times kept it loose in order to accentuate her curves or leave them to her spectators' imaginations. These women, Chrysostom concluded, do far more to provoke desire than women resplendent in gold ornaments.[163] Knowing the power they held over their spectators, Chrysostom accused some ascetics of stationing themselves in their doorways "to lure the passersby" (an allusion to the "foolish woman" of Prov. 9).[164]

In sum, while the Christian ascetic was counseled not to dress lavishly so as to forestall desirous attention from onlookers, her modest appearance was regularly construed as equally seductive, so much so that ascetics were accused of intentionally devising their simple and humble looks with womanly seduction in mind.[165] It is difficult to know how the chaste virgin could fashion a look that could not be interpreted in some way as an expression of her womanly vice. If she revealed too much skin, she would be labeled immodest, and if she properly covered herself, spectators might still conclude that she merely feigned modesty in an attempt to seduce through the alluring concealment of her best features. Such interpretations were plausible for two reasons. First, because desirous spectators controlled the interpretation of ascetics' appearance. They could place the blame for their arousal on female ascetics, who they claimed possessed an innate desire to seduce. Second, because the feminine vice of seduction was presumed to lie at the center of every woman's nature—not in particular forms or features of dress—and thus could be expressed in any number of appearances, lavish or simple.

Because Christian ascetics' public display was so fraught with desire and because Christian leaders were aware that chaste women ought not be overly exposed to the public's gaze, they regularly counseled female ascetics to stay out of public view.[166] Many writers who elsewhere commended the public veiling ceremonies, or who instructed ascetics to visit mentors and guides, urged ascetics to remain out of sight whenever possible.[167] Jerome, for example, frequently counseled female ascetics (or their custodians) to guard the degree to which they appeared in public.[168] Likening ascetics to the vessels and sanctuary of the Temple, "which priests alone are permitted to behold," ascetics' guardians were urged to monitor carefully their exposure to immodest eyes.[169]

Although we read numerous appeals for female ascetics to stay out of sight, their removal from the public sphere did not necessarily make them invisible. Reports about them, as well as public letters addressed to them, kept them in the public eye even if they were unseen.[170] It was precisely the combination of discourse about ascetics and ascetics' conspicuous absence that served to awaken public curiosity and desire.[171] Bishop Ambrose, for example, relates just such an instance in Antioch: "Not long ago there was a certain virgin at Antioch who kept from public view. But the more she avoided the gaze of men, the more she enflamed them. *For a beauty that is heard of but not seen is all the more desirable.*"[172] From this passage it is clear that Christians were busy broadcasting the virtue (and beauty?) of unseen ascetics, so that (whether intentional or not) Christian leaders' advice to closet female ascetics along with their public reports about these ascetics worked together to heighten the public's awareness and desire for them.[173]

In fact, even holy men expressed desire for inaccessible and unseen female ascetics. Jerome compares the plethora of Roman women "in silk dresses, glowing gems, rouged faces, [and] displays of gold" with the virtuous Paula, writing:

> Of all the ladies in Rome, but one had power to subdue me (*meam posset domare mentem*), and that one was Paula. She mourned and fasted, she was squalid with dirt, her eyes were dim from weeping . . . *The only woman who took my fancy (nulla me alia potuit delectare) was one whom I had not so much as seen at table.*[174]

Although we know that Jerome was in regular correspondence with Paula, here he claims not to have seen her often.[175] We are left to wonder if it was Paula's *absent presence* that had such a seductive effect on Jerome.

In the end, the female ascetic's appearance garnered attention and acclaim through a play between visibility and invisibility, through a conspicuous presence as well as a conspicuous absence. It was the inaccessibility of the Christian ascetic—both sexual and visible—that proved alluring and, in turn, attracted attention to Christian asceticism. Whether seen or unseen, unattainable Christian ascetics conferred prestige in two ways. First, they were evidence of Christianity's superior sexual ethic, an ethic that could produce a class of moral elite. Second, their virtuous inaccessibility heightened the allure of Christian asceticism. Thus, Christians could boast a higher degree of piety and moral restraint by exhibiting the manliness of female ascetics, while the image of the female ascetic drew attention by culling notions of female strategies of seduction.

Despite the fact that female ascetics were still regarded in terms of feminine display and allure as they performed their newfound piety, their changes in attire clearly distinguished them from other women. As female ascetics altered their dress—dress that in the past had *made* them women—they created space for a renegotiation of their gender identity. Here, we see the roots of the crises over gender and dress to be discussed in the next chapter.

# 3 Performance Anxiety
## Dress and Gender Crises in Early Christian Asceticism

A woman shall not wear a man's apparel, nor shall a man put on a woman's garment; for whoever does such things is abhorrent to the Lord your God.

Deut. 22:5

[Do not be like some women who] change their garb and assume the attire of men, ashamed to be as they were born—women. They cut off their hair and shamelessly flaunt the appearance of eunuchs.

Jer., ep. 22.27 (CSEL 54.184)

Women who cut off their hair, contrary to divine and human laws, at the instigation and persuasion of some professed belief, shall be kept away from the doors of the churches. It shall be unlawful for them to approach the consecrated mysteries, nor shall they be granted, through any supplications, the privilege of frequenting the altars which must be venerated by all.

Cod. Theod. 16.2.27 (trans. Pharr, Theodosian Code, 445)

Late ancient Christian leaders hoped that by imbuing ascetics' appearance with biblical, theological, and moral significance, they might persuade their audiences to fashion particular looks that visibly demonstrated their advanced moral and spiritual states to spectators. It is impossible to know how convincing their arguments were or how many ascetics adjusted their dress in response. Although we possess extant texts in which Christian leaders praise particular female ascetics for dressing according to their counsel, indicating that some ascetics may have heeded their leaders' advice, such praise is consistently presented as a model for other ascetics to follow, so we must be aware of the rhetorical function of these anecdotes.[1] We might assume that ascetics who were supervised by clerics, ascetic mentors, or monastic leaders were more likely to conform to their wishes than those who practiced forms of asceticism that lacked direct oversight, such as those who remained in the family home or lived in a "spiritual marriage" with an ascetic partner.[2] It is clear, though, that not all ascetics dressed as Christian leaders wished. We possess a handful of texts in which ascetics' dress and grooming are condemned and censured. In these texts, Christian leaders deploy new strategies of persuasion and, in one case, enforce their sartorial prescriptions through conciliar edict in an attempt to bring these unruly ascetics into the fold.

In this chapter, I analyze several debates that arose over ascetics' dress. In each case, the trouble stemmed from the way the ascetics (female and male) performed their ascetic and gender identities through their dress. Some ascetics purportedly claimed that by becoming an ascetic they were no longer to be regarded as women or men and thus they were no longer bound by conventionally gendered modes of dressing that marked them as such. Others appealed to their new ascetic look as justification that they had transcended their former gender status. Why were these dress performances and assertions of gender so distressing to male Christian leaders? As we shall see in the case studies that follow, it was because these ascetics muddled a category of difference used to regulate social relations within their Christian community. Namely, when they troubled one aspect of gender difference—proving that, to some degree, they could achieve masculine virtue—they undermined the justification that social roles and hierarchies were based on stable gender categories, male and female. The axis of gender was inextricably connected to several axes of social difference and rank. Thus, when gender difference was blurred for the sake of signaling Christians' difference from their pagan neighbors, it simultaneously threatened internal hierarchies based on gender difference, producing a ripple effect of category crises.[3]

In the cases that follow, issues of power and authority persistently rise to the surface. Christian leaders rebuke subversively dressed ascetics for merely seeking attention and influence. It is, in fact, unclear whether these ascetics sought additional social privileges or power, but we quickly surmise that this was the fear of the men in charge. It is also not coincidental that most of the debates relate to the improper presentation of an ascetic's head. Because the head was the symbolic location of agency in Roman society, it was an important site for the expression of an individual's status.[4] Female ascetics' acts of unveiling and cutting their hair short, as well as men's decision to grow long hair, should be understood as particularly significant assertions of ascetics' identity and status. As Howard Eilberg-Schwartz and Wendy Doniger have noted, one could diminish women's agency and signal their secondary status by either eroticizing or covering women's heads. When women styled their hair, donned jewelry, and wore cosmetics, they extended the sexuality and allure of their "lower parts" upward to their now hyper-sexualized head. This eroticization "turns the head into a symbol of desire rather than a symbol of identity," an *object* to be seen rather than a *subject* that sees.[5] Covering a woman's head (or face) was another way of stifling her agency, especially when head coverings are perceived to be an expression of submission.[6] Head coverings, though, also further eroticize, because that which is "forbidden to the gaze is that much more tantalizing to the imagination . . . covering the female head . . . simultaneously presupposes and creates its eroticism."[7] Because customary practices of ornamenting and covering women's heads were integrally related to regulating women's submission and, by extension, sustaining cultural ideas about natural gender difference and hierarchy, the disruptive dress performances of the ascetics discussed in this chapter posed noteworthy problems to traditional gender expectations, behavior, and roles.

In each of the cases examined below, we can only see ascetics' dress performances and hear the logic behind their dress choices through the very texts that censure them. Thus we can not know precisely how the ascetics themselves understood the connection between their dress and gender and we must be wary of the representations of their logic given by their opponents. Additionally, we should not assume that each group of ascetics' claims were identical. Each case analyzed in this chapter represents the localized negotiation of sexual, moral, and gender codes. For this reason, we should not collapse them into coordinated acts of gender resistance and logic. When read together, however, these several debates demonstrate broadly how ascetics could strategically configure their physical appearance to make *material* declarations that resisted and challenged conventional boundaries of gender, declarations that were forceful enough to necessitate responses from Christian leaders and councils.[8] In other words, they demonstrate the power of dress performances, a power that rivaled the discourse of Christian leaders.

Although Christian leaders did not have the power to police the dress habits of all ascetic women, they could interpret the significance of ascetics' dress in ways that supported their notions of gender. First, they reduced the significance of ascetics' transgressive dress by redirecting attention to the discursive—theological or hermeneutical—arguments presumed to lie behind such looks. If they could defeat ascetics' reasoning, they hoped in turn to compel ascetics to dress in ways that supported their versions of gender difference and hierarchy. Second, they reinterpreted the signs of their dress, arguing that, because gender was so natural, they could identify elements of ascetics' femininity even when ascetics' dressed in ways that transgressed gender conventions. Third, they redefined the basis of gender difference. Because female ascetics' gender could not be understood according to the partners of heterosexual intercourse nor defined unproblematically in terms of traditionally gendered virtue and vice, they relied on other gender models based on the order of Creation. Finally, they designated new features of appearance to be constitutive markers of gender difference (e.g., hair and breasts) in order to ensure that even subversively dressed ascetics were bound to categories of gender difference and hierarchy. In each of these ways, Christians attempted to reinforce notions of gender difference, difference that could be read from an ascetics' dress and physical appearance, at the same time when they used the slipperiness of gender boundaries to their advantage in competition with their pagan neighbors.

## TERTULLIAN—UNVEILING THE CARTHAGINIAN VIRGINS

From his writings, it is clear that Tertullian carefully monitored the lifestyles of the Christians in his Carthaginian community.[9] He sought to restrict their participation in public events (*De spectaculis, De idolatria*), to order their diet (*De ieiunio adversus psychicos*), and to direct how they prayed, repented, and handled persecution (*De oratione, De paenitentia, Ad martyras, De fuga in persecutione*).[10] Tertullian also had a lot to say about Christian dress. He addressed the topic periodically throughout his writings and devoted four treatises specifically to the subject (*De corona, De pallio, De cultu feminarum, De virginibus velandis*). In most of these texts, he counseled Christians on what to wear and how to present their Christian identity through their material presence.

In his treatise *De virginibus velandis* (*On the veiling of virgins*), however, we find Tertullian responding to a crisis crystallizing around ascetic dress, this time having to do with ascetics' proper performance of gender.[11] The debate centered on the veil. According to Tertullian, women past the age of puberty (those old enough to marry, whether they were married or not) were required to wear veils in public.[12] They were additionally to remain veiled in church, demonstrating that the early veiling controversy attested to by Paul in his letter to the Corinthians had been settled by the beginning of the third century in Tertullian's community.[13] Whether dedicated virgins—vowed ascetics past the age of puberty—were to remain veiled in church, however, was an unresolved matter. Although the Carthaginian virgins certainly were to be veiled in public, they had the option of attending church veiled or unveiled, as there was precedent in the Christian churches for both customs.

Some time at the end of Tertullian's career, the virgins in his community united and, in a *tour de force*, refused to wear veils in church. Although Tertullian gives us no information about these virgins, we could hazard a few guesses as to their background. Because Tertullian opens the work by remarking that the treatise is a Latin version of a Greek original, we could assume that the first Greek version was a letter addressed to the virgins, who either belonged to North African families wealthy enough to educate their daughters in Greek or to Greek families who immigrated to North Africa. If the latter is the case, these women may have removed their veils in church because this was the custom of their previous community. A Greek background would also explain why Tertullian takes pains to debate certain Greek words in scripture and, as Geoffrey Dunn points out, why Tertullian sought to find examples of Greek communities who advised their virgins to remain veiled in church.[14]

Tertullian suggests that the virgins first based their actions on the veiling customs of neighboring Christians and pagans. The Christian virgins of Carthage were exposed to a range of veiling practices within their North African context.[15] While the Jews in Carthage wore a distinctive veil,[16] other women bound or covered their head only partially with "turbans and wool" hats or "strips of linen."[17] These might be the same virgins whom Tertullian elsewhere describes as "going around with their foreheads distinctly uncovered . . . in contrast with the [Christian] virgins of God."[18] According to Tertullian, the "pagan women of Arabia" outdid them all, wearing not only a head covering, but also a face covering "such that they may be content with one eye free to enjoy half the light, rather than to prostitute the whole face."[19] Finally, Tertullian admits that there was precedent for wearing or removing the veil within Christian churches, and thus individual virgins had the right to choose which custom to follow.

Tertullian reports that the Carthaginian virgins next appealed to Paul's first letter to the Corinthian church to support their decision to remain unveiled. In this letter, Paul directed the γυνή to keep her head covered in church. Playing on the linguistic ambiguity of the Greek word, which could be translated either as "wife" or "woman,"[20] the Carthaginian virgins purportedly claimed that the essential criterion for being a "woman" was to be a "wife," that is, to be heterosexually active. It is "union with a man that makes a woman."[21] Because the virgins had renounced sexual activity, they no longer belonged to the category woman and should be thought of only as virgins (i.e., a third gender).

In fact, they argued that Paul too categorically distinguished women/ wives from virgins, as he stated that the groups' interests were distinct and therefore addressed different advice to each group.

> To *the unmarried and the widows* I say that it is well for them to re-main unmarried as I am. But if they are not practicing self-control, they should marry. For it is better to marry than to be aflame with passion. To *the married* I give this command—not I but the Lord—that the wife should not separate from her husband . . . Now *concerning virgins*, I have no command of the Lord, but I give my opinion as one who by the Lord's mercy is trustworthy. I think that, in view of the impending crisis, it is well for you to remain as you are.[22]

When Paul offered instructions to virgins in chapter seven of his letter, he plainly addressed the παρθένοι. Because Paul's veiling directives later in chapter eleven were addressed only to the γυναῖκες—virgins were not explicitly named—Paul's instructions, the virgins' concluded, must not apply to them.[23] Tertullian summarizes:

> [The Carthaginian virgins argue that] no mention of virgins (*virginum*) were made by the apostle when he made a ruling about the veil, but that only women (*mulieres*) were named. If he had wanted virgins to be covered as well, he would also have written something about the "virgins" when the "women" were mentioned. Just as in that [other] passage where he handles the issue of marriage, he declares what ought to be observed concerning virgins as well. And thus those [virgins declare that they] are not included in the law about the veiling of the head since they have not been named in this law, but on the contrary, from this [omission, they are allowed] to be unveiled. They who are not named are not commanded by it.[24]

With their change in sexual status, the Carthaginian virgins purportedly maintained that they had achieved a corollary change in gender status. *As virgins* they were no longer bound by regulations for women, including the veiling requirement set out in the letters to the Corinthian church. Thus, they discarded their veils, conspicuously performing a collective departure from femininity by relinquishing a conventional marker of that gender status.[25] It was this material act of protest—and their alleged interpretation of that act—that necessitated Tertullian's response.[26]

Tertullian first responds to their argument from custom. Although Tertullian allows that there is precedent in the Christian churches for remaining veiled or unveiled in church, his vituperative choice of words reveals his disdain for those who preferred the latter: *"Tamen tolerabilius apud nos ad usque proxime utrique consuetudini communicabature; arbitrio commissa res erat, ut quaeque voluisset, aut tegi aut prostitui . . . "*[27] He clearly implies that choosing to be exposed is like choosing to be "prostituted." Moreover, he argues that the common practice of not only the majority of Christian churches, but of the most important, apostolic churches, was to remain veiled. He concludes that, because all Christian communities throughout the Mediterranean belonged to one body, it would be ecclesiastically divisive to deviate from convention.[28]

Next, Tertullian found the virgins' definition of gender completely unacceptable. Although he admitted that women and men would share "the same angelic nature" in the heavenly kingdom,[29] he firmly supported gender distinctions in the earthly present. Adopting Aristotelian principles of categorization, Tertullian contends that, in the here and now, women of all sexual states share a common essential nature. Virgins, widows, and wives are several *species* (*specialis*) that belong to the *genus* (*generalis*) woman, which is distinct from man.[30] He argues that Paul too understood there to be an overarching category of woman, a category that linked wives and virgins according to their "shared condition (*condicionis communionem*)."[31] Although he agrees with his ascetic opponents that Paul could at times clearly distinguish between wives, widows, and virgins, he contends that Paul made such distinctions, explicitly addressing each group, only when the groups were to receive different sets of advice. At all other times when he addressed women in general, the virgins should consider his advice to pertain to them as well. Tertullian concludes: "Therefore by saying nothing about those whom he has not divided, he has united [them] with the other [type]."[32]

Further, Tertullian notes that the two groups were differentiated in 1 Cor. 11 *for a stated reason*: virgins are anxious about the things of the Lord whereas matrons are anxious about the things of the world, especially pleasing their husbands. The married Christian woman and ascetic Christian woman are differentiated only on the basis of their "cares" and not on an ontological level. Tertullian writes: "This will be the interpretation of that division, which has no place in that [eleventh] chapter, in which [there is] mention neither about marriage nor about the life or the thinking of a virgin and a woman."[33] If Paul does not state reasons for which to distinguish matrons and virgins, Tertullian concludes, readers should assume they are bound together.

Tertullian next argues that famous virgins, Eve and Mary, were both referred to as "women" in the biblical narratives in order to prove that the Carthaginian virgins also belong to the *genus* woman. He begins by analyzing the Genesis narrative in which Adam names Eve "woman" directly after her creation, before the couple had a chance to consummate their relationship and thus while Eve was still a virgin.[34] Tertullian anticipates (or perhaps responds to) his opponents' interpretation of this passage: that Adam referred not to Eve's *present* virginal state with the name "woman," but to her *future*—married and sexually active—state because the biblical narrative uses the future tense ("she *shall* be called 'woman' ") and pairs the naming with a description of marriage and sexual intercourse ("on account of this, a man leaves father and mother and will be joined together with his woman, and the two will be in one flesh").[35] None of the names Adam assigned to other creations, Tertullian counters, were predicated on their future status. By analogy, then, this could not be the case when woman was named. Tertullian further argues that it was not the natural name "woman" that announced her future, married status, but rather her personal name, "Eve," which means "mother of the living."[36] Finally, Tertullian adds that the reference to future marriage and sexual intercourse that follows the naming must be a prophecy for all later human marriages, not related directly to Adam and Eve because Adam had no parents from whom to leave![37]

Tertullian reminds readers that another famous virgin, Jesus's mother, Mary, was also called "woman" in the biblical texts. In fact, Paul, whose categories were under dispute, called Mary a woman in his letter to the Galatians, writing "God sent his son, born of a woman" (Gal. 4:4). And although the gospel author reports that the angel Gabriel was sent to a "virgin" (Luke 1:26–27), Tertullian stresses that Gabriel himself called her "blessed among women"—not among virgins—concluding that "the angel knew that even a virgin is called a woman."[38] (Here Tertullian mistakenly attributes Elizabeth's proclamation in Luke 1.42 to Gabriel.) Tertullian's opponents (allegedly) argued that Mary's status as "woman" could likewise be predicated on her future marriage to Joseph. The biblical narrative, in fact, announces that she was "betrothed" and "a betrothed woman is in some sense a married woman."[39] But, Tertullian retorts, if Mary is to be considered only a woman, then Christians could no longer claim that Jesus was born of a *virgin*![40] It may be that Tertullian here hoped to sully his opponents by aligning them with the heretical side of a newly emerging controversy over Mary's virginity. At the beginning of this treatise, in Tertullian's definition of the "rule of faith," he includes the declaration that Jesus was "born from Mary the virgin," possibly demonstrating what had become right doctrine at least in his community by that time.[41]

Tertullian then replaced the virgins' definition of gender (based on heterosexual activity and marriage) with his own model that categorized women and men according to gendered descent: women were properly women because they drew their lineage from women of the past. Thus, women of all sexual states shared a common essential nature passed on through descent from Eve. This lineage model is made evident most clearly, Tertullian argues, in the naming scene of Gen. 2:

> . . . the name of the new female, which is "woman" . . . is separate from the person herself, such that [Scripture here] does not speak in fact about Eve herself, but about those future females, whom [Adam] has named in [she who is] the origin of the female population.[42]

According to Tertullian, therefore, gender difference derived from the order of creation as opposed to sexual status or activity.

Through his interpretations of scripture, Tertullian shifted the debate to the realm of theology and hermeneutics that supposedly undergirded the ascetics' dress choices. He pit the virgins' interpretations of Paul and Genesis against his own. By reducing the dress performances to the terrain of discourse, Tertullian turned attention away from the force of the dress performances that originally caused a stir. As Patricia Cox Miller has aptly argued: "By making [the] practice of the body a cipher for theological and philosophical ideas, the tangible physicality of the practice tends to recede in importance, if not to disappear altogether."[43] In this way, the meaning (or multiple possible meanings) of the virgins' dress performance was overwritten and controlled by Tertullian's intellectual expertise.

But Tertullian's argument was not completely discursive. He claimed to be able to prove that women's gender was derived from their lineage by pointing to aspects of women's appearance, which, he argues, exhibit essential traits belonging to all women and which signal their connection to famous biblical women of the past. He attempted to elucidate a female nature that was made material in "testimonies of the body"—long hair, cosmetics, and the veil—taking up each of these markers of the female in turn.[44] First, Tertullian returns to 1 Cor. 11, in which Paul identifies women's long hair as a natural sign of her inferiority in the order of creation.[45] Paul argues that it is dishonorable for a man's head to be covered (because he is the image and reflection of God) and it is dishonorable for a woman's head to remain uncovered (because she is the reflection of man). Although Paul's logic here is somewhat obscure, it is clear that he bases his veiling instructions on the idea that gender, as well as the gender hierarchy, is naturalized in the body. Paul asks, *"Does not nature itself teach you* that if a man wears long hair, it is degrading to him, but if a woman has long hair, it is her glory? For her hair *is given to her* for a covering."[46] Following Paul's logic, Tertullian infers that *every* woman's long hair locates her in the category of woman, which is determined by the order of creation. Because it is inherently shameful for a virgin, as much as for a matron, to have a shaven head, and because virgins naturally have an "excess of hair" like other women (and unlike men), virgins undoubtedly belong to the category woman. Tertullian contends that hair length is a definitive bodily marker of difference between men and women of all ages and sexual states.[47]

Next, Tertullian points to the use of cosmetics as proof that all virgins participate in the essence of womanhood. Although elsewhere Tertullian rails against female ascetics who use beautification products—at those moments lamenting such artificial enhancements to women's created and natural bodies[48]—here Tertullian argues that such accoutrements give expression to and thus properly belong to women's natural condition. He claims that *all* women, including virgins,

> . . . change their hair [e.g., through dying], and implant their coiffure with an outlandish hairpin, asserting open womanhood by parting their locks of hair from the front. And then they seek beauty advice from the mirror and they torment their more fastidious face with washing, perhaps they even falsify it with some rouge, fling a mantle around themselves, cram [their foot into] an oddly-shaped shoe, bring more implements to the baths.[49]

Tertullian insists that these "obvious preparations alone proclaim [virgins'] complete womanhood."[50] Although the Carthaginian virgins wished to exhibit their virgin status by relinquishing their veil—"one single item of dress"—they more forcefully revealed their full participation in women's nature and pursuits through their preening and beautification.[51]

Finally, Tertullian returns to the veil. The veil, for Tertullian, reminds contemporary women that they all are equally linked to the sins of their predecessors, the "daughters of men" and Eve, proving that women of every sexual state shared a common essence.[52] He first calls to mind the Watcher myth of Gen. 6.[53] In the Genesis story (and expanded versions of the myth in later Jewish pseudepigraphal literature), the "sons of God," who are later understood to be fallen angels, are seduced by the "daughters of men" and so took them as wives. From this mismatched coupling, the race of Giants was produced, who in turn introduced all sorts of evils into the world. Some versions of the story claim that the Giants introduced cosmetics and beauty products,[54] whereas other versions claim that women's cosmetics helped them seduce the sons of God.[55] Tertullian understands the daughters of men to be virgins because they were referred to in relation to fathers rather than husbands. The story thus demonstrates to Tertullian that these virgins of ages past possessed the power to seduce even heavenly beings. All women, including and especially virgins, have worn veils from that day forward, both in penance for this past transgression and to prevent such crimes from occurring again. Just as past virgins with "such perilous faces" had the ability to seduce angels so as to "cast stumbling blocks as far as heaven,"[56] so too did contemporary virgins retain the power to seduce.[57] Because all women, no matter what their sexual state, shared this threatening power of seduction, the veil was imposed as a safeguard, and could be read equally as a marker of women's common condition.[58]

In other treatises, Tertullian also posits that the veil is a reminder of every woman's participation in Eve's first sin. In *De cultu feminarum*, Tertullian argues that Eve was the first to forsake the divine law and to cause humanity's fall from Paradise. He goes so far as to blame Eve, the one who brought death into the world, for the death of Jesus. Again, the veil was to be considered an aspect of her "penitential garb," a constant reminder of every woman's participation in that sin by virtue of her gendered lineage from Eve.[59]

Tertullian constructed a reading of the ascetics' appearance that highlighted their lineage from shared character with other women in order to prove the naturalness and stability of femininity. Because all women were created inferior, because all women shared the power to seduce, and because all women bore mutual shame for the transgressions of Eve and the daughters of men, they were distinguished with long hair and the veil. Additionally, all women's use of cosmetics, hair dyes, and adornments proved their participation in common womanly traits of vanity, hyper-sexuality, and exhibition.[60]

In a tautological manner, Tertullian implored the Carthaginian virgins to dress like women by claiming that their natural gender was *already* evident in their appearance. The problem with this argument is that Tertullian relied on women's compliant dress and grooming practices—keeping their hair long, wearing cosmetics, and wearing the veil—in order for his version of natural gender categories to remain viable, indeed to appear natural.[61] Because he attempted to root his version of gender in particular *aspects* of dress (rather than in particular *manners* of dress, as we will see below), his argument would fail whenever the virgins proved able to manipulate their appearance in purportedly unnatural ways.[62]

But this was not Tertullian's only strategy for appealing to the virgins' appearance. He also pit the virgins' performance of their new gender status against their performance of true asceticism. When the Carthaginian virgins contended that their dress performances communicated their new gender status as virgins, Tertullian warned them that such innovations in dress puts their status as virgins in jeopardy. He argued that the impiety of the act precluded them from being deemed virgins, the very category upon which their new gender identity relied. The immodesty demonstrated by a virgin who removed her veil, he argued, effected a real change in her ascetic status: "[When] you have laid bare a girl by her head, she already has become known to herself not as a virgin; *she is made something else* (*Denudasti puellam a capite et nota iam sibi virgo non est, alia est facta*)."[63] Here, Tertullian reinterprets the ascetics' transgressive dress choice to be at odds not only with his own conception of gender but also with the definition of asceticism.

Why did Tertullian labor so strenuously to induce the Carthaginian virgins to remain veiled and to appear as women? Through their unveiling, the virgins challenged broader conventional understandings of natural gender difference, throwing into disarray social structures that relied on gender distinctions. If there were no longer simply men and women, but now a third class of virgins, one is left to wonder: Which rules of social behavior apply to them? Would they be allowed to teach, to baptize? Should they be honored more or less than a presbyter, clergyman, or bishop? How did they fit into the order of Christian communities that relied at least in part on gender to distinguish and rank individuals?

It seems that such social upheaval is precisely what was at stake for Tertullian. We know from Tertullian's other treatises that he was indeed confronted with Christians who argued for women's right to baptize.[64] Whether or not these virgins claimed those or similar entitlements is unclear.[65] Tertullian accuses them of being motivated by an impious desire to be "notable and distinguished," although in what specific way he leaves unspecified.[66] It is clear, however, that Tertullian was anxious that, if these virgins were recognized as possessing a new and different gender, they might likewise unsettle the conventional roles that had been defined by gender. He responds by inverting the presumed logic of his opponents. While virgins and their allies might make an argument for ascetics' expanded liberties and roles from *genus* to function—that is, their sexual/gender status informs the social rules that regulate their behavior—Tertullian constructs an argument from function to *genus*. He asks first if virgins are accorded the liberty to teach, baptize, offer sacrifices, or "to claim a share of any male function (*ullius virilis muneris*)."[67] Because the answer is undoubtedly "no"—that virgins must be humbly submissive to men like Christian matrons—then they must belong to the same *genus* as Christian matrons.[68] By posing his argument from function to *genus*, Tertullian attempted to forestall any such disruptions to church order in order to stabilize the thoroughly gendered organization of his Christian community.[69]

## EUSTATHIUS OF SEBASTE—ONE SIZE FITS ALL

Not all Christian leaders were hesitant to complicate ascetics' gender status and dress. Reports about Eustathius of Sebaste's monastic communities, for instance, immediately stand out.[70] Flourishing in the first half of the fourth century, Eustathius was famous (or infamous) for his monastic program that spread throughout Asia Minor, as well as his tangles with other members of the ecclesial hierarchy. Eustathius grew up in Cappadocia with his father Eulalius, the bishop of Caesarea. After being sent to school in Alexandria, he returned to Armenia Minor (in the late 320s or early 330s), where he was ordained a presbyter[71] and founded groups of ascetics throughout Armenia, Paphlagonia, and Pontus, directing their discipline with his own set of *Rules*.[72] Eustathius's monastic program became famous throughout Asia Minor,[73] even inspiring the young Basil, who was eager to meet him in the mid-350s.[74] Eventually, Eustathius made his way to Basil's monastery on the river Iris and to the Annisa estate of Basil's mother and sister, spending a great deal of time discussing spiritual matters with Basil and his family.[75] (So influential was Eustathius on the young Basil, Sozomen even alleges that Eustathius might be the author of ascetic treatises commonly attributed to Basil.[76])

Because we do not possess any works claiming to be authored by Eustathius (although Basil states that he was a "voluminous" writer[77]), we must rely on ancient historians' recollections, as well as his opponents' indictments against him, to reconstruct his monastic ideals. From the descriptions of Socrates and Sozomen, as well as the synodical letter from his opponents at the council of Gangra, we gather that Eustathius advocated a strict and "zealous" ascetic routine. According to the church historians, Eustathius imposed dietary restrictions and condoned unusual fasting and feasting practices.[78] He purportedly welcomed (or "seduced") runaway slaves into his communities, granting them equal rank with all other members.[79] Eustathius is best known, however, for censuring marriage.[80] He compelled those who communed with him to dissolve their marital relationships and further forbade them from participating in Christian services held in the homes of married couples.[81]

From these reports, it seems that Eustathius believed that all distinctions of status were to be abolished when one adopted the Christian way of life. Members' equal status was made evident through the communities' identical attire: men and women donned the same clothing, the philosopher's coat (φιλοσόφου σχῆμα).[82] The practice of common clothing presumably extended in part from Eustathius's view of gender. It seems that Eustathius saw a connection between the renunciation of sexual activity and the obliteration of gender difference. If gender categories functioned only to demarcate members of heterosexual marital relationships, then, for his community, gender ceased to be useful.[83] Thus, Eustathius purportedly saw no need for female ascetics to continue to dress in conventional ways; rather, he directed them to cut their hair short and to wear the same clothing as the men in the community.[84] In the end, the flattening of gender—which was particularly significant for the communities' women, for whom the change was most patent—was related to the flattening of other hierarchical categories (e.g., slave and free) and expressed materially through the communities' "strange and extraordinary garb."[85]

The Eustathian communities' distinctive dress set them apart from other Christians as visible detractors who wore "strange clothes in subversion of the common kind of clothing."[86] The synodical letter suggests that the ascetics' changes in clothing reflected Eustathius's views of ascetic identity and status, but the relation between dress and identity was circular because the ascetics new modes of dressing impelled them to reimagine their status and identity, as well as to alter their behavior:

Slaves withdraw from their masters and, *because of their strange dress,* become disdainful toward their masters. Women too disregard the customary clothing of women, and instead take up men's clothes, *thinking they are justified by these.* Many of them, under a pretext of piety, cut off their hair, which is natural to women.[87]

Changes in clothing allegedly functioned to liberate slaves and women from a demeaning status and to deem their previous status denigration as unjust and unwarranted. Common clothing not only *conveyed* but *created* a notion of equality among members of Eustathius's communities.

Even while the community flattened some categories of difference, they fortified others. The Eustathian monks were charged with repudiating married presbyters and breaking company with other married Christians, refusing to meet in house churches belonging to married couples. As Jean Gribomont suggests, Eustathius made the church authorities around him anxious precisely because they understood him to be a reformer of church structures.[88] As in the case of the Carthaginian virgins, this subversion of traditional hierarchies was likewise understood to trouble ecclesial structures, clerical authority, and communal order. In this case, though, the ascetics were not threatening to infiltrate the ranks and roles of the clergy, but rather, they allegedly set the ascetic community apart from and above the clerical order.

In response to his "strange" ascetic program, Eustathius was condemned by the bishops of Paphlagonia at the Gangra synod around the mid-360s.[89] Although Eustathius was accused of Arian tendencies at this time in his career, it is striking that the bishops deemed his controversial "monastic philosophy"—and the material expressions of that philosophy in his communities' dress—more threatening and in need of censure than his alleged heresy. The council of Gangra produced twenty canons and a synodical letter that was to be circulated to the bishops of Armenia in order to prevent the spreading of Eustathius's ascetic ideals and practices.[90]

First and foremost, the bishops of Gangra were troubled by Eustathius's denigration of the hierarchies of marriage, master/slave relations, and gender.[91] Furthermore, they condemned the ways in which categories of difference were erased from the ascetics' physical appearance. The bishops focused their fiercest critiques on the cross-dressing women in Eustathius's community. The bishops admitted that it was not always problematic for an ascetic to shave her head or to cut her hair short. It was in fact a common occurrence for female ascetics to cut their hair upon entering a monastery. Cross-dressing too had an appropriate time and place: in the theater. They found the Eustathian customs of dress problematic because they were interpreted as signifying the dissolution of gender difference and hierarchy. Whereas orthodox female ascetics might properly shave their head to signal their renunciation of beauty, Eustathius's ascetics understood (or were perceived to have understood) their short hair to be a sign of their rejection of marital or gendered subjection. Likewise, they dressed in male attire not to entertain (like stage players) but to muddle gender categories. These interpretations ran contrary to the divinely created order of society, which the bishops claimed to be clearly explicated in scripture (alluding to 1 Cor. 11). In the end, the bishops wished to regulate not only ascetics' dress and grooming but even more their interpretations of their looks.[92] Thus the council concluded: "If a woman, from supposed asceticism, cuts off the hair given to her by God as a reminder of subjection, *as if to annul the commandment of subjection,* let her be anathema."[93]

The bishops at the council made it clear that they did not oppose asceticism altogether, but merely "those who make asceticism a pretext for pride, who exalt themselves against those who lead simpler lives and who introduce innovations contrary to the Scriptures and the canons of the Church."[94] From this passage we see that the bishops, like Tertullian, wished to shift the focus from the material dress performances to the biblical and theological premises presumed to lie behind their dress habits. They argue that Eustathian ascetics improperly interpret scripture and deviate from Christian tradition, motivated by their impious pride. Given the bishops' counterarguments, Susanna Elm has argued that Eustathius and his followers were condemned at Gangra because they interpreted certain passages of scripture too literally. The bishops "felt obliged to condemn Christians who did nothing but insist on a literal interpretation" of passages[95] that caused "socially explosive repercussions": selling all they owned and giving it to the poor, leaving home and family and fatherland, abandoning marital relations like the angels in heaven, and affirming that there is indeed no Jew nor Greek, slave nor free, male nor female.[96] In my view, however, we should resist reducing this crisis to theology or biblical interpretation alone, which seems rather to have been a strategy employed by the Christian authorities attempting to deal with unruly ascetics' dress and grooming. Rather, we should consider how the disruptions to social order stemmed from the hermeneutical and theological positions *made material* in the communities' dress and physical appearance, an appearance that could further signify a proliferation of potentially troubling hermeneutical and theological positions.

Indeed, we should not underestimate the importance of Eustathius's dress and grooming regimes because this was not the first time that Eustathius caused a stir with his dress choices. Eustathius seems to have regularly drawn on unconventional dress in order to communicate his particular vision of Christian discipline. Years earlier, when Eustathius was a presbyter, his father Eulalius, then bishop of Caesarea, censured him "for dressing in a style unbecoming of the sacerdotal office."[97] Eustathius was again condemned at the council of Neocaesarea for inappropriate dress (although the specifics of this impropriety are not known).[98] The dress innovations that alarmed the bishops at Gangra, therefore, were part of a larger pattern of behavior. Eustathius commonly manipulated his dress in order to communicate his Christian ideals and identities.

In response to Eustathius, the Gangra bishops aimed to reaffirm gender difference and rank in two ways. First, they used Eustathius's sartorial means of communicating identity against him. They called his monks' attention to dress "arrogant," "over-fastidious," and "effeminate."[99] Even though his female ascetics dressed like men, it was precisely their plan to express their identity through exhibition and display, the bishops argued, that demonstrated aspects of their natural femininity. Although a female ascetic who cut her hair short and dressed as a man violated what was conventionally read as the natural look of femininity, her appearance still could be understood to affirm gender categories that connoted the feminine as vain, excessive, and overly concerned with display. Here gender was read not only from particular appearances but also from the *manner* of dressing and grooming. Unlike Tertullian's, their interpretations did not reply on particular appearances to remain viable. Rather, they sought to identify gendered motivations, desires, and inclinations that could be read from a number of different looks, even from those that deviated markedly from dress conventions. Thus the Gangra bishops retrained spectators' interpretations of Eustathian ascetics' physical appearance in order to bolster their assertions of natural gender categories and difference.

Additionally, whereas Tertullian could only hope to persuade his opponents, the Gangra bishops possessed the power to enforce their censure. The bishops developed regulations of dress that they deemed orthodox and enforced those regulations with a series of anathemas. Female ascetics who cut their hair short and dressed as men as an expression of a newfound gender identity violated divinely created order and were thus condemned.[100] The anathemas of Gangra were reiterated in later years. In 390, Valentinian and Theodosius issued a similar edict on dress:

> Women who cut off their hair, contrary to divine and human laws, at the instigation and persuasion of some professed belief, shall be kept away from the doors of the churches. It shall be unlawful for them to approach the consecrated mysteries, nor shall they be granted, through any supplications, the privilege of frequenting the altars which must be venerated by all. Moreover, if a bishop should permit a woman with shorn head to enter a church, even the bishop himself shall be expelled from his position and kept away, along with such comrades. Not only if he should recommend that this be done, but even if he should learn that it is being accomplished by any persons, or finally, that it has been done in any way whatsoever, he shall understand that nothing will exonerate him. This shall indisputably serve as a law for those who deserve correction and as a customary practice for those who have already received correction, so that the latter may have a witness, and the former may begin to fear judgment.[101]

Given the repeated censure of this sort of ascetic dress and grooming, however, it appears that Eustathius's prescriptions remained influential long after he died.

It is interesting to see the influence of Eustathius—as well as the influence of Eustathius's censure—on Basil of Caesarea's ascetic program. According to Basil's own admission, Eustathius provided a model on which he and his family patterned their ascetic regime.[102] In some ways, Basil followed Eustathius's concern to flatten hierarchy. In his shorter *Rule*, composed shortly after the council, all of the brothers and sisters were considered—at least theoretically—to be of equal status.[103] But what of dress? In his *Rule*, Basil explicitly commands the monks to wear clothing appropriate to their gender.[104] I agree with Anna Silvas that this is evidence that, after the Gangra censure, Basil wished to distinguish his ascetic regimen from that of his mentor and that one of the clearest ways to do so was through the physical appearance of his ascetics.[105]

In fact, it seems that Basil's insistence on supervising a double monastery—which distinguished gender even *structurally* according to living conditions—may also have been a reaction to the censure of Eustathius. As Daniel Stramara has explained, monasteries in Asia Minor could be organized in one of several ways: mixed monasteries in which male and female ascetics cohabited closely, most notably sharing common sleeping quarters; double monasteries that housed both male and female ascetics who were segregated within the monastic compound; and neighboring or twin monasteries that were separate, though connected, dwellings for male and female ascetics and that had separate supervisors.[106] Stramara and Gribomont find Basil's living arrangements—the double monastery—to be a structural expression of his agreement with the egalitarian "ascetic principle—neither male nor female in Christ—[that] permeated the monastic spirit throughout Asia Minor in the fourth century."[107] While Basil certainly shows a tendency toward *spiritual* egalitarianism, he does not go as far as he might because he had the option to set up mixed monasteries, resembling others in Asia Minor.[108] I propose that Basil's decision to run a double monastery stemmed not only from his loyalty to the egalitarian principles, as Stramara and Gribomont argue, but also from his concern to distinguish his views of gender from more radical positions, particularly those espoused by his mentor, Eustathius.

We might even wonder if Basil's accusations of Eustathius's Arianism was yet another strategy by which he could distance himself from his former mentor.[109] It may be that Basil launched his attack on Eustathius's Arian and Sabellian heresies in order to focus more attention on his doctrinal than on his ascetic failings, of which Basil himself could be implicated. In fact, it is only from Basil that we hear about Eustathius's tutelage under Arius,[110] leading us to question the validity of this charge.[111]

Basil's family members, though, seemed not to have been as wary of Eustathius's ascetic practice and even his dress prescriptions than the Caesarean bishop. According to the *Life of Macrina*, not only did Basil's mother

Emmelia and sister Macrina put themselves "on a level with the community of virgin maids so that [they] shared with them the same food and lodging and all other things one needs in daily life, and there was no difference between [their] lives," but they also allowed (or ordered?) the virgins in their household to wear garb very reminiscent of Eustathian communities.[112] Emmelia, Macrina, and the virgins were said to have worn dark undyed garments that could have been the philosophers' coats worn by Eustathian ascetics.[113] It is very plausible that the women were convinced to dress according to Eustathius's recommendations at the time of his visit to the family estate in Annesi in 358.[114]

In the ascetic programs of the Carthaginian virgins and Eustathius's communities, dress made material new understandings of ascetic gender and authority. The ascetics in these communities, however, contested conventional notions of gender to different degrees. The Carthaginian virgins attempted to break out of traditional gender categories by creating a new category, virgin. Thus their renunciation of the veil made material their move away from femininity and into a liminal state beyond or between male and female. The women of Eustathius's communities also purportedly refused to dress like women, but ultimately they did less to destabilize the traditional categories. By cutting their hair short and adopting traditionally male garb, they challenged only *who* could fit into which category, promoting certain women into men. Eustathius's female ascetics, somewhat ironically, strengthened gender categories because they patterned their dress on a conventional male appearance, thus fortifying the domains and looks of male and female and perpetuating the gender hierarchy that positioned men above women.

Moreover, although in their responses to these crises Tertullian and the Gangra bishops aimed to retrain spectators' interpretations of the ascetics' dress and physical appearance, they did so in slightly different ways. Both reinterpreted the looks of the transgressive ascetics to bolster their understanding of gender: Tertullian focused attention on aspects of their physical appearance that could be associated with a stable category of femininity (e.g., hair, cosmetics, the veil), whereas the bishops at Gangra deemed the violations of gendered dress codes to be proof of gender (i.e., femininity was evidenced by their manner of dressing, namely their over-fastidiousness). Finally, the bishops at Gangra relied on their power more so than persuasion. Unlike Tertullian, the bishops were, at least theoretically, able to compel ascetics to dress in ways that were commensurate with their notions of gender by deeming violations "heretical" and censuring improper dress as *anathema*.

## AUGUSTINE AND THE "WIDOW" ECDICIA— WHO WEARS THE PANTS IN THE FAMILY?

Scholars of Augustine have long been interested in the bishop's reply to the matron Ecdicia's letter.[115] From his letter, we understand that Ecdicia was so taken by the ascetic movement that she decided to abstain from sexual relations with her husband. Eventually, she convinced him to pursue a sexless marriage as well. Soon thereafter, Ecdicia gave a cache of clothing, gold, and silver to wandering monks as a further expression of her ascetic pledge.[116] When he discovered that his wife disposed of these possessions, Ecdicia's husband was enraged. His anger broke his will to remain sexually chaste and he committed adultery.

Ecdicia wrote to Augustine presumably seeking comfort for her husband's indiscretion and encouragement in her chosen life of asceticism.[117] Augustine's reply is unexpected in that he offers no such consolation, but rather blames Ecdicia for neglecting to perform the wifely duties that would have preserved her husband's marital and ascetic fidelity. Appealing to 1 Cor. 7, Augustine reminds Ecdicia that a husband has the right over his wife's body and he blames her refusal to grant his sexual desires—even after he pledged to abstain from sex—for his adultery.[118] If she would have given in to his desire, the couple would be grieving only a broken vow of continence, not the far more serious transgression, adultery.[119]

Interpreters of this letter often comment on the clash here between ascetic practice and marital obligations. Joyce Salisbury, for instance, argues that Ecdicia, like other ascetically inclined women, "believed that by renouncing the marriage debt and taking control over her own body, she could also control other aspects of her life."[120] It is clear from Augustine's response that this transgression of order is precisely what concerned him. He feared wives who, justified by their ascetic pledge, claimed too much independence in determining how they might structure their life. In his opinion, their ascetic pledge ought not interfere with marital concord nor with the divinely ordained gender hierarchy that structured marital relations.[121] In fact, Augustine argues, ascetic spouses are even more wedded than those who indulge in sexual activity because he privileges the spiritual aspects of marriage over the carnal bonds. Augustine writes:

> He did not cease to be your husband because you were both refraining from carnal intercourse; on the contrary, you continued to be husband and wife in a holier manner because you were carrying out a holier resolution, with mutual accord.[122]

Through this logic, Augustine strengthened husbands' authority in marriages in which the couple had renounced sexual activity.[123]

Ecdicia's actions not only violated traditional familial roles and relations but, as Kim Power notes, they were "incompatible with Augustine's ideas of social order, in which the properly governed family is the microcosm of the state and the church."[124] Peter Brown concurs: "Ecdicia's gesture [of independence] was intolerable in a region where the security of the Catholic church depended on the authority of male heads of households."[125] Thus, for Augustine, Ecdicia must first and foremost be a wife. Her ascetic pledge must always be filtered through her marital status and responsibilities so that gendered social and ecclesial hierarchies might not be upset.

Although several scholars have been attentive to this conflict between Ecdicia's ascetic and marital commitments, they have undervalued the role that dress played in the conflict.[126] Ecdicia made two significant decisions regarding dress: she gave away clothing, gold, and silver (the latter of which were likely in the form of jewelry because it would not have been unusual for much of her wealth to be laid up in her gold and silver jewelry and ornamentation[127]) and she adopted "widow's garb" (*uiduali ueste*). Both decisions seem to have been deeply linked to her resolution to live an ascetic life. As discussed in the previous chapter, ascetics were urged to cast aside superfluous adornments in order to communicate their renunciation of both wealth and sexual activity. We must see Ecdicia's gift to the wandering monks, therefore, not only as a hospitable and charitable act but also a sign of her ascetic renunciation of wealth and of her disdain for womanly sexual allure. It seems that Ecdicia further desired to communicate her new sexual state—withholding conjugal rights from her husband—by adopting a "widow's garb."[128] Through these acts, Ecdicia proficiently signaled her ascetic commitments. The problem, however, was that she was unable to exhibit simultaneously her marital standing. In fact, the ascetic identity expressed in her new look directly confounded her married state: by donning a widow's garb, she accurately conveyed her sexual status and religious vow, but obscured the fact that her husband remained alive! Although her "distinct garb" would "not offend religious decorum," Augustine asserts that her husband might not appreciate Ecdicia "flaunt[ing] yourself as a widow during his lifetime."[129] The conflict centered not merely on ascetic and marital identities but also on how an ascetic wife properly performed these two identities through the same dress signs, how clothing became the site of expression for the ascetic vow, as well as wifely submission.

Augustine first responded by framing the problem as a mismanagement of household goods. He argued that Ecdicia's husband had every right to be upset with her rash gift to the wandering monks because she neglected to take into consideration the livelihood of her husband and son. Augustine here implicitly characterizes Ecdicia as a typically irrational woman whose inclination is to spend the household's money wastefully and carelessly (even though she gave the money to worthy recipients rather than spending it on frivolous luxury goods). Although the gift may have been an appropriate course of action for an ascetic, it was not appropriate behavior for an ascetic *wife*. The good wife would have consulted with her husband in order to decide "what treasure is to be laid up in heaven and what is to be left as a means of support for yourselves, your dependents, and your son."[130] For Augustine, Ecdicia is guilty of disregarding the health of the household and circumventing gendered decision-making processes, which was unbecoming of a Christian matron, whether she had vowed continence or not.[131]

In addition to criticizing Ecdicia's financial independence, Augustine further condemned her sartorial independence. By making autonomous decisions about how to dress, she acted as if her husband was indeed dead. Again, as an ascetic she might be praised for donning new garb, but as an ascetic wife she violated the proper order of the household. Even though Ecdicia traded her expensive clothes for simpler dress, Augustine paradoxically accuses her of "extravagance," claiming that this act did nothing more than demonstrate her womanly rashness.[132] It was nothing more than her desire to stand out—to show off her zealous commitment to abstinence according to her womanly vanity and pride—that prompted her to dress in ways that obscured her marital relations.[133] Here Augustine reads Ecdicia's womanly nature—and thus also her need to be controlled—from her dress practices. The good wife, on the contrary, would receive her husband's approval before making any drastic changes to her appearance, especially because what constitutes holy dress is not explicitly covered in scripture and thus needs to be determined by the more rational spouse, the husband (as was proven to be true by this situation).[134]

If Ecdicia sought her husband's counsel regarding her dress, Augustine claims, she would very likely have been allowed to dress discreetly, consistent with her ascetic commitments. Her Christian husband would not have required her (presumably like non-Christian husbands) to wear excessively ornate clothing and adornments. And even if he did wish for her to wear luxury items, Augustine argues, Ecdicia must submit to her husband's wishes, because her ascetic pledge did not free her from her wifely obligation to submit to her husband's control. Just like Queen Esther, who continued to adorn herself in glorious apparel for the sake of her husband, a foreign king, but who "regarded her royal attire as a menstruous rag," Ecdicia would still be free to "wear" a humble heart that would please God.[135] Her attitude and composure, rather than her clothing, would be the true sign of her ascetic pledge. Besides, Augustine adds, it would only be through pious submission to her husband that Ecdicia could hope to sway him to a more rigorous state of asceticism, a state in which he might presumably allow her more latitude to dress in ascetic garb.[136]

Augustine concludes that a wife should relay her submissive relation to her husband both *in her dress*—in that her clothing should incorporate markers of her marital status—and *through her dressing*—in that decisions about how she dresses should be always guided by her husband's wishes. To support these claims, Augustine appeals to 1 Pet. 3:5–6, seizing on the link between clothing and submission:

"After this manner," as the Apostle Peter says, "certain holy women who trusted in God adorned themselves, being in subjection to their own husbands; as Sara obeyed Abraham, calling him lord, whose daughters" he says "you are."[137]

Ironically, in this citation Peter is arguing against excessive adornments and rather for the adornment of the "inner self": "a gentle and quiet spirit." Peter uses Sara as an example of a woman who figuratively "adorned" herself in virtue, demonstrating proper submission to her husband. Augustine rereads the passage rather to imply that chaste matrons ought to literally "adorn" themselves if that is what their husbands wish.[138]

In order to preclude any confusion in the future, Augustine distinguishes versions of dress appropriate for different types of ascetics. The virgin and widow wear distinctive styles of dress to communicate their sexual commitments: the *uiduali ueste* and *indumentum monachae*. The matron, whether continent or not, should wear a Christian adaptation (i.e., a simplified version) of the "matronly attire" (*habitus matronalis*).[139] Each look, Augustine argues, communicates Christian modesty, whereas the matronly costume also conveys a woman's relation and submission to her husband. For Augustine, this is the only garb that could suitably communicate both aspects of Ecdicia's sexual and marital identity without conflict. Although the matronly garb might not evidence her decision to renounce sex within marriage as clearly as the virgin or widow's garb, for Augustine it is better to obscure the degree of her ascetic commitment than her marital relationship. The chastity communicated through the matronly costume, Augustine concludes, should be sufficiently honorable for the ascetic wife who has properly quashed her pride and cultivated her humility.

In this letter Augustine employs strategies we have seen in the other debates analyzed in this chapter. Like the bishops at the council of Gangra, Augustine reinterprets Ecdicia's dress performance as evidencing not her ascetic commitments but rather her base womanly impulses. He charges her with "flaunting" her humility with typical feminine flair and seeking honor and attention through her appearance. Augustine complains that such drives run counter to true asceticism no matter how proficiently a woman might be able to fashion a look of piety on the surface. Sounding like Tertullian, Augustine attempts to shame Ecdicia into heeding his advice by linking certain forms of dressing to the definition of true asceticism. If Ecdicia dresses as a widow, he argues, she proves that she does not possess the virtue of either a true ascetic or a good wife.

In the end, I acknowledge, with other scholars, that this incident indeed arises from a clash between ascetic ideals and marital order. Yet, I wish to stress that the controversy is grounded in Ecdicia's material expression of her identities. While it is easy to understand conceptually or discursively the double identity of an ascetic wife, it was far more complicated to manifest both identities in one's physical appearance. In this case, Ecdicia's renunciation of extravagant clothing—a decision that combined her desires to denigrate wealth and to renounce sexual activity and allure—failed to simultaneously perform her gendered marital status and submission.

## AUGUSTINE AND THE LONG-HAIRED MONKS

Disputes over ascetic dress and gender concerned not only female ascetics but male ascetics as well. Around 401, Augustine wrote a letter to several monks in Carthage reproving them for their bad behavior.[140] These monks rejected manual labor, claiming to emulate "the birds" of Matt. 6:25–26 ("Look at the birds of the air; they neither sow nor reap nor gather into barns, and yet your heavenly Father feeds them. Are you not of more value than they?"), and relied wholly on Christian alms for their livelihood.[141] Others in the community objected to their seeming laziness and appealed to Paul's pronouncement to the Thessalonians: "Anyone unwilling to work should not eat" (2 Thess. 3:10). When Aurelius, bishop of Carthage, noticed that pro- and anti-labor factions were dividing the community, with one group appealing to Matthew and the other appealing to Paul, he petitioned Augustine to help resolve the issue by writing a letter to the monks.[142]

Although most of Augustine's letter, *De opere monachorum* (*On the work of monks*), concentrated on the question of monastic labor, Augustine also used the opportunity to rebuke the monks for growing their hair. From Augustine's response, we ascertain that the monks wore long hair for three reasons. First, they wished to be associated with long-haired men from scripture, such as Samuel and other Nazarites.[143] Just as Tertullian attempted to link the Carthaginian virgins to the sins of biblical women of the past by pointing to particular features of their appearance, these monks hoped that their long hair would call to mind their association with the virtue of biblical men of the past. Second, their long hair was a gesture to their liminal gender status.[144]

Augustine counters each argument in turn. First he must disallow the monks from emulating the biblical forefathers while being careful not to criticize their practices. Augustine manages this tricky situation by arguing that long hair served a function in the past that was no longer necessary in the present. The prophets lived in a time without the mediator, Jesus. For this reason, they were unable to endure the glory of God directly, nor to understand the will of God. Their long hair either functioned as a protective covering for them when they were in God's presence or symbolized their hard hearts and minds that were unable to comprehend or receive God's commands.[145] In terms of the latter symbolism, Augustine likens the long hair of Israel's "saints" with the "prophetic veil" worn by Moses because both head coverings were necessary for the Israelites to receive the messages of God at this time.[146]

Augustine cleverly pairs passages from the Hebrew bible about long hair with passages about the veil so that he can use New Testament indictments of the veil to censure the monks' long hair. Augustine first turns to 1 Cor. 11. As we have already seen, here Paul links the customary coverings of women's heads, the veil, to the covering provided them by nature, long hair. Augustine argues that a similar connection between hair and veil existed for biblical men of the past: the confounding veils of their minds and hearts were replicated in their long hair. As Paul asserts in his second letter to the Corinthians, however, in the new Christian era this veil has been taken away.

> When you shall go over to Christ, *the veil shall be taken away* . . . And all of us, *with unveiled faces*, seeing the glory of the Lord as though reflected in a mirror, are being transformed into the same image from one degree of glory to another, for this comes from the Lord, the Spirit.[147]

With the coming of Christ and the endowment of the Holy Spirit, Augustine argues, Christians were now able to stand before the glory of God with receptive hearts and minds. For this reason they no longer needed a veil and, by extension, the natural, external covering, long hair. The Carthaginian monks, therefore, should cut their hair if they wished not to scandalize the work of Jesus and the Holy Spirit.[148] Augustine adds that Paul's prescriptions regarding male and female veiling and hair length were not merely opinions drawn from Paul's "cleverness," nor were they suggestions. Rather, Paul orders his readers to heed his directions, concluding the section: "Now this I command."[149] If the Carthaginian monks continued to wear their hair long, he concluded, they would be directly challenging the apostolic authority of Paul.[150]

The Carthaginian monks found a way around the 1 Corinthians' "command" through careful intertextual exegesis, reading the Corinthian pronouncement—that long hair on a "man" is disgraceful—through the famous eunuchs passage of Matt. 19 ("There are eunuchs who have made themselves eunuchs for the sake of the kingdom of heaven"). They argued that because they had renounced sexual activity—because "with respect to their masculine sex they do nothing (*quia masculino sexu nihil operantur)*"— they should be considered no longer to be men, but rather those have "made themselves eunuchs."[151] In fact, they argued, in Gal. 3:27–28 Paul flattened *all* social distinctions—ethnic and economic, as well as gendered—for those Christians who were baptized.[152] Whether the monks claimed to have overcome gender by appealing to their eunuch status or by arguing that their gender was transformed—as it was for all Christians—once they were baptized, either way, they were no longer to be considered men. Thus they ought also to be released from Paul's proscription against long hair because that ban was directed squarely at men.

Augustine quickly counters the monks' interpretation of Matt. 19 and Gal. 3, guided in large part by his reading of two other passages: "The apostle declares . . . strip off the old man with his deeds and put on the new one that is being renewed unto perfect knowledge of God according to the image of Him who created Him" and "with regard to your former manner of life, you are to put off the old man which is being corrupted through its deceptive lusts. But be renewed in the spirit of your mind,

and put on the new man which has been created after God ['s image]."[153]
According to Augustine, the human contains two parts: the rational and
the concupiscential. Baptism renews the human mind and will by enabling
the rational part to regulate concupiscence. This transformation takes
place equally in Jew and Greek, slave and free, and men and women and
is a more significant commonality between the groups than anything else
the might divide them. This transformation, though, occurs only in the
"inner man (*interiore homine*)"; it does not affect material differences of
the body. Since creation, the male body has been a signifier for the mind,
whereas the female body signified concupiscence: "What, therefore, in
one person are mind and concupiscence (for the one rules and the other
is ruled; the one dominates and the other is subdued), is figured in two
human beings, man and woman, according to the sex of the body."[154]
Augustine adamantly asserts that gendered bodies persist as signifiers of
these two parts even after the baptismal transformation that equalizes all
Christian minds and wills. Augustine thus can not tolerate the monks'
claim that they cease to be men because of their body.[155] (Here Augustine's claim that bodies can still signify the ordering of the fallen human
even after s/he has been released from her fallenness seems to run counter
to his earlier argument about the link between outer and inner: Christians
ought to cut their hair short to physically and outwardly denote a lifting
of the "inner veil" in the new age.)

In this treatise, Augustine asserts a material limit to the gender transformations associated with asceticism. Although he might be perfectly willing
to admit that these monks have experienced a spiritual transformation and
a renewal of the mind-body-will, he stops short of endorsing (at least in the
case of men's hair) a physical appearance that confounds conventionally
materialized gender categories. Like Tertullian, Augustine cements masculinity and femininity in the body. Unlike Tertullian, though, he does not
explicitly state *which* aspects of the body are the chief signifiers. This may
work to Augustine's advantage. By not delimiting gender to one particular
body sign, he allows spectators the freedom to identify one of many signs
available to them as evidence of natural gender difference. He need merely
direct them to begin the search.

Also like Tertullian, Augustine attempts to bolster his claim that gender
persists after baptism, even for ascetics, by culling biblical passages that
label famous male virgins "men." He demonstrates that Paul, for instance,
speaks of himself as a man twice: "When I was a child, I spoke as a child,
I sensed as a child, I thought as a child. Now that I have become a man,
I have put away childish things" (1 Cor. 13:11) and "I would that you all
were as I am myself" (1 Cor. 7:7).[156] In fact, he continues, even Jesus was
referred to as a man in Paul's letter to Ephesians: Let us "attain the unity
of faith and the deep knowledge of the son of God, the perfect man (*uirum
perfectum*), the mature measure of the fullness of Christ so that we may be
now no longer children."[157]

What was at stake in this controversy? Besides causing a divide in the community, these monks also jeopardized the reputation of Christianity among her neighbors. Matthew Keufler has convincingly argued that Christian men could flex the conceptual boundaries of masculinity, even going so far as to call themselves "brides of Christ," but they could not present an unmanly appearance, which made them far more vulnerable to attack.[158] But as we have seen, with the right interpretation any appearance could be regarded as either manly or effeminate. The male monk could renounce the flashy dress of the pagan aristocrat (which he deemed effeminate), don the simple garb of a monk (to demonstrate his superior manly virtue and self-control), yet be charged with effeminacy if he seemed to be too overattentive to his appearance (like the Carthaginian monks).[159]

In this chapter we have identified several strategies by which early Christian leaders attempted to limit the influence of transgressively dressed ascetics. They turned subversive dress practices that illustrated the malleability of gender into contests of theology and hermeneutics. Moreover, they reinterpreted ascetics' appearances so that spectators would still see elements of the ascetics' allegedly natural gender, stabilizing categories that had been thrown into crisis. At a time when they allowed flexibility with regard to ascetics' gendered virtue, they policed more vigilantly physical manifestations of gender, pointing to certain features of the body that they hoped would keep gender difference intact. In the next chapter, we will see how this turn to the body would develop more fully in the narratives of cross-dressing saints.

# 4 Narrating Cross-Dressing in Female Saints' *Lives*

No matter how willing early Christian leaders were to attribute spiritual virility to ascetic women, they rarely wished them to represent such manliness in their outward dress and physical appearance. As we have just seen, dress performances that proved too significant a challenge—or potential challenge—to conventional gender categories were censured by Christian leaders or, when possible, forcefully suppressed by Christian councils. In light of the widespread criticism in the third through fifth centuries, we might be puzzled by the popularity of the numerous legends of female cross-dressing saints in the fifth through seventh centuries.[1] We might find it odd that we find no objections from ascetic leaders whose disciples circulated and elaborated these stories and that only rarely do the characters within these narratives express concern about the protagonists' cross-dressing.[2]

Some contemporary scholars have concluded that by the fifth century we do not see the anxiety about gender confusion detailed in the previous chapter. The authors of these legends, they argue, were perfectly comfortable portraying the female ascetics as having overcome their femininity because they evaded the world of heterosexual marriage and reproduction and denounced their worst feminine vices. That the saints of these legends join male monasteries and adopt male garb was apt because they symbolize Christian repentance and spiritual progress, notions that coded masculine, and thus properly fit in the more spiritual world of male asceticism. The cross-dressing motif works symbolically to demonstrate a transitional moment in which the ascetic's femininity is dissolved and she is granted entry into the realm of the masculine.[3]

Stephen Davis amends this view slightly by arguing that the authors did not masculinize the cross-dressing protagonists so much as they blurred their gender. Davis bases his reading primarily on the "crossed" biblical allusions within the *Lives*. He observes that the legends frequently evoke comparisons of the cross-dresser with women in gospel parables, as well as with male bishops and the suffering Christ.[4] The end result, argues Davis, is not that these cross-gendered allusions "cancel each other out," but rather that the cross-dressing saint occupies a liminal state between genders and "the bipolar view of human gender . . . is ultimately destabilized."[5]

While I agree that the legends of cross-dressing saints provide important moments of gender confusion and that the saints' dress was used to symbolically mark their spiritual progress, I argue that the authors of these narratives were as wary as their predecessors of subversions to gender and gendered dress practices. I demonstrate that they were consistently intent on diffusing the potent performance of cross-dressing. They absorbed the transgressive dress performance into their narratives not to uphold it as a model for readers to follow but rather to control, domesticate, and harness the dress practice, as well as claims of radical gender transformation, that were troubling to them. They used dress to symbolize only the saints' spiritual state, while they simultaneously inscribed and naturalized femininity onto the saints' hidden bodies and character. In so doing, they depicted the protagonists' masculinity as secondary, temporary, and—at least while in this earthly realm—always still incomplete. It is for this reason, I believe, that, in late antiquity when gendered dress was so closely scrutinized, these texts received little censure: because they worked to strip real cross-dressing of its transgressive nature—of its threat to undermine gender categories—through narrative discourse.[6]

The authors of these legends understood that not all cross-dressing would disrupt traditional gender categories. Although the cross-dresser who is able to pass beyond spectators' recognition might remake and newly understand her/his *own* gender identity, s/he is still understood by *viewers* to fit within conventional gender categories and in turn s/he stabilizes the stereotypes of masculinity or femininity that s/he mimics. So too does the cross-dresser who recognizably parodies the opposite gender by drawing on formulaic male and female appearances, while simultaneously revealing an underside that does not fit.[7] In order to resist and upset the rigid categories of masculinity and femininity, the cross-dresser must be perceived as ambiguous (What is *that*? A man? A woman?); spectators must be unable to fit the cross-dresser into either category, demonstrating the failure of the categories themselves. Cross-dressing can also pose a challenge to the utility of gender categories when spectators realize that they have been duped, when they discover that a person they thought fit in one category belongs in another. These two situations most challenge the categories of male and female by forcing spectators to expand the boundaries of existing gender categories in order to accommodate persons and appearances that do not properly fit. The cross-dressing saints of early Christian legends do not force the reader to modify or expand gender categories. A close analysis of these legends shows that they ultimately and forcefully locate the saints' identities within conventional categories of gender.

Modern commentators, however, are certainly right to see some moments in which the saints' gender is blurred. The simultaneous blurring and stabilizing of gender categories correlates with two levels of gender performances or passing related to the narratives. On the one hand, the cross-dressing saints are regularly able to pass successfully as men (or more often as eunuchs) within the stories. On the other hand, readers of the legends nearly always understand that the cross-dressing saint is in disguise; readers know that the cross-dresser's true gender identity is to be found underneath the disguise. The narratives ensure that readers are not deceived like the spectators within the stories by using a common set of narrative techniques. First, nearly every legend opens with a description of the saints' former lives and their adoption of male garb, marking the saints' original and primary gender status which is dissonant with her disguise. Second, the narratives accentuate the saints' true gender by including scenes in which there is a threat that her real gender will be discovered and in which they craftily escape detection. These scenes heighten readers' awareness and anxiety that the holy woman is living in a place where she would not normally be allowed because of her true gender. Third, the *Lives* commonly include false charges of rape and paternity, which, punctuated by dramatic irony, enlivens readers' hope for the saints' true femininity to be revealed in order to prove her innocence. Finally, the narratives regularly conclude with a scene in which the ascetic's body is undressed and her true gender is ultimately revealed. Through these narrative conventions and readerly expectations, the saint's body—whether obscured, misunderstood, or exposed—ultimately verifies her true femininity. Regardless of her ability to pass within the legend, she remains throughout a woman in the reader's mind, thus reinforcing traditional categories of male and female.

Readers, including even those modern commentators who argue that the legends muddle ascetics' gender, intuitively understand these separate levels of reading. Even when describing the protagonists' new gender (i.e., masculinity) or confused gender (i.e., liminal state), they continue to represent the saints in feminine terms and not in terms of the new gender they argue the narratives evoke. For instance, they continue to call the cross-dressers "women," "heroines," or "female saints," and continue to refer to them with their female pronouns and names (not the male names they adopted as part of their guise).[8] Moreover, scholars regularly point out the difference between "disguise" and "true identity," implicitly admitting the secondary quality of the saints' transformed gender.[9] For this reason, I argue, the cross-dressing depicted within these legends did not pose the same threat to gender categories as some real dress performances could.

The *Lives* further domesticated the threat of cross-dressing by delimiting the contexts in which cross-dressing was deemed appropriate, thereby restricting readers' imitation of the practice. They frame cross-dressing as a practical necessity for those ascetics who must hide from a sexually voracious husband or suitor, obscuring any other motivation behind this form of dressing (e.g., transgressing gender). Additionally, the initial act of cross-dressing is often regulated by male clergy or ascetic leaders and is never entered into on the sole discretion of the woman. By casting appropriate cross-dressing as such, few women would be able to appeal to the legends to justify their own wish to cross-dress because it is unlikely that their situation would mirror that of the legends.

In the end, the narrativization of cross-dressing worked both for and against stable notions of gender. Even while the narratives attempted to undermine cross-dressing's ability to muddle gender categories, the *writing* of cross-dressing nonetheless served to confuse the protagonists' gender. Authors were required to mix gendered names and pronouns in scenes in which the ascetic was successfully passing, creating many examples of confused, mixed, and blurred gendered language (e.g., "When the porter entered and related *her* business to the Abbot, [the Abbot] commanded *him* to enter"[10]). After describing the common authorial moves that aimed to construct distinct categories of male and female in the *Lives* of cross-dressing saints, I briefly discuss how the writing of cross-dressing could also muddle the very gender distinctions and boundaries the authors attempted to create.

## *LIVES* OF CROSS-DRESSING SAINTS[11]

It is extraordinarily difficult to situate the legends of cross-dressing saints in their original contexts. Because the stories were so popular, they triggered multiple editions and translations, which have obscured the earliest versions' provenance.[12] Most scholars agree, however, that the majority of the *Lives* were originally composed in Greek in the fourth and fifth centuries. Having been circulated throughout the Mediterranean world by travelers, the legends were translated into Coptic, Syriac, and Latin in the sixth and seventh centuries, also prompting the composition of new variations of the stories.[13] Although many versions of the same *Lives* are closely related, and therefore we can assume that translators had access to an earlier version of the text, others do not seem to be textually related. Thus, some stories about the same saint could be disseminated in slightly different forms. Given the distinct traditions, it is most appropriate to deal with each version on its own terms. When I discuss versions of these legends side by side in this chapter, I will frequently note similarities and differences among the versions.

I have chosen to analyze *Lives* of cross-dressing saints that derive from the fourth through the seventh centuries (although the assortment of versions may date to later periods) because they present the most elaborate narrativization of cross-dressing and demonstrate the most focused strategies for fixing the saints' femininity. Although there are a number of discrete scenes of cross-dressing in earlier Christian literature (see, for example, second- and third-century *Apocryphal Acts of the Apostles,* in which several female protagonists are depicted cutting their hair short and donning men's garments[14]), these earlier narratives do not employ the strategies I outline in this chapter, and for this reason, the cross-dressing scenes elicited much more criticism than the later *Lives* of cross-dressing saints. Most of the *Lives* were written around the same narrative premise: a woman, usually from a noble family, desires to live an ascetic life but is often trapped by familial obligations, such as pending nuptials or an existing marriage.[15] To hide from those who wish to force her into a secular life, the woman cuts her hair short and dons male garb in order to join a male ascetic community. While there, she conducts herself in a noble and disciplined way and, as a reward for her piety, often receives accolades and sometimes a leadership role within the monastery. Her true identity, however, is eventually discovered either when she is charged with rape or paternity (and she must reveal her secret in order to prove her innocence) or when her body is prepared for burial upon death.

## FIXING THE FEMININITY OF THE CROSS-DRESSING SAINTS

Several narrative movements in the *Lives* unsettle the cross-dressing saint's perceived masculinity no matter how successfully she might pass within the narrative. In this section, I describe each of these narrative techniques in detail and demonstrate how they were used to inscribe and naturalize the femininity of the cross-dressing saints.

### Marking the Disguise

Through the typical chronology of the *Lives*, the authors underscore the cross-dressing saints' primary gender identification. The narratives are regularly organized to follow the progress of the saint from her secular life, in which she is trapped by familial obligations (either a marriage or engagement) into a life of asceticism. Nearly every narrative includes a scene from the saints' past life and pays careful attention to the moment in which she adopts her disguise.[16] From these scenes, readers are led to believe that the saint's real gender is not consonant with the gender of her disguise, but rather can be found beneath the cover of her clothing. Moreover, as the women of these narratives construct their disguises, they could be understood by readers to be dressing in a thoroughly feminine manner. As we recall from the non-Christian and Christian invectives detailed in previous chapters, women were regularly understood to be driven by feminine impulses as they constructed artificial and deceptive looks and as they put those looks on display. Even though these saints dressed like men, their act of "dressing up" could still secure a feminine identification.[17]

Although the act of disguise is supposed to conceal the monk's gender identity among her community, these scenes function to reveal to readers the secondary quality of her masculinity. For example, in the *Life of Pelagia*,[18] after Pelagia dons bishop Nonnus's garments, the narrative reports that "she left dressed as a man and secretly went off without our being aware of it."[19] There is nothing secret about this moment in the reader's mind. The cross-dressing saints' ability to pass within the narrative is based on spectators' ignorance of their former lives and of their newly adopted disguise, an ignorance not shared with readers. Rather, readers are in on the secret that each woman is simply playing a man.[20]

The story of Anastasia/Anastasios is one of only two known stories in which the reader is fooled by the monk's disguise alongside the characters in the story.[21] Set within a larger sixth-century narrative recording the journeys of Abba Daniel, Abba Daniel directs his disciple to visit an old eunuch, who lived in the desert of Scetis, bringing him water once a week.[22] One week, the disciple finds a message from the eunuch foretelling his own death and requesting that the disciple bring burial equipment on his next visit. Daniel and his disciple quickly return to the eunuch before he dies. During this visit, the eunuch asks that his clothes not be removed when he dies "so that others may not learn of my secret."[23] Readers have yet to understand of what "secret" the eunuch speaks until the disciple, when preparing him for burial, "saw that there were breasts (nipples ܪܶܬ) in the likeness of two dried-up leaves."[24] Only after the discovery does Daniel tell his disciple (and the readers) how the monk, formerly the patrician Anastasia, came to live in the desert after fleeing emperor Justinian's sexual advances.[25] This story of a cross-dressing ascetic is peculiar in that it discloses the saint's gender at the end rather than the beginning of the story. This unconventional form may be explained by the fact that the story of Anastasia/Anastasios is not a freestanding legend but rather makes up a scene in the larger *Life of Abba Daniel*. The divergent structure, however, underscores the common mode by which the cross-dresser's gender is known to readers from the start.

In addition to the conventional narrative structure that begins with the cross-dressing saint's former life and highlights the donning of her/his disguise, the perpetual threat of discovery further reminds readers that the cross-dresser is not who s/he appears to be.[26] For example, in the *Life of Matrona*,[27] readers become anxious when some of the brothers began to suspect Matrona's/Babylas's identity: "For the Lord very nearly revealed her secret to those who shared in the contest with her, but she quickly diffused suspicion with the wisdom of her soul, and contrived to escape everyone's notice."[28] Certainly Matrona/Babylas's wisdom here could be read as an indication of the masculinity she had achieved, but ultimately the threat of discovery reminds readers that s/he is not really or wholly a man.

As in the case of Matrona/Babylas just cited, most often the threat of discovery lies in the cross-dressing saints' inability to pass *completely*. In the fifth century *Life of Mary*,[29] the narrative calls attention to the fact that the brothers were not convinced that Mary/Marinos was a man because of her bodily characteristics: she was beardless and had a soft voice. Mary/Marinos escapes discovery only because her brothers assume that she is a eunuch.[30] So too in the sixth-century Coptic *Life of Hilaria*,[31] Hilaria's/ Hilarion's brothers attribute her beardlessness to her eunuch status, which serves to protect her hidden femininity.[32] While several scholars have argued that this conflation between cross-dressers and eunuchs works to accentuate the gender ambiguity of the cross-dressing ascetic,[33] I argue that likening the saint to a eunuch also reminds readers that the cross-dresser fails to achieve a *wholly* masculine physiology, marked by facial hair and a deep voice, and evokes readers also to recall other bodily failings, such as the lack of male genitalia. Ultimately, then, masculinity is defined according to features of the body, features that the eunuch does not possess. Although the eunuch category allows the cross-dresser to be perceived as a "not woman," it is a category that also marks the saint as being an incomplete man.[34] By casting the cross-dressers as eunuchs, therefore, the narratives create the impression that masculinity can only be fully achieved by *real* men and that women disguised as men can pass only partially and under much suspicion.

Labeling the cross-dressing saints' "eunuchs" also might have been an attempt to link them to other infamous cross-dressing eunuchs: the *galli* priests of the Mother goddess cult. Immediately following their self-castration ritual, the *galli* were reputed to have run through the streets with their testicles in hand. If they threw them at one's doorstep, the woman of the house was obliged to give him her clothing and jewelry.[35] Thus, once the *galli* were emasculated according to their bodily form, they adopted clothing that was better suited to their newly conceived gender. Although the *galli* and the Christian saints crossed their dressing in different ways— the cross-dressing saints used clothing to mask rather than disclose their true femininity—the authors of the *Lives* could cull the image of the cross-dressing eunuch to make the point that both failed to possess the body parts that would make them real men. Additionally, the comparison also pointed to the effeminate nature of cross-dressing, a point made by Firmicus Maternus as he ridicules the priests of the Carthaginian goddess:

> They nurse their tresses and pretty them up in the manner of woman; they dress in soft garments; they can hardly hold their heads erect on their languid necks. Next, being thus divorced from their masculinity, they get intoxicated with the music of flutes and invoke their goddess to fill them with an unholy spirit so that they can ostensibly predict the future to fools. What sort of monstrous and unnatural thing is all this? They say they are not men, and indeed they aren't.[36]

Not only did the cross-dressers' lack the body parts that would firmly root them in the male category, but they displayed bodily signs that traditionally identified them as women. For example, one of Matrona's/Babylas's brothers noticed that both of the monk's ears had been pierced. Matrona/ Babylas escapes discovery by shaming the brother for being preoccupied with frivolous matters: "You should be paying attention to the ground, not to me."[37] She escapes detection by playing a man who pursues manly, ascetic knowledge in contradistinction to her fellow monk who exhibits womanly curiosity.[38] Although Matrona/Babylas is able to evade suspicion, the idea is reinforced in readers minds that such near detection is to be expected because a woman could never completely imitate a man's appearance. There will always be traces of her femininity. In fact, in this very moment in the story, Matrona/Babylas is made to remember the warning of her mentor, Eugenia, who earlier cautioned her: "It is a difficult thing . . . and indeed impossible for a woman to enter a male monastery or, once entered, to escape notice."[39]

Scenes that demonstrate the saints' inability to fully pass are paired with scenes that depict the saints' evading detection. The latter scenes highlight the deception of her guise and underscore that she is someone other than she seems. Once Hilaria successfully poses as a eunuch and is accepted into the monastery, for instance, the narrative notes the deception: "For [the abbot] did not know that she was a woman."[40] Other narratives merely make passing mention of the saint's ability to fool those around her, such as the *Acts of Eugenia*, which writes: "Eugenia disguised as a man remained in the monastery."[41] On numerous occasions, the saints are undetectable to even friends and family members who come to the monastery for help or healing. By noting the cross-dresser's ability to fool those who should recognize them, the narrator can juxtapose the saints' false appearance with her true, gendered identity. In the *Life of Euphrosyne*,[42] when Euphrosyne's father Paphnutius arrives at the monastery in which she is hiding, the narrative notes that, despite Euphrosyne's/Esmeraldus's fear of being discovered, "he did not recognize her in the very least."[43] Likewise, in the *Life of Hilaria*, when Hilaria's/Hilarion's sister arrived at the monastery in search of healing, the narrative notes that she no longer recognized her kin:

> The blessed Hilaria, when she saw her lay sister, knew her; but the lay sister knew not her sister, the monk. How should she know her since her flesh had withered through mortification and the beauty of her body had altered, and her appearance, she being naught but skin and bone? Besides all this she was wearing a man's garb.[44]

In the Syriac *Life of Pelagia*, when Pelagia's old companion Jacob encounters her now as the monk Pelagius, he himself admits (retrospectively) to having been duped by the monk's appearance:

> The next day I, Jacob, went out to ask where the monk Pelagius lived. After a great deal of inquiry, I learnt that he dwelt on the Mount of Olives . . . Accordingly, I went up to the Mount of Olives and kept on asking until I discovered his cell . . . I knocked, and Pelagia, the

handmaid of God, opened it. She was dressed in the habit of a vener-
able man. She came up and greeted me with great humility, clasping
my hands and kissing them from within. She was overjoyed at my ar-
rival, for the moment she saw me she recognized me . . . and *I failed
to recognize her* because she had lost those good looks I used to know;
her astounding beauty had all faded away, her laughing and bright face
that I had known had become ugly, her pretty eyes had become hollow
and cavernous as a result of much fasting and the keeping of vigils.[45]

Although Jacob confesses to being fooled, the attention he draws to being
fooled disallows readers from making the same mistake. Moreover, the
narrator signals Pelagia's true gender identity with a sudden change in gendered language. When Jacob initially searches for "Pelagius" on the Mount
of Olives, the narration follows his understanding (and the understanding
of those in the area) that the monk is male. Once Jacob comes into contact
with the monk, however, he immediately switches to feminine language
(although the narrator *claims* not to have recognized her at the moment
they meet). The language choices here do not follow the typical rules that
guide the narration of cross-dressers (see my discussion of these rules below)
for a particular reason: the narrator aims to uncover Pelagia's true identity.
Through Jacob's retrospective awareness of Pelagia's hidden identity and
a concerted effort to stabilize her gender through the gendered terms in
which he narrates the story, the disguise is interrupted and revealed before
it has a chance to mislead readers as well.

## False Accusations of Rape and Paternity

The *Lives* also construct the saints' femininity through false accusations of
rape or paternity.[46] These accusations feminize the cross-dressing saints in
two ways. First, they rely on the *topos* that women inherently exude sexual
allure; they can not shake their hyper-sexualized femininity and, therefore, pose sexual problems when they enter the male monastery.[47] While
the cross-dressing saint is a symbol of sexual renunciation in that she does
not project her own sexual desires, she still attracts to herself sexual vice
and accusations of sexual indiscretions. Thus, she is cast as the alluring and
deceptive feminine presence that produces sexual anxiety for those around
her (whether explicitly within the narrative or in the mind of the reader).
Furthermore, because the cross-dressers are the objects of other *women's*
desire, sexual vice is conveniently kept within the realm of the feminine.

At the beginning of the *Life of Mary*, for example, Mary's father refuses
to bring his young daughter with him when he joins a male monastery,
reasoning that "it is through those of your sex that the devil wages war on
the servants of God."[48] When the child offers to cut her hair short and dress
as a man, the problem is temporarily evaded; for the time, it seems that
the *appearance* of a woman is more troubling in a male monastery than

her actual *presence*. Sexual temptations and vice, however, soon follow Mary as she is accused of fathering a child with an innkeeper's daughter.[49] Although Mary has had no contact with the innkeeper's daughter, who became pregnant by a soldier and later named the monk as the father, the desire between this couple is displaced onto Mary, through whom the devil indeed wages war on the monastery, casting it into disrepute. Likewise, Abba Pambo agrees to allow Hilaria to stay in the monastery as long as she does "not let anyone know that you are a woman."[50] Again, Pambo assumes that the woman is only a threat if the brothers detect her true identity. This assumption is proven false later in the narrative when Hilaria is charged with committing sexual indiscretions with his/her sister (who did not recognize her) when she came to their monasteries for healing, sullying the reputation of her brothers.[51]

In addition to casting the cross-dressing saints as gateways to sexual vice and disrepute, the false accusations further feminize them by leading readers to assume that the saints could not possibly be guilty because they do not possess the body parts presumed to be necessary to rape a woman or to father a child. The narratives presume—and call readers to imagine—a body that links the saints innocence to their femininity.[52] For example, in the *Life of Mary*, when the monk Mary/Marinos is charged with fathering a child with the innkeeper's daughter, the accusation leads readers to consider the monk's body parts in order to thereby determine her guilt or innocence.[53] Readers are led to presume that Mary/Marinos is innocent because they know that she is incapable of insemination or that she is incapable of insemination because they know that she is innocent. Either way, the saint's body is tied to her blamelessness.

Likewise, in the *Acts of Saint Eugenia*,[54] the narrator combines a spectator's misunderstanding of Eugenia's true gender with a false accusation as a way to induce readers to imagine the real female body under the saint's clothing. A local woman, Melania, "*not knowing that [Eugenia] was a woman*, longed to behold Eugenia from a corrupt motive; and not because she had been healed by her intercession, but *because she believed her to be a man*."[55] This narration leads readers to suppose Melania is misguided in thinking that Eugenia/Eugenios could sexually satisfy her, thus creating an image in readers' minds of the saints' feminine body. Then, when Eugenia is accused of having an affair with Melania, the eparch, Philip (who is her biological father), charges her with adopting the "guise of a Christian" in order to perpetrate sexual crimes. The dramatic irony of this scene calls upon readers' knowledge of the *true* guise of the story—which is not religious, but rather gendered—so that the accusation produces a different effect on readers. Namely, it draws attention to the cross-dresser's true secret and increases readers' expectation that the monk must disclose *her* body in order to absolve herself of guilt.[56]

The accusations prompt readers to link the saints' bodies with their gender and encourage their desire that the saints' natural, bodily femininity be exposed. In many legends, readers wishes are fulfilled: Eugenia and Susanna reveal their gendered bodies to prove their innocence. In the *Life of Mary*, however, the monk humbly submits to the charges of sexual indiscretion and accepts the punishment of raising the child she allegedly fathered. In fact, Mary confesses that she had transgressed and committed fornication; both the Greek and Syriac versions put the following confession into Mary's mouth: "Forgive me father for I have sinned as a man/human (ὡς ἄνθρωπος; ܐܝܟ ܒܪܢܫܐ)."[57] Because readers know that the confession of sexual indiscretion is false, they are led to believe that so too is the confession of the monk's gender. The acceptance of blame further heightens readers' anxiety over the misperception of the saint's innocence and gender, as does Mary's excruciating punishment: "But it was not enough for Mary that he had borne this accusation, but the boy [child] stained his clothes with much weeping. And the blessed Mary endured this pain and this grief for three years."[58] By aligning the saint's innocence with the female body, the authors of these legends ensure that the saint be vindicated *as innocent* only when it is discovered that she is *truly a woman according to the body*.

## Discovering and Exposing the Saints' Naked Bodies

Scenes of discovery and revelation of the cross-dressers' bodies, usually found at the end of the narratives, ultimately cement the saints' true gender again in certain body parts, particularly the saints' breasts or nipples. No matter how convincing her disguise was in the preceding narrative, in the end her physical appearance is shown to be a temporary façade that obfuscated her true, material femininity underneath. Moreover, these discovery scenes are spiked with the allure of the exposed body, further feminizing the saint. Whether as part of a trial to prove their innocence or as part of burial preparation, the cross-dressers are often undressed and their bodies are put on display for multiple characters to see and readers to imagine.[59] For example, when Eugenia is charged with the attempted rape of a senator's wife, in order to prove her innocence, she throws open her garments to expose her breasts before the crowd.

> . . . [Eugenia] rent the garment with which she had attired herself from her head downwards, and exposed her hidden countenance and her beautiful virginal breasts. But for one moment only and then she hastily veiled them again with her rent garment.[60]

The narrative presents Eugenia/Eugenios as somewhat modest—she exposes herself only momentarily—but also eroticizes the act by commenting explicitly on her "beautiful virginal breasts." The Syriac version adds: "And when she had done this [i.e., exposed her body], she convinced everyone *what she was*."[61] By combining the disguise with the accusation, and the erotic disclosure with the proof of her innocence, the narrative suggests that Eugenia is not only innocent as a woman, but moreover *as a woman exposed.* Her identity—"what she was"—is grounded in her female body, a body that is sexualized according to typical tropes of femininity.

Likewise, in the *Life of Susanna*,[62] Susanna also exposes her body to prove that she did not rape a female ascetic. Unlike Eugenia, Susanna discreetly reveals her body to only two deaconesses and two virgins rather than to the entire crowd.[63] Although she discloses her body modestly in this scene, the narrative later returns to focus on her body in another miraculous scene. Years later, when she is persecuted for refusing to perform pagan sacrifice, the prefect ordered her breasts to be cut off. Miraculously, angels retrieved her breasts and restored them to her body. God has found her worthy of divine intervention, an intervention that restored her feminine parts to their proper place.[64]

Additionally, several cross-dressing legends depict the exposed bodies of saints as they were being prepared for burial. According to the Syriac and Latin versions of the *Life of Mary*, the monks first discover that Mary is a woman when they clothe her for burial. The narrative describes the tremendous effect this discovery had on the monks: "And when they saw her, their limbs became weak, and the light of their eyes was troubled. And immediately when they had rested a little, they began crying out, *Kyrie eleison.*"[65] After reporting the news to the Abbot, he too "came and saw her," indicating yet another exposure of the saint's naked body.[66] The Abbot then rebuked the innkeeper for bringing charges of sexual impropriety against the monk, who was now proven innocent by her body. When the innkeeper remained incredulous, "the Abbot led him by the hand and showed him."[67] Only after three exhibitions of the naked corpse did they "dress her sacred body," which readers are to presume had been on display until this point.[68] Likewise, when the monks were preparing Pelagia's body for burial, they uncovered her body and her true gender. Although they "wanted to hide this astonishing fact from the people, [they] were unable to do so" for, according to the Latin version, the crowd gathered around the body had already caught sight of her.[69]

> They wanted to keep such a wonder hidden but they could not, because of the crowds of people thronging around (*sed populum ipsum latere non poterat*), who cried out with a loud voice, "Glory to you, Lord Jesus Christ, for you have hidden away on earth such great treasures, women as well as men." So it was known to all the people (*Divulgatum est autem omni populo*) . . .[70]

We cannot ignore that it was the saint's body on display "to all the people" through which this "wonder" was made known.

Although the *Life of Euphrosyne* does not contain an exposure of the monk's body, her body is the object of physical affection at her death. When Euphrosyne prepared to die, she disclosed her identity to her father,

Paphnutius (who had become her disciple) and asked him to shroud her corpse so that none of the brothers would discover her secret. Paphnutius, on the contrary, could not restrain his emotion and divulged his daughter's identity at her death. Once the brothers learned that Euphrosyne was a woman, several of them handled the corpse in hopes of receiving a blessing or healing: the abbot and another monk were said to have "fallen upon her body" and "embraced her body," while another monk pressed his face against hers.[71] Similarly, when Abba Daniel's disciple was preparing Anastasia/Anastasios for burial, he was shocked to notice her breasts. Later, when the pair is walking away, the disciple tells Daniel, "As I was putting on the burial garment, I *felt* and noticed that she had breasts (nipples) hanging down like two withered leaves."[72] This vivid confession of not only seeing the woman's body, but also touching her breasts, adds to the sexual charge of the scene.[73]

These episodes, in which the saints don their disguise, are fearful of and threatened by near detection, bear false accusations, and expose their bodies, function to ground the cross-dressing saints' femininity in a body that readers are consistently called to imagine alongside her disguise, a body that the reader longs to be exposed. Although the cross-dressers had renounced sexual activity (i.e., the sexual use of that body), appeared as men, and lived a disciplined, manly monastic life, the *Lives* make the female body a constitutive component of the saints' femininity. The male disguise, on the contrary, is constructed to be secondary, temporary, and always incomplete. In this way, narrativization trains the proper reading of clothed bodies, so that readers might even be able to imagine the gendered bodies of ascetics in their midst.

## BLURRING THE GENDER OF CROSS-DRESSING SAINTS

Although I argue that the authors of these legends took great care to reinforce gender categories and to decisively locate the cross-dressing saints within the category of the feminine through the narrative techniques described above, the language in which the narratives were written could at times muddle the very gender the authors wished to secure. The authors of the *Lives* were regularly forced to make decisions about the gendered names and pronouns they used to refer to the saints. While a few narratives use the protagonist's female name and pronouns throughout, it was more typical for the authors to move back and forth between masculine and feminine names and pronouns, corresponding to two levels on which the stories were told. When the events of the story were narrated by a detached, omniscient observer or a character who memorialized the saint, the narrator—who knew the cross-dresser's true gender—narrated the story using feminine terms. When the narratives related the direct speech of characters within the story—who believed the cross-dresser to be male—the narratives used masculine terms in order to relate the characters' perception of the cross-dresser's gender. Simply put, the narratives generally used feminine terms when writing from the omniscient voice and used masculine terms in direct speech between the cross-dressing monk and those who considered her to be male.

This oscillation between gendered terms no doubt contributed to readers' understanding of the saints' liminal gender identity. Furthermore, there are moments in the legends when narration runs up against direct speech, when the rules dictate that the author switch gendered terms midstream. In these scenes, the writing of the cross-dresser's written gender becomes even more porous. For example, in *Life of Euphrosyne*, after Euphrosyne cuts her hair and adopts male garb, she poses as a eunuch and attempts to gain admittance into a male monastery. From the beginning of the narrative, Euphrosyne is consistently referred to by her feminine name and pronouns, but when she comes into contact with monks who understand her to be male, the narrative begins to blur the gendered writing of the scene:

> And *she* talked with the porter and *she* said to him, "Brother, if it please you, go and say to the Abbot that a certain eunuch from the palace is at the door outside and *he* desires to speak to you." And when the porter had entered and related *her* business to the Abbot, [the Abbot] commanded *him* to enter. And when *he* had entered, *he* threw *himself* down and *he* did penance. And after a prayer had been offered they sat down. The Abbot said to *her*: "Why has the love of God that is in you (*m.*) made you (*m.*) trouble yourself with us?" *She* replied to him, "Father, I am from the palace, and I had a love for the garb of hermits . . . and I heard about your Holiness and about this monastery, and I am come to be with you if it please you to accept me" . . . The Abbot said to *him*: "You have done well in coming, my *son*." . . . And again the Abbot said to *him*: "My *son*, what is your name?" "*Esmeraldus*, sir" *he* replied.[74]

Although the narrator understands that Euphrosyne is a woman in disguise, the author also attempts to reflect the porter's and abbot's perception of the monk's gender, resulting in compound sentences that merge the monk's male and female identities: "And when the porter had entered and related *her* business to the Abbot, [the Abbot] commanded *him* to enter."[75]

Directly after this scene, we find an interesting lapse in the conventional rules for narrating gender: once the monk declares his name to be "Esmeraldus," the omniscient narrator begins to refer to "him" in masculine terms. He is caught up in Euphrosyne's passing. Thus, we see that the perception of the cross-dressing monks' gender could persuade not only the characters within the story but also the authors who composed the stories. Even when Euphrosyne's feminine allure peeps out from behind the disguise, proving to be a temptation to the brothers in the monastery, the narrative continues to use masculine language:

And when *he* [Esmeraldus] came into the refectory Satan made many to stumble at *his* beauty, so that they complained against the Abbot, that he had received such a fair and beautiful face into the monastery, and when the Abbot learnt it he called for *Esmeraldus* and said to *him*, "The fair beauty of thy face has occasioned many falls to those who are not well-established. I therefore desire thee to dwell in a separate cell at some distance from [the monastery]" . . . [76]

Although readers, trained to understand sexual charm and temptation to be coded feminine, might presume that the monk is alluring precisely because she is a disguised *woman*, it is curious that here her allure is gendered masculine.[77]

The narrative reverts back to feminine descriptors for Euphrosyne once her father, Paphnutius, arrives at the monastery in order to seek prayers for his missing daughter's safe return.[78] Once reminded of Euphrosyne's past life and past gender, we (and the author?) recall that she is a woman in disguise. When Paphnutius is sent to his daughter for spiritual guidance— another scene in which narration and direct speech, as well as the monk's past and present gender identities, merge—the gendered language of the narrative again becomes confused:

. . . the Abbot sent and called Agapius his chief [monk] and said to him, "Take my lord Paphnutius and lead him to *brother Esmeraldus*, so that he may profit by *him*. And he took him and conducted him to *him*." But when *Euphrosyne* saw *her* father *she* was all bathed in tears. But *her* father imagined that penitence was the reason of *her* tears. He did not recognize *her* in the very least . . . When they had engaged in prayer he sat down and *she* began to talk to him about mercy and righteousness and love and chastity, and about the freedom of souls,[79] and while *Esmeraldus* was speaking the heart of Paphnutius was moved, and he was full of tears.[80]

To add to this gender confusion present in this legend, the narrative announces the end of the story with the pronouncement: "Here ends the story of Esmeraldus of Alexandria."[81] This is the only instance in which the saint is remembered by her male name. More often, as Susan Ashbrook Harvey points out, the cross-dresser is sainted as a woman.[82]

We also find lapses in the conventions of gendered narration in the Greek *Life of Mary*. Once Mary accepts the charge of paternity, the narrator muddles the gendered terms he uses to refer to Mary: "But it was not enough for *Mary* that *he* had borne this accusation [of paternity], but the boy [child] stained *his* clothes with much weeping. And the blessed *Mary* endured this pain and this grief for three years."[83] Additionally, once Mary has died and her body was undressed, the brothers announce, "Brother Marinos is a woman (ὁ ἀδελφὸς Μαρῖνος γυνή ἐστιν; ‏ܡ ܪܚܠܕܘܪ ܪܚ.ܝܕ ܪܚܘܪ‎)."[84]

After—and perhaps in response to—this startling pronouncement of blurred gender, the narrative reverts to using feminine terms.[85]

Even in legends in which the narrator chooses to represent the monk with feminine terms throughout, there are moments of slippage. The *Life of Matrona*, for instance, consistently refers to Matrona with feminine terms. Even when Matrona is introduced to the abbot of the monastery, having been "completely transformed into a man and bore a man's name, Babylas," the narrative continues to call her by her given name, Matrona, and uses feminine pronouns to reference her. Although the omniscient narrator is consistent in narrating the monk in feminine terms, at one point in the narrative the author inadvertently slips, using masculine participles to describe the ascetic practice and virtue of the monk.

ἤδη δὲ καὶ ἀγωνιζόμενον, ἐθαύμαζε τὸ τῶν ἀδελφῶν πλῆθος...οὐκ ἐξισοῦσθαι αὐτοῖς μόνον ἐν τοῖς ἀσκητικοῖς πόνοις ἐσπούδαζεν, ἀλλὰ καὶ πλέον τι ἔχειν ἐφιλονείκει, νηστεύων μὲν καρτερικῶς, τροφῆς δὲ μεταλαμβάνων ὀλίγης, θυμοῦ τε κρατῶν καὶ ἐπιθυμίαις μὴ ἀπαγόμενος, προσευχῇ προσκαρτερῶν, τῇ ἀγάπῃ πλουτῶν, πρὸς ὑπακοὴν εὐπρόθυμος, τοῖς δὲ πόνοις τῆς γῆς ἐγκαρτερῶν καὶ τὸ μεῖζον τούτων τῇ πολεμούσῃ τοῖς ἐγκρατευομένοις ἀκηδίᾳ μὴ χαυνούμενος· καὶ βασκαίνειν μὲν οὐκ εἶχον αὐτῇ...μιμεῖσθαι δὲ ἔσπευδον καὶ ὡς διδασκαλίᾳ μεγίστῃ προσεῖχον τῇ αὐτῆς πολιτείᾳ

The multitude of the brethren there marveled at [Matrona/Babylas's] struggles . . . [that Matrona/Babylas] endeavored not only to vie with them in ascetic labors, but strove to do yet more, fasting patiently and taking little nourishment, tempering anger and resisting desires, abiding in prayer, abounding in love, most eager in obedience, persevering in labors of the earth and, greater than all these things, not giving in to the despair that besets those who practice continence. Nor did they envy her . . . they strove to imitate and gave heed to her way of life as to a most important lesson.[86]

Even in this text, in which the protagonist is linguistically feminized throughout, the author is momentarily persuaded by the monk's ability to pass as a man within the story as his language reflects.[87] Here we see that performances of masculinity even within a discursive story can be compelling, even enough for the authors themselves to be forgetful of the rules of narrating the protagonists' gender.

The narratives that seem to maintain the conventions of gendered language the best are those in which the cross-dressing saint is least able to fool other characters, such as the *Acts of Saint Eugenia*. This legend records the story of the daughter of an Alexandrian proconsul, Eugenia, who sought to avoid marriage by cutting her hair, adopting the garb of a man, and fleeing with her two eunuch servants to live a life of asceticism. When the three sought admission into the monastery of bishop Helenus, the bishop immediately perceived that Eugenia was a woman in disguise.[88] He allowed her to stay as long as they told no one the "real facts." In time, Eugenia became well-known for her piety and ability to heal and eventually succeeded Helenus as head of the monastery. Eugenia is said to have been wary of taking over leadership: "Her conscience admonished her that she was a woman, and it was not fitting that she should be commander [and] governor to the men of God. And moreover she was afraid lest she might cause the minds of the brethren to stumble who were advising and persuading her to do this."[89] Even when her successful passing allowed her access into the community and even a position of power, the narrative repeatedly marks these moves as transgressive, normally not allowed for those of Eugenia's gender, by placing such thoughts in Eugenia's own conscience. Once abbot, Eugenia spurned the advances of a local woman and the woman accused her of attempted rape. The proconsul of Alexandria accordingly brought the monk before the court to investigate the matter. Eugenia exposed her breasts to reveal her true (gender and familial) identity, at which time she was acquitted of the charges and reunited with her family. This narrative consistently reminds readers of the saint's femininity and consistently depicts Eugenia in feminine terms. There is less gender confusion in the language of the narrative, I believe, because the monk was unable to pass completely throughout the narrative.

From the above examples, we see that the gendered language used to refer to the cross-dressing saints was terribly confusing. Even when the *Lives* developed rules to keep the saints' true and perceived genders straight, these rules were often broken. Thus, although the authors of the *Lives* made a significant effort to naturalize femininity according to the bodies of cross-dressing protagonists, the narrativization of cross-dressing could never entirely achieve this goal because gendered language was the medium through which the stories were told.

## LIMITING THE INFLUENCE OF FAMOUS CROSS-DRESSING SAINTS

While the disguise of the cross-dressing saint was meant to mislead characters within the legend into believing that the saint was a man, the deception was meant to be recognized by readers. The disguise functioned to imbue the saints with the spiritual and moral qualities of maleness while keeping their bodily femaleness intact. In other words, it allowed for two distinct readings of the cross-dresser's gender: one that was constructed as natural and the other as acquired. These two distinct registers were necessary because, as several scholars of late antiquity have shown, a female model of sanctity was incongruous with the consistent devaluation of the feminine. Susan Ashbrook Harvey succinctly writes:

Early Byzantine hagiography displays full awareness of its inherent self-contradictions on the subject of women. It tells us that women are unworthy by nature, become worthy by what they do, and nonetheless remain unworthy because of who they are. It tells us women can do and be the very things it tells us they are incapable of doing and being; and it declares this irresolvable conundrum the basic fact of women's lives.[90]

Because virtue was understood in male terms (*virtus* and *andreia* in fact derive from the very words for maleness, *vir* and *andros*), in order to venerate female saints, they had to be imparted with a degree of masculinity.[91] This explains why we find references that connect the cross-dressing saint's gender with manful spiritual progress. Bishop Helenus confirms, "You [Eugenia] are rightly called a man, since, although you are a woman, you act manfully (*recte vir diceris, quia, cum sis femina, viriliter agis*)."[92] Likewise, at Euphrosyne's death, the abbot prays that the saint might intercede for the brothers so that they might "manfully (*viriliter*)" gain entrance into heaven like the saint.[93] While the saints themselves are to be praised for achieving such a state, we cannot ignore that they accomplished this feat alongside men, within the presumably virtue-rich environments of male monasteries. Moreover, as has been confirmed in previous chapters, male virtue was not merely an abstract concept but was manifested through particular styles and manners of dress. The men's clothing worn by the cross-dressing saints worked as the transferential object that brought with it notions of superior masculine characteristics; male clothing became the metaphor, code, and signifier of (male) virtue.[94] In fact, that the female saints adopt not only men's garments but men's monastic or clerical garb marks their supremely pious state even more.[95]

The *Lives'* depictions of masculine virtue and spiritual progress through men's garments were not as menacing as the controversies described in the previous chapter for two reasons. First, they concurrently *inscribed* a bodily register of gender. The cross-dressing saints' masculinity was perpetually cast as an addition that did not erase the body underneath. The reader is forever reminded that beneath the male garments, the saint is always still a woman, as her body—particularly her breasts or nipples—repeatedly affirms.[96] By pointing to a *hidden* difference underneath the saints' appearance, the authors directed the proper reading of bodies both within the narrative and in the world of their readers. Even if spectators could not *perceive* bodily difference in the female ascetics in their midst, they could still be persuaded that there was indeed an obscured body beneath that proved the stability of gender categories and they could be induced to *imagine* such bodily difference in their minds. This interpretive guidance was not only useful for cross-dressers, but likewise for ascetics whose natural feminine body (e.g., breasts and curves) became less perceptible as a result of rigorous ascetic practice.[97] In the end, indeed, the bodies of female ascetics need never physically resemble these ideas of a conventionally gendered body because spectators could always adjust incommensurate appearances using their imagination.

Second, these legends domesticated cross-dressing's ability to contest gender boundaries by limiting the interpretive significance of the sartorial act. The narratives determine the boundaries of meaning imparted to the sign of cross-dressing by directing and focusing the reading of such clothing.[98] The saints' cropped hair or male garb is not interpreted through 1 Cor. 11—as a challenge to the natural order of gender—but rather it is always framed as a practical and necessary disguise that hides the cross-dresser from the secular world that pursues her.[99] Because the texts regularly assert that the saints adopt male clothing for purely practical reasons, other possible interpretations of their dress performance (especially the gender-bending interpretations found in the previous chapter) are elided and the story achieves "narrative closure."[100] By isolating one "explanatory structure"—the overriding principle that directs and assigns significance to the chosen image—over all others, authors control the interpretation and ultimately the meaning of cross-dressing.[101] The narrative then masks its construction by appearing to recount real events of history.

Just as the *Lives* demarcate suitable excuses for female ascetics' cross-dressing, so too do they ally cross-dressing women with ecclesial and monastic leaders, making sure to underscore the proper—i.e., gendered—order and hierarchy of Christian communities. From our examination of the controversies over dress in North Africa and Asia Minor, we saw that cross-dressing could cause a rift (or reflect a preexistent rift) between ascetics and Christian leaders. In these legends, however, such competition for power is smoothed over and female ascetics are consistently depicted following the counsel of their superiors, both abbots and bishops.[102] In fact, male monks and church leaders are frequently implicated in the initial act of cross-dressing. In the Syriac *Life of Pelagia*, Pelagia seeks permission from Bishop Nonnus not only to dress like a man but to wear his clothing: a hair shirt and a woolen mantle.[103] Euphrosyne's hair is cut short and she is dressed in a robe by a local hermit. In fact, Euphrosyne makes a point of saying that she does not want to be tonsured by a "layman," seeking out the holy man instead.[104] Anastasia was said to have been aided in her disguise by the famous Abba Daniel.[105] Moreover, when the saints' true gender is discovered, they are persistently shown to comply with the orders of their superiors.[106]

We should not underestimate the importance of these scenes that describe the cross-dressing as a practical necessity and tether the cross-dressing saint to a male leader in the Christian community. From these scenes, readers understand that ascetics are allowed to dress as men only in extenuating circumstances and only when sanctioned by a male ecclesial or monastic superior.[107] It is only with men's help that such women have access to and find solace in a life of male monasteries.

In the end, it becomes clear that the *Lives* of cross-dressing saints domesticated the radical cross-dressing that worried church leaders. The legends foreclosed the interpretive possibilities of the dress performance so that cross-dressing spoke only to a notion of symbolically transcended gender, to her spiritual manliness rather than any real change in gender status, thus diffusing cross-dressing's transgressive potential. At the same time, the legends simultaneously constructed a realm of physical bodily differences that worked to naturalize gender categories. Finally, the *Lives* retrained readers' interpretation of the ascetic appearances in their midst, so that even if aspects of bodily difference were not present or immediately evident (i.e., they had disappeared due to rigorous ascetic practice or were hidden beneath clothing), gender difference could—and should—still be imagined in the minds of spectators.

# Conclusion

The central aim of this book was to analyze late ancient bodily performances and texts together in order to understand how the two worked in concert to create, consolidate, and contest the interconnected notions of gender, piety, and authority. In the end, how does this study nuance our understanding of gender? As noted in the Introduction, in the past few decades scholars have argued that gender in antiquity was not definitively measured by biological features such as genitalia; rather, notions of masculinity and femininity were linked to a range of extracorporeal characteristics (e.g., reason, discipline over passions, domination/submission). For this reason, gender was never truly stable. Gender—particularly masculinity—needed to be repeatedly asserted (or defended) though deliberate and calculated public performances, such as oration, athletic contests, military pursuits, proper fiscal management, and virtue. Such public performances of gender were necessary because gender status and difference undergirded social hierarchies and, in turn, played a prominent role in social competition. So too individuals were to craft their physical appearance with great care since such appearances could be scrutinized by others, above all by adversaries hoping to justify their claims of moral superiority and sanction their positions of power.

This study has drawn attention to the role of dressing and grooming in the public performance of gender. Moreover, while much of the past research has studied performances of masculinity, my focus has been on the extent to which a noble and pious Christian woman ought to perform her femininity. For men, the goal was clear: to perform masculinity through a well-groomed appearance that did not show signs of too much careful attention. The danger lay in failing to achieve a fully masculine performance, leaving men vulnerable to charges of effeminacy. Women faced danger in every direction. On the one hand, women's typically feminine looks were denigrated as demonstrating their innate vice. On the other hand, even though women were to aspire to acquire masculine virtues and character, they were also critiqued for overstepping their place in the order of society (and the order of creation). Women were criticized for performing too much femininity or too much masculinity. The ideal performance for women seems to have been largely contradictory: the virtuous woman should strive to achieve masculine traits in a way that never troubled her firm identification with femininity. Christians and non-Christians alike hoped to maintain two distinct registers of gender so that a woman's progress on one level might not dissolve gender categories and difference altogether.

While it might be relatively easy to praise a woman—especially a female ascetic—*in writing* by holding together these two registers of gender, it was much more difficult for a woman to communicate both in her dress and physical appearance, because dress signs were read to signal her manly virtue and spiritual state as well as her female nature and bodily form. The difficulty could be managed through a carefully crafted reading of female ascetics' dress and physical appearance, which explains the exhaustive work of Christian leaders to identify aspects of masculinity, and especially femininity, in ascetics' looks. Although Christian leaders argued that ascetics' simplified dressing and grooming exhibited their ascetic discipline and advanced spiritual standing, they likewise guided spectators to see expressions of feminine impulses, such as the overriding vanity and pride that prompted women to assert their identity—even their ascetic identity—through display. Even when female ascetics dressed as men, Christian leaders pointed to their manner of dressing, which, contrary to outward appearance, exhibited their true female nature.

In addition to locating femininity in ascetics' unconventional dress and physical appearance, we find that Christian leaders were prompted to identify new modes of defining femininity in order to prove that female ascetics continued to fit within the category "woman." Christian leaders could no longer define gender according to gendered character traits or partners of heterosexual intercourse because female ascetics undermined both of these premises. Moreover, once female ascetics renounced conventional female dress, they no longer looked like typical women. Thus, the boundaries of femininity needed to flex in order for female ascetics to continue to fit within its parameters. Tertullian accordingly outlined a lineage model of gender that identified even female ascetics to be women according to the created order and descent from Eve.

The next strategy was to locate new aspects of the body that could be read as certain signs of all women's shared femininity. This turn to bodily criteria of gender is not terribly surprising because ascetics' rejection of marriage, heterosexual intercourse, and reproduction already focused attention on the corporeal aspects of gender *through renunciation*. Once female ascetics departed from women's conventional lifestyle—and no longer made use of body parts and functions that distinguished them as women—new body parts needed to be found to fill the vacuum. By calling attention to female ascetics' bodily form, Christian leaders counterbalanced attributions of virility and manliness (in terms of their piety and spiritual maturity) in order to maintain the stability of gender categories. Thus, we find Christian leaders appealing to ascetics' bodies as proof of their female status regardless of their ascetic discipline or dress: Tertullian and Augustine point to hair length, whereas the *Lives* of the cross-dressing saints pay greater attention to women's breasts and nipples, as constitutive markers of bodily gender, initiating a step in the trajectory toward modern understandings of biological sex categories. These bodily markers need not even be evident for them to be meaningful criteria of difference. Christian leaders and authors of the cross-dressing saints' *Lives* could direct specta- tors' reading of ascetic appearances in such a way that even if such bodily markers of difference were not present or visible (i.e., if they had disap- peared due to rigorous ascetic practice or were hidden beneath clothing), they could still be imagined in the minds of viewers. In fact, the *Lives* could be read as pedagogical literature that trained readers to locate gender in even ambiguously dressed bodies, diffusing the impact of ambiguous bod- ies to dissolve gender categories, as discussed in the Introduction.

No matter how proficiently Christian leaders signified the looks of female ascetics, their interpretive enterprise was made more difficult by female ascetics who refused to fashion looks that complied with Christian leaders' interpretations or who offered alternative interpretations of their new forms of dress and grooming. Much to the chagrin of most Christian leaders, some ascetics argued that they had indeed overcome their gender— either claiming a new genderless or masculine status—and claimed that their dress and grooming (e.g., relinquishing the veil and cross-dressing) confirmed their new gender status. They buttressed these arguments and looks with scriptural reasoning that could not be easily dismissed. Ascetics' dress and interpretations of their dress, therefore, resisted an easy identifi- cation of them as "virile women" hoped for by the Christian leaders around them, presenting them rather as full-fledged men, a "third sex," or some state between or beyond gender.

Christian leaders and councils hoped to reduce the significance of ascet- ics' dress performances as challenges to existing gender categories by redi- recting attention to the theological or hermeneutical arguments presumed to lie behind such bodily acts. If they could best ascetics' reasoning, they hoped in turn to constrain ascetics to dress in ways that corresponded with their understanding of gender. When all else failed, as in the case of the council of Gangra, they exerted their ecclesial power, censuring troubling dress as anathema and branding sartorial violators heretics.

Why did Christians and non-Christians labor so hard to assert gender difference even for female ascetics and to compel individuals to demon- strate that difference in their dress and grooming? Because difference is the basis of hierarchy. In the early Imperial period, women's dress was read to signify differences between Roman and non-Roman, as well as between Roman men and women. Elite women's decadent dress was a sign of wom- en's natural vice, vice that was safely distanced from Roman men, who were understood to possess a far greater degree of self-mastery and ratio- nality. At the same time, women's decadent dress and adornments—which were imported from abroad—were also a sign of Roman power, gesturing to her dominance over the peoples of the Mediterranean. This association between femininity and foreignness was not lost on elite Roman men, who hoped to dominate both outsiders and women. By linking feminine looks with foreign luxury goods—and by extension feminine and foreign vice—elite Roman men justified their need to control both populations as a moral prerogative. In this way, women's ornate dress secured elite Roman men's individual and political social capital.

So, too, women's dress was publicized by Christians, who jockeyed for influence and authority in the Mediterranean. The simple and unadorned dress of female Christian ascetics was interpreted as a symbol of Christianity's moral superiority, which set Christians apart from their pagan neighbors. The Christian ascetic exhibited not the typical feminine vice of other women—the vain and hyper-sexual desire to be alluring and attract attention—but rather exhibited humility and restraint. This difference was then mobilized as evidence of Christianity's exceptional piety and moral superiority.

Even while ascetics' dress and grooming constructed *difference* between Christian women and their non-Christian counterparts and created a moral hierarchy in which Christians appeared to surpass pagans, it simultaneously threatened to *flatten* distinctions of gender that, in the minds of male Christian leaders, constructively ordered Christian communities. In order to exhibit her difference from the women around her, the female Christian ascetic demonstrated a lack of feminine vice by deviating from the conventional feminine look. If fact, in several instances, she dressed and looked like her ascetic brothers. I have attempted to highlight Christian leaders' efforts to continually keep these women in check by imposing a material limit to ascetics' total gender transformation. Most Christian leaders and counsels insisted that female ascetics continue to *appear* as women. Christian men, along with non-Christian men of the early Imperial period, wished to identify women as distinct and used clothing as a principal indicator of women's difference. Roman men—Christian and non-Christian—strove hard to assert this difference between men and women in order to suppress the influence of ever more powerful women, whether women of the early Imperial period whose wealth and influence was on the rise or early Christian ascetic women whose status within their communities was elevated beyond that of other women and threatened to impinge upon the realm of Christian men.

# Notes

NOTES TO THE INTRODUCTION

1. For example, Ambr., *Virg.* 3.1.1 (PL 16.219); Jer., *ep.* 23.2 (CSEL 54.212); Jer., *ep.* 24.5 (CSEL 54.217).
2. Ben., *Reg.* 55 (CSEL 75.140–44). Likewise, in Shenoute's community, the *Canons* stress that common clothing should be worn for the sake of equity within the community, although no specific style of dress is described (*Canon* 9 [FM 192]). On descriptions and prescriptions of dress in coenobitic *Rules* and other Patristic writings, see Maria Boulding, "Background to a Theology of the Monastic Habit," *DRev* 98.331 (1980): 119–22; Gillian Clark, *Women in Late Antiquity: Pagan and Christian Lifestyles* (Oxford: Clarendon Press, 1993), 105–18. Although beyond the scope of the present project, the significance of Christian men's dress likewise deserves attention. Lynda Coon offers a preliminary analysis in *Sacred Fictions: Holy Women and Hagiography in Late Antiquity* (Philadelphia: University of Pennsylvania Press, 1997), 52–70. Additionally, Maria Boulding devotes a section to male ascetics' use of the *pallium* in "Monastic Habit," 119–20.
3. The natural gray or black color—*pullati* (dark-clad)—signified the working class because the poor were unable to bleach their garments. Dark colors were also worn during periods of mourning (Gillian Clark, "Women and Asceticism in Late Antiquity: The Refusal of Status and Gender," in *Asceticism*, ed. Vincent Wimbush and Richard Valantasis [New York: Oxford University Press, 1995], 36).
4. Clark, "Women and Asceticism," 36.
5. The terms "pagan" and "heathen"—employed by early Christians to designate non-Christian and non-Jewish Romans—have come under scrutiny in recent years. Michele Salzman and Maijastina Kahlos have shown, however, that alternative terms, such as "polytheists" or "adherents of Greco-Roman cults and religion," are equally problematic and imprecise (Michele R. Salzman, "Pagans and Christians," in *The Oxford Handbook of Early Christian Studies*, ed. Susan Ashbrook Harvey and David G. Hunter [Oxford: Oxford University Press, 2008]), 187–89; Maijastina Kahlos, *Debate and Dialogue: Christian and Pagan Cultures, c. 360–430* [Aldershot: Ashgate, 2007], 17–18). For that reason, these scholars have elected to continue to use the term "pagan" to designate the non-Christian Other, while always attentive of the term's rhetorically derogatory and differentiating function. I, too, follow this convention.
6. Teresa Shaw, "*Askesis* and the Appearance of Holiness," *JECS* 6.3 (1998): 488, 491, 493.
7. John Carl Flügel, *Psychology of Clothes* (London: Hogarth Press, 1930), 15.

8. Lou Taylor, *Establishing Dress History* (Manchester: Manchester University Press, 2004), 4–43, 66–104.
9. As cited in Christian Feest, "European Collecting of American Indian Artefacts and Art," *JHC* 5.1 (1993): 3.
10. Conversely, photographs of converted "natives," who had changed their clothing—or in many cases had merely clothed their exposed bodies—were used as signs of the civilizing triumph of Christianity over "savage religions" (Taylor, *Dress History*, 73–75).
11. Taylor, *Dress History*, 84–85.
12. Tony Bennett, *The Birth of the Museum: History, Theory, Politics* (London: Routledge, 1995), 177–86; Edwina Taborsky, "The Discursive Object," in *Objects of Knowledge*, ed. Susan Pearce (London: Athlone Press, 1990), 50–77; Susan Pearce, "Objects as Meaning; or Narrating the Past," in *Objects of Knowledge*, 125–40.
13. Thorstein Veblen's 1899 *The Theory of the Leisure Class* was the first full-length academic study of dress. Veblen's work, entrenched in an economic debate of the time, argued that the chief motivation for acquiring private property was not purely to meet subsistence (as was the prevailing opinion of nineteenth-century economists), but also to demonstrate "pecuniary superiority" over other members of the community: "If, as is sometimes assumed, the incentive to accumulation were the want of subsistence or of physical comfort, then the aggregate economic wants of a community might conceivably be satisfied at some point in the advance of industrial efficiency; but since the struggle is substantially a race for reputability on the basis of an invidious comparison, no approach to a definitive attainment is possible" (*The Theory of the Leisure Class: An Economic Study in the Evolution of Institutions* [New York: The Macmillan Company, 1912], 32, cf. 24–25).
14. Veblen, *Leisure Class*, 73–74. Veblen argues that society's definitions of beauty and "taste" are grounded in costliness and rarity (*Leisure Class*, 130f; cf. Tert., *Cult. fem.* 1.7).
15. Veblen, *Leisure Class*, 170. Veblen offers the French heel, corset, Chinese foot-binding, and the "general disregard of the wearer's comfort which is an obvious feature of all civilized women's apparel" as examples of incapacitating fashions that exhibit individuals' inability to be productive and instead demonstrates their pecuniary ability to live a life of leisure (*Leisure Class*, 171–72, 181–82). Veblen admits that although women might put on a show of conspicuous leisure, they more often than not still engaged in some form of productive labor. Their productivity was merely obscured by an appearance that communicated leisure (*Leisure Class*, 43–44, 82–83).
16. Although Bourdieu concludes that both forms of capital go hand in hand, he asserts that an understanding of cultural capital helps scholars identify subtleties of classed consolidations of power missed by many Marxist sociologists (Pierre Bourdieu, *La distinction. Critique sociale du jugement* [Paris: Éditions de Minuit, 1979], 1–8, 293–364).
17. Veblen, *Leisure Class*, 181–82, emphasis added; cf. 53–65, 81–85.
18. So too did servants whose dress reflected the prestige and power of their master (Kelly Olson, *Dress and the Roman Woman: Self-Presentation and Society* [London: Routledge, 2008], 43–44).
19. Roland Barthes, *The Fashion System*, trans. Matthew Ward and Richard Howard (New York: Hill and Wang, 1983), 13. Elsewhere Barthes writes: "Is there any system of objects, a system of some magnitude, which can dispense with articulated language? Is not speech the inevitable relay of any signifying order? . . . [C]an clothing signify without recourse to the speech that

describes it, comments upon it, and provides it with signifiers and signifieds abundant enough to constitute a system of meaning?" (*Fashion System*, xi).

20. Barthes, *Fashion System*, 9.

21. Butler follows the lead of feminist film theorists, who, in the words of Jane Gaines, have cleared up "the confusion caused by the success of the moving image at putting itself over as the same as the reality to which it refers . . . the work cut out for feminist film theorists has been the continual rescue of this image which tends to dissolve into a mist of naturalness—to hold it up for further scrutiny, and to make its constructedness evident—to turn it inside out so that the stitching shows" (Jane Gaines and Charlotte Herzog, eds., *Fabrications: Costume and the Female Body* [New York: Routledge, 1990], 1).

22. As Butler dismantles the assumptions that sex categories exist coherently and naturally apart from discursive appendages, it is important to note that she does not intend to ignore what many consider to be real material differences. She agrees that there might be "parts, activities, capacities, hormonal and chromosomal differences" between bodies, but "to 'concede' the undeniability of 'sex' " is to ignore the sheer arbitrariness of criteria used to constructed sex categories. Classifications, for instance, could be made according to earlobe formation, eye color, or nose length. But, "we do not ask when a child enters the world what species of earlobe it has. We immediately ask about certain sexually differentiated anatomical traits" ("Variations on Sex and Gender: Beauvoir, Wittig and Foucault," in *Feminism as Critique: On the Politics of Gender*, ed. Seyla Benhabib and Drucilla Cornell [Minneapolis: University of Minnesota Press, 1987], 135; cf. Butler, *Bodies That Matter*, 10–11, 28). When her critics argue that certain aspects of sex are indeed "real" and "natural," therefore, they perform the very work of categorization that Butler wishes to expose. Sex difference, she concludes, is never simply a function of material, physical difference, "which is not in some way both marked and formed by discursive practices" (*Bodies That Matter*, 1).

23. Butler concludes: "My suggestion is that the body becomes its gender through a series of acts which are renewed, revised, and consolidated through time . . . [O]ne might try to reconceive the gendered body as the legacy of sedimented acts rather than a predetermined or foreclosed structure, essence or fact, whether natural, cultural, or linguistic" ("Performative Acts and Gender Constitution: An Essay in Phenomenology and Feminist Theory," in *Performing Feminisms: Feminist Critical Theory and Theatre*, ed. Sue-Ellen Case [Baltimore: Johns Hopkins University Press, 1990], 274). Sex is therefore no longer a prediscursive, corporeal given, but rather is "one of the norms by which the 'one' becomes viable at all, that which qualifies a body for life within the domain of cultural intelligibility" (Butler, *Bodies That Matter*, 2). This is not, however, a unilateral process, whereby the discursive realm invests the material realm with meaning and forces it to comply. Rather, the compliance of material bodies is necessary for the ideal to be upheld. In Butler's words, "The ideal that is mirrored, depends on that very mirroring to be sustained as an ideal" ("Performative Acts," 272). So, on the one hand, the regulatory ideal of a sex binary structures expectations about sexed bodies, whereas on the other hand, the performance of sexed practices and appearances reinforces the regulatory ideals of sex through repeated citations. Gender performativity enacts and produces the sex that it repeatedly cites.

24. Butler, "Performative Acts," 273. Although Butler recognizes that "sex" difference is based on materiality, she completely rethinks materiality. Butler writes, "What constitutes the fixity of the body, its contours, its movements, *will be fully material*, but materiality will be rethought as the *effect* of power,

as power's most productive effect" (*Bodies That Matter*, 2, emphasis added). Material performances of language, gesture, and dress do not merely represent sex difference, but actually make sex (Butler, *Gender Trouble*, 171–90; idem, "Performative Acts," 270–82; idem, *Bodies That Matter*, 12–16).

25. Other gender theorists note that we have become so proficient at dressing our parts that "clothing delivers gender as self-evident or natural and then recedes as 'clothing,' leaving the connotation 'femininity' " (Gaines and Herzog, eds., *Fabrications*, 1; cf. Joanne Entwistle, *The Fashioned Body: Fashion, Dress and Modern Social Theory* [Cambridge: Polity Press, 2000], 141).

26. Here I also follow a current historiographical trend. With the so-called literary and linguistic turns, many historians have begun to acknowledge our limited access to "real" events of the past because such events are accessible only through texts that are laden with literary and rhetorical strategies, and are furthermore mediated through complex language systems and signs. This acknowledgment has prompted many historians to shift their focus to the "text" itself rather than to the historical events and figures "behind" or "beyond" the text. The questions these historians ask are qualitatively different. Rather than asking only "what happened?" "to whom?" "when?" "why?" many historians now also ask "how": "How does this text define and categorize groups?"; "how does this text produce a normative understanding of the subject or object discussed?"; "how does this particular production of knowledge delimit social realities?"; and "how does the text reinforce and perpetuate systems and institutions of power?" For a detailed discussion of shifts in historiographical method, see Elizabeth A. Clark, *History, Theory, Text: Historians and the Linguistic Turn* (Cambridge: Harvard University Press, 2004), 9–28, 119–24; Averil Cameron, "Redrawing the Map: Early Christian Territory after Foucault," *JRS* 76 (1986): 266–71.

The discursive analysis of the text has not replaced a concern for material realities but rather has defined a new approach to studying material realities. Historians have become interested in how a text's logic is connected to broader cultural ideologies and how such ideological systems had very real material and political consequences. (See, for example, Andrew Jacobs, *Remains of the Jews: The Holy Land and Christian Empire in Late Antiquity* [Stanford: Stanford University Press, 2004].) For a growing number of late ancient historians, therefore, language, textuality, and discourse provide the lens through which to focus on historical, material realities.

27. Here, though, we must proceed with caution. Not every performance described in late ancient texts can be read as evidence of "real" bodily acts and "real" agency. As we know, writers frequently deployed stylized performances of women to meet their own literary goals. For instance, as Elizabeth A. Clark has demonstrated, Gregory of Nyssa models his portrait of Macrina on Diotima and Sophia not only to honor his deceased sister, but also to score theological points for orthodoxy. Likewise, Gregory's portrayal of Macrina's "sisters," who are wildly emotional at her death, follows conventional social codes of mourning that are meant to convey the degree of honor that Macrina deserved ("The Lady Vanishes: Dilemmas of a Feminist Historian after the 'Linguistic Turn' " *CH* 67.1 [1998]: 22–30; cf. idem, "Holy Women, Holy Words: Early Christian Women, Social History, and the 'Linguistic Turn,' " *JECS* 6.3 [1998]: 413–30; idem, "Sex, Shame, and Rhetoric: En-gendering Early Christian Ethics," *JAAR* 49 [1991]: 221–45).

28. Recent studies of dress and adornment using material and visual evidence include Cynthia S. Colburn and Maura K. Heyn, "Introduction: Bodily

Adornment and Identity," in *Reading a Dynamic Canvas: Adornment in the Ancient Mediterranean World*, ed. Cynthia S. Colburn and Maura K. Heyn (Newcastle: Cambridge Scholars Publishing, 2008); Michael Koortbojian, "The Double Identity of Roman Portrait Statues: Costumes and Their Symbolism at Rome," in *Roman Dress and the Fabrics of Roman Culture*, ed. Jonathan Edmondson and Alison Keith (Toronto: University of Toronto Press, 2008), 71–93; and Silvia Schroer, ed., *Images and Gender: Contributions to the Hermeneutics of Reading Ancient Art* (Göttingen: Vandenhoeck & Ruprecht, 2006).

29. Laqueur, *Making Sex*, 25–26. Several contributors to the recent volume *Mapping Gender in Ancient Religious Discourses*, ed. Todd Penner and Caroline Vander Stichele (Leiden: Brill, 2007) further explicate this notion of a gender spectrum. See especially Virginia Burrus, "Mapping as Metamorphosis: Initial Reflections on Gender and Ancient Religious Discourse," 1–10, and Diana M. Swancutt, "*Still* before Sexuality: 'Greek' Androgyny, the Roman Imperial Politics of Masculinity and the Roman Invention of the *Tribas*," 18–19.

30. Laqueur, *Making Sex*, 29, cf. 26; cf. Maud Gleason, "The Semiotics of Gender: Physiognomy and Self-Fashioning in the Second Century C.E.," in *Before Sexuality: The Construction of Erotic Experience in the Ancient Greek World*, ed. David Halperin, John Winkler, and Froma Zeitlin (Princeton: Princeton University Press, 1990), 390. I do not intend to undervalue the bodily aspects of ancient gender. There remained a functional reality to classifying "male" against "female" according to the body. As Lesley Dean-Jones notes, even if medical writers did not distinguish men and women wholly according to anatomical difference, they did distinguish their different physiological *processes*, namely menstruation (which marked women's bodies as less efficient and thus inferior to men's bodies), pregnancy, and childbirth (Lesley Dean-Jones, *Women's Bodies in Classical Greek Science* [Oxford: Clarendon Press, 1994], 55–65). More generally, the association of body with "the feminine" and reason with "the masculine" was such a well-attested trope in antiquity so that even if women were not exclusively defined by particular parts of the body, they were characterized as "bodily" in contradistinction to "rational" men (Elizabeth V. Spelman, "Woman as Body: Ancient and Contemporary Views," *Feminist Studies* 8.1 [1982]: 108–31; Genevieve Lloyd, *Man of Reason: "Male" and "Female" in Western Philosophy* [Minneapolis: University of Minnesota Press, 1993], 18–33).

31. Virginia Burrus has observed that proving one's virility depended upon carefully crafted and "flawlessly embodied performance" (*"Begotten, Not Made": Conceiving Manhood in Late Antiquity* [Stanford: Stanford University Press, 2000, 19). "Masculinity in the ancient world," Maud Gleason similarly concludes, "was an achieved state" (*Making Men: Sophists and Self-Presentation in Ancient Rome* [Princeton: Princeton University Press, 1995], 59). Both Burrus and Gleason are careful to note, however, that the performance of masculinity was malleable and that men could strategically transform typically "feminized" performances, attributes, and roles into the realm of the masculine. On this point, see also Chris Frilingos, "Wearing It Well: Gender at Work in the Shadow of Empire," in *Mapping Gender in Ancient Religious Discourses*, ed., Todd Penner and Caroline Vander Stichele (Leiden: Brill, 2007), 338.

32. See Elizabeth Castelli, "Virginity and Its Meaning for Women's Sexuality in Early Christianity," *JFSR* 2.1 (1982): 61–88; Carlin Barton, *The Sorrows of the Ancient Romans: The Gladiator and the Monster* (Princeton: Princeton

University Press, 1993); Gleason, *Making Men*, xxii (who writes: "Rhetoric was a calisthenics of manhood"); Catharine Edwards, "Unspeakable Professions: Public Performance and Prostitution in Ancient Rome," in *Roman Sexualities*, ed. Judith P. Hallett and Marilyn B. Skinner (Princeton: Princeton University Press, 1997), 66–95; Craig Williams, *Roman Homosexuality: Ideologies of Masculinity in Classical Antiquity* (New York: Oxford University Press, 1999), 141; Bettina Bergmann and Christine Kondoleon, eds., *The Art of Ancient Spectacle* (New Haven: Yale University Press, 1999); Burrus, *Conceiving Manhood*, 18–22; Mathew Kuefler, *The Manly Eunuch: Masculinity, Gender Ambiguity, and Christian Ideology in Late Antiquity* (Chicago: University of Chicago Press, 2001); Jaclyn L. Maxwell, *Christianization and Communication in Late Antiquity: John Chrysostom and His Congregation in Antioch* (Cambridge: Cambridge University Press, 2006), 42–64; Michael Carter, "(Un)dressed to Kill: Viewing the *Retiarius*," in *Fabrics of Roman Culture*, 113–35; L. Stephanie Cobb, *Dying to Be Men: Gender and Language in Early Christian Martyr Texts* (New York: Columbia University Press, 2008), 60–66.

33. The earliest modern researchers of the historical dress of Greece and Rome were eighteenth-century French politicians hoping to use ancient dress as a symbol of political ideals and nineteenth-century British costume designers hoping to provide accurate depictions of historical figures for their theater productions (Aileen Ribeiro, *The Art of Dress: Fashion in England and France 1750 to 1820* [New Haven: Yale University Press, 1995]; Thomas Hope, *Costumes of the Greeks and Romans* [New York: Dover Publications, 1962]).

At the beginning of the twentieth century, on the heels of economic and psychological studies of dress (Veblen, *Leisure Class*; Flügel, *Psychology of Clothes*), there was a surge of interest in the dress of antiquity among classicists. From this time, a number of scholars compiled pictorial catalogues of ancient dress, often organized by ethnic group or geographical region and time period (e.g., section titles might include: "Roman empire—early period," "Iberia—fourth–second centuries BC," "Persia—second century BC–second century CE"). Using archaeological remains, art and monumental depictions, and literary descriptions of dress and ornaments, these catalogues intended mainly to illustrate and describe the material aspects of dress, such as available textiles, construction patterns, and draping methods. See James Laver, *Costume in Antiquity; 480 Illustrations* (London: Thames and Hudson, 1964); Léon Alexandre Heuzey, *Histoire du costume antique d'après des études sur le modèle vivant* (Paris: É. Champion, 1922); Karl Köhler and Emma von Sichart, *Praktische Kostümkunde* (London: G.G. Harrap, 1928); Mary Evans, *Costume throughout the Ages* (Philadelphia: J.B. Lippincott, 1930); Margarete Bieber, "Stola," *RE* (1931), 56–62; Lillian May Wilson, *The Clothing of the Ancient Romans* (Baltimore: Johns Hopkins University Press, 1938); Mary G. Houston, *Ancient Greek, Roman and Byzantine Costume and Decoration* (London: Adam & Charles Black, 1947); J. P. V. D. Balsdon, "Women's Daily Life: Dress, Coiffure, Make-up and Jewels," in *Roman Women: Their History and Habits* (London: Bodley Head, 1962), 252–65; Larissa Bonfante, *Etruscan Dress* (Baltimore: Johns Hopkins University Press, 1975); Alexandra T. Croom, *Roman Clothing and Fashion* (Gloucester: Tempus, 2002); Lloyd Llewellyn-Jones and Sue Blundell, *Women's Dress in the Ancient Greek World* (London: Duckworth, 2002).

Comprised mostly of illustrations with short captions, these publications provided little accompanying analysis of the complex social significance of dress. These treatments rarely addressed intragroup distinctions, such as clothing variations that characterized economic, political, or social groupings within a region. While they did frequently distinguish "men's dress" from "women's dress," these commentaries provide a glimpse less into ancient notions of gender and gendered clothing than into early twentieth-century stereotypes and prejudice. For instance, F. H. Marshall unabashedly asserts that "Roman ladies were passionately fond of jewellery," ignoring the many depictions of richly adorned men in Roman art and literature, such as the Prima Porta statue of Augustus adorned in an ornate breastplate, the Ravenna mosaics of Justinian and his entourage, and the well-attested decorative costumes of Persian men ("Dress," in *A Companion to Latin Studies*, ed. John Edwin Sandys [Cambridge: Cambridge University press, 1929], 199).

These catalogs were furthermore preoccupied with the group boundaries thought to be reflected in such appearances and, thus, overlooked how visual and textual depictions of dress participated in the creation of those very boundaries. In other words, these catalogues failed to consider how particular visual or textual representations were strategically employed in order to construct and convey particular aspects of group identity and to participate in social competition. Later generations of classicists, understanding this oversight, have sought to address the rhetorical implications of visual and textual representations. In 1988, a group of scholars convened a seminar in Rome on "The Religious, Social, and Political Significance of Roman Dress." Although these scholars continued to focus mainly on the construction of national and ethnic identities, and analyzed mostly men's dress, they diverged from their predecessors in the field by revealing the calculated ways in which dress was used to assert identity and difference. (Many of the papers from this conference can be found in Judith Lynn Sebesta and Larissa Bonfante, *World of Roman Costume* [Madison: University of Wisconsin Press, 1994].) Since then, a new wave of studies has been published that continue to focus on the "use of [dress] and bodily adornment as a means of shaping and communicating identity, and thereby facilitating interaction, negotiating difference, and creating or crossing boundaries" (Colburn and Heyn, *Dynamic Canvas*, 1; cf. Olson, *Dress and the Roman Woman*; Jonathan Edmondson and Alison Keith, eds., *Fabrics of Roman Culture*; Liza Cleland, Mary Harlow, and Lloyd Llewellyn-Jones, eds., *The Clothed Body in the Ancient World* [Oxford: Oxbow Books, 2005]).

34. The notable exception is Kelly Olson's recent book *Dress and the Roman Woman*.

35. See, for example, *Gos. Thom.* 114 (NHC II, 2, 51:18–26); Jer., *Ephes.* 3.5 (PL 26.533); Ambr., *Luc.* 10.16 (PL 15.1938); Aug., *Conf.* 13.9.4 (CCSL 27.137); Gr. Nyss., *v. Macr.* 1 (SC 178.138); Bas., *inst. ascet.* (PG 31.624D-625A); Pall., *hist. Laus.* 9 (Dom Cuthbert Butler, *The Lausiac History of Palladius*, vol. 2 [Cambridge: Cambridge University Press, 1898], 29); Geront., *v. Melan. Junior.* 39 (SC 90.200–2); *Apophth. Patr.*, Sarah (PG 65.419–22). For discussions of the "manly woman" trope, see Kerstin Aspegren, *The Male Woman: A Feminine Ideal in the Early Church* (Stockholm: Almqvist and Wiksell, 1990); Gillian Cloke, *This Female Man of God: Women and Spiritual Power in the Patristic Age 350–450* (New York: Routledge, 1994), 212–21; Kuefler, *Manly Eunuch*, 221–38; Jane Tibbetts Schulenburg, *Forgetful of Their Sex: Female Sanctity and Society, Ca. 500–1100* (Chicago: University of Chicago Press, 1998).

36. This perspective is based on a paired reading of the Genesis creation myths and myths of the primal androgyne. Daniel Boyarin finds this perspective represented most strongly in Paul, the *Apocryphal Acts of the Apostles*, and Clement of Alexandria, whereas Mathew Kuefler demonstrates that Origen and Tertullian likewise hold this position (Daniel Boyarin, "Paul and the

Genealogy of Gender," *Representations* 41 [1993]: 1–33; idem, "Gender," in *Critical Terms for Religious Studies*, ed. Mark C. Taylor [Chicago: University of Chicago Press, 1998], 117–35; Kuefler, *Manly Eunuch*, 225–29; cf. Wayne A. Meeks, "The Image of the Androgyne: Some Uses of a Symbol in Earliest Christianity," *HR* 13.3 [1974]: 185–97). Augustine too represents this position in *De Genesi ad litteram* 9.3–11 (CSEL 28/1.271–81).

37. For discussions of the theological significance attributed to baptismal clothing, see Boulding, "Monastic Habit," 115–19; Meeks, "Image of the Androgyne," 180–89. For a collection of baptismal texts that reference disrobing and clothing, see Thomas M. Finn, *Early Christian Baptism and the Catechumenate: West and East Syria* (Collegeville: Liturgical Press, 1992), 43, 47, 75, 78–79, 83–84, 87, 104, 107, 117, 127–28, 168; and idem, *Early Christian Baptism and the Catechumenate: Italy, North Africa, and Egypt* (Collegeville: Liturgical Press, 1992), 16–17, 49, 57, 60, 65, 87–88, 117, 157, 218, 233.

38. Boyarin, "Genealogy of Gender," 4, 10; idem, "Gender," 125–26; cf. Peter Brown, "Bodies and Minds: Sexuality and Renunciation in Early Christianity," in *Before Sexuality: The Construction of Erotic Experience in the Ancient Greek World*, ed. David Halperin, John Winkler, and Froma Zeitlin (Princeton: Princeton University Press, 1990), 483–90.

39. Boyarin writes: "It was only in virginity, that is only in a social acting out of a disembodied spiritual existence, that gender parity ever existed. Female humans could escape being 'women' by opting out of sexual intercourse" ("Gender," 124, 132; cf. Boyarin, "Genealogy of Gender," 17–18; Graham Gould, "Women in the Writings of the Fathers: Language, Belief and Reality," in *Women and the Church*, ed. W. J. Sheils and D. Woods [Oxford: Blackwell, 1990], 1–13).

40. "Sexual differentiation was thus envisioned as a principal effect of a human sin, not yet 'historically' committed but foreseen by God and consequently accounted for in that unique event of creation which extended to two distinct ontological levels," writes Giulia Sfameni Gasparro in "Image of God and Sexual Differentiation in the Tradition of *Enkrateia*," in *The Image of God: Gender Models in Judaeo-Christian Tradition*, ed. Kari Elisabeth Børrensen (Minneapolis: Fortress Press, 1995), 148–49, 150–55. For full discussions of this position, as well as primary source references, see also Kari Elisabeth Børrensen, "Male-Female, a Critique of Traditional Christian Theology," *Temenos* 13 (1977): 32, 36; Jo Ann McNamara, "Sexual Equality and the Cult of Virginity in Early Christian Thought," *Feminine Studies* 3.314 (1976): 145, 148–51; Giulia Sfameni Gasparro, "Asceticism and Anthropology: *Enkrateia* and 'Double Creation' in Early Christianity," in *Asceticism*, ed. Vincent L. Wimbush and Richard Valantasis (New York: Oxford University Press, 1995), 136–38; Clark, *Women in Late Antiquity*, 122.

41. As Gregory contends, "those who refrain from procreation of death by preventing it from advancing further" are a sort of "boundary stone between life and death" and are able to live in accordance with their nongendered spiritual essence (Gr. Nyss., *virg.* 13 [PG 46.377]; trans. McNamara, "Sexual Equality," 151–52). See also Peter Brown, *The Body and Society: Men, Women, and Sexual Renunciation in Early Christianity* (New York: Columbia University Press, 1988), 222–24.

42. Following Luke 20:27–40, esp. 34–36: "Jesus said to them, 'Those who belong to this age marry and are given in marriage; but those who are considered worthy of a place in that age and in the resurrection from the dead neither marry nor are given in marriage. Indeed they cannot die any more,

because they are like angels and are children of God, being children of the resurrection.'"

43. Verna Harrison, "Male and Female in Cappadocian Theology," *JTS* 41.2 (1990): 441, 451; Margaret R. Miles, *Carnal Knowing: Female Nakedness and Religious Meaning in the Christian West* (New York: Vintage Books, 1989), 66; Sfameni Gasparro, "*Enkrateia*," 134–36; idem, "Sexual Differentiation," 146–47. Even within this position, though, there was significant debate over whether angels and resurrected humans possessed "sexed" bodies. See Elizabeth A. Clark, "The Celibate Bridegroom and His Virginal Brides" *CH* 77:1 (2008): 21–22.

44. Sfameni Gasparro, "*Enkrateia*," 138; idem, "Sexual Differentiation," 136; Clark, *Women in Late Antiquity*, 123–25.

45. Boyarin, "Gender," 122; cf. Franca Ela Consolino, "Female Asceticism and Monasticism in Italy from the Fourth to the Eighth Centuries," in *Women and Faith: Catholic Religious Life in Italy from Late Antiquity to the Present*, ed. Lucetta Scaraffia and Gabriella Zarri [Cambridge: Harvard University Press, 1999], 11.

46. Elizabeth A. Clark, *Ascetic Piety and Women's Faith: Essays on Late Ancient Christianity* (Lewiston: E. Mellen Press, 1986), 180; cf. Ross Kraemer, "The Conversion of Women to Ascetic Forms of Christianity," *Signs* 6 (1980/81): 298–307; Meeks, "Image of the Androgyne," 182.

47. Clark admits that social liberation stemmed not only from female ascetics' vows of sexual renunciation, but also from the privileged backgrounds whence they came (*Ascetic Piety*, 175–80, 185–88; cf. Virginia Burrus, "Chastity as Autonomy: Women in the Stories of the Apocryphal Acts," *Semeia* 38 [1986]: 101–17).

48. Clark, *Ascetic Piety*, 180.

49. See discussions of patristic examples in Pauline Nigh Hogan, *No Longer Male and Female: Interpreting Galatians 3:28 in Early Christianity* (London: T. & T. Clark, 2008), 85–121; Kari Vogt, " 'Becoming Male': A Gnostic and Early Christian Metaphor," in *The Image of God: Gender Models in Judaeo-Christian Tradition*, ed. Kari Elisabeth Børrensen (Minneapolis: Fortress Press, 1995), 174–79.

50. Castelli, "Virginity," 74; cf. Ingvild Sælid Gilhus, "Male and Female Symbolism in the Gnostic *Apocryphon of John*," *Temenos* 19 (1983): 40.

51. Boyarin, "Gender," 126; cf. McNamara, "Sexual Equality," 152–54; Vern L. Bullough, "Transvestites in the Middle Ages," *AJS* 79.6 (1974): 1381.

52. Clem., *Str.* 6.12.100–1 (PG 8.321).

53. Jer., *Ephes.* 3.5 (PL 26.533); trans. Ronald E. Heine, *The Commentaries of Origen and Jerome on St. Paul's Epistle to the Ephesians* (Oxford: Oxford University Press, 2002), 237–38, adapted.

54. Castelli refines this point later in the essay. Recognizing how the paradigm both corroborates the traditional gender hierarchy, while at the same time flexes gender categories, she writes, "These discourses do not simply rearticulate the hegemonic gendered order, nor do they simply deconstruct it; rather, they stretch its boundaries and, if only for a moment, call it into question— even if, ultimately, things return to 'normal' " (" 'I Will Make Mary Male': Pieties of the Body and Gender Transformation of Christian Women in Late Antiquity," in *Body Guards: The Cultural Politics of Gender Ambiguity*, ed. Julia Epstein and Kristina Straub [New York: Routledge, 1991], 33; cf. Dale Martin, *The Corinthian Body*. [New Haven: Yale University Press, 1995], 230–32).

55. Jo. Eph., *vita* 28 (PO 17.559); trans. Susan Ashbrook Harvey, *Asceticism and Society in Crisis: John of Ephesus and the Lives of the Eastern Saints*

(Berkeley: University of California Press, 1990), 121. See also John's introduction to Susan's *Vita*, which reads: "Not only is the mighty strength of Christ God apt to show its activity in men who are powerful in appearance and mighty and forceful, but also in weak, feeble, frail women" (PO 18.541); trans. Harvey, *John of Ephesus*, 121. Basil similarly praises the martyr Julitta: "If indeed it is fitting to call 'woman' one whose great nature of her soul overshadowed the weakness of female nature" (Bas., *Hom. Mart. Julittam* [PG 31.237]). Gregory Nazianzus too says that his mother displayed "in female form the assertiveness of a man" (*De vita sua* 1.60 [PG 37.979]; cf. *De rebus suis* [PG 37.1469]). Finally, Gregory of Nyssa wonders how the label "woman" could apply to his sister, Macrina, because she had clearly overcome her weak womanly nature (*v. Macr.* 1 [SC 178.138]).

## NOTES TO CHAPTER 1

1. For discussions on how consumption and wastefulness are still thoroughly feminized and linked to the realm of dress, see Gaines and Herzog, eds., *Fabrications*, 15; Jennifer Craik, *The Face of Fashion: Cultural Studies in Fashion* (New York: Routledge, 1994), 70–73, 161, 210.
2. See, for instance, the Pandora myth in which Pandora was dressed and adorned by the gods to be an alluring punishment to men. Pandora's beauty was wholly constructed by the gods: they clothed her, draped golden jewelry around her neck and other ornaments on her body, crowned her head with flowers and an embroidered veil. She was thusly deemed a "beautiful evil" (καλὸν κακὸν) because men would be unable to resist her beauty, which would ultimately undermine their dominance and self-control. From this myth we find several themes about women's nature and appearance that remained prevalent in early Imperial Roman literature. First, Pandora's irresistible beauty was depicted as a sham, an unnatural artifice constructed by the gods. Although her beauty was a pretense, her predilection for seducing men through illusion and deception was considered to be a perfectly natural trait in women. Second, Pandora's allure threatened men's dominance by prevailing over men's self-control. Just as Prometheus had unsettled the proper hierarchy of the gods and humans, woman was sent as a punishment that would endanger the proper gendered order of the human realm. Third, woman's extravagant nature would undermine the health of the household. Men needed women in order to produce heirs—to continue the family name and maintain the family's property—yet women's penchant for greed and consumption would continually threaten to deplete the household wealth, undermining the ultimate stability of the family line (Hes. *Theog.* 603–5 [LCL 122]; cf. idem, *Op.* 72–77).
3. In recent years, several new studies have helpfully catalogued and commented upon the literary discussions of male and female dress in the early Imperial period. In this section, I endeavor only to present illustrative examples of how women's dress was signified in order to highlight how these significations recast the concept and appearance of Roman gender in the early Imperial period. For a list of full treatments of the sources, see note 33 in the Introduction.
4. Andrew Dalby, *Empire of Pleasures: Luxury and Indulgence in the Roman World* (New York: Routledge, 2000), 227. For a discussion of the novel products resulting from new trade routes, see p. 266.
5. Mary Harlow, "Dress in the *Historia Augusta*: The Role of Dress in Historical Narrative," in *Clothed Body*, 149–50; Croom, *Roman Clothing*, 21.

6. Aristid., *Rom. Or.* 11–13 (Bruno Keil, *Aelii Aristidis Smyrnaei Quae Supersunt Omnia*, 2nd ed. [Berlin: Weidmann, 1957], 94–95); trans. Charles A. Behr, P. *Aelius Aristides: The Complete Works*, vol. II (Leiden: Brill, 1981), 75.

7. Catharine Edwards, *The Politics of Immorality in Ancient Rome* (Cambridge: Cambridge University Press, 2002), 28, 176–80.

8. Plin., *HN* 37.6 (LCL 10.172–74). Compare Ambrosiaster's concern that Saxon tunics (*saxonicia*) were unfitting for Roman senators in *Qu. test.* 127.36 (CSEL 50.416). For detailed discussions of this argument, see Dalby, *Empire of Pleasures*, 10–12; Jacqueline Dangel, "L'Asie des poètes latins de l'époque républicaine," *Ktèma* 10 (1985):175–92.

9. Edwards, *Politics of Immorality*, 9. See also Donald C. Earl, *The Moral and Political Tradition of Rome* (Ithaca: Cornell University Press, 1967), 11–43.

10. Edwards, *Politics of Immorality*, 2, 19.

11. Edwards, *Politics of Immorality*, 22–24. See also Jennifer Wright Knust, *Abandoned to Lust: Sexual Slander and Ancient Christianity* (New York: Columbia University Press, 2006), 27; Dangel, "L'Asie des poètes latins," 175–92.

12. Edwards, *Politics of Immorality*, 3–4, 19, 25; Knust, *Abandoned to Lust*, 11–12. Edwards and Knust also find moral accusations functioning among individual Roman writers, orators, and leaders who vied for social and political power. Because immoral behavior was linked to the feminine and the foreign, and these associations undermined one's right to lead, morality made for a compelling means of attack. Knust writes: "Designed to marginalize and exclude, moralizing accusations about the decadence, prodigality, and self-indulgence of target members of the male Roman elite justified the dominant position of some—said to embody proper Roman virtue—at the expense of others" (*Abandoned to Lust*, 7, cf. 1–13, 15–25; cf. Earl, *Moral and Political Tradition*, 14–17, 19–21).

13. Knust notes: "The main thing that such slander signified, therefore, was that someone was an opponent" (*Abandoned to Lust*, 6; cf. Edwards, *Politics of Immorality*, 7).

14. Edwards, *Politics of Immorality*, 5–6, 8, 16; Earl, *Moral and Political Tradition*, 17–18; Judith Lynn Sebesta, "Women's Costume and Feminine Civic Morality in Augustan Rome," *G&H* 9.3 (1997): 529–41.

15. Ria Berg, "Wearing Wealth: *Mundus Muliebris* and *Ornatus* as Status Markers for Women in Imperial Rome," in *Women, Wealth, and Power in the Roman Empire*, ed. Päivi Setälä et al. (Rome: Institutum Romanum Finlandiae, 2002), 18–31; Leslie Shumka, "Designing Women: The Representation of Women's Toiletries on Funerary Monuments in Roman Italy," in *Fabrics of Roman Culture*, 177–78.

16. See Maria Wyke's groundbreaking article "Woman in the Mirror: The Rhetoric of Adornment in the Roman World," in *Women in Ancient Societies: An Illusion of the Night*, ed. Léonie J. Archer, Susan Fischler, and Maria Wyke (New York: Routledge, 1994), 134.

17. For estimates of women's wealth in this period, see Kate Cooper, *The Fall of the Roman Household* (Cambridge: Cambridge University Press, 2007), 112–13; Janne Pölönen, "The Division of Wealth between Men and Women in Roman Succession (ca. 50 BC–AD 250)," in *Women, Wealth and Power*, 178.

18. Here I follow the lead of scholars who read late ancient arguments as negotiations between speakers and listeners. Jaclyn Maxwell, for example, has recently analyzed how John Chrysostom delivered sermons that aimed to reorient "his followers' practices and beliefs to align better with his own conception of orthodoxy" (*Christianization and Communication*, 119). This approach

builds on Averil Cameron's *Christianity and the Rhetoric of Empire: The Development of Christian Discourse* (Berkeley: University of California Press, 1991) and Peter Brown's *Power and Persuasion in Late Antiquity: Toward a Christian Empire* (Madison: University of Wisconsin Press, 1992).

19. Jonathan Edmondson, "Public Dress and Social Control in Late Republican and Early Imperial Rome," in *Fabrics of Roman Culture*, 24; Kunst, "*Ornamenta Uxoria*," 127–42. In fact, the same moralists who read women's vice from their attire also used dress terms as shorthand for womanly virtue, implicitly recognizing the many ways one might interpret dress signs (Olson, *Dress and the Roman Woman*, 31, 41, 50).

20. Olson, *Dress and the Roman Woman*, 5–6, 96–112; Berg, "Wearing Wealth," 15–73; Christiane Kunst, "*Ornamenta Uxoria*: Badges of Rank or Jewellery of Roman Wives?" *MHJ* 8.1 (2005): 135; Alicia Batten, "Clothing and Adornment," *BTB* 40.3 (2010): 154–55.

21. Donald Earl, for example, writes: "The influx into Rome during this period of Asiatic luxury and Greek manners on a scale far greater than anything that had gone before provoked, according to our tradition, a double reaction. On the one hand, the youth of the city, particularly the young men of aristocratic family, eagerly embraced the innovations and tended to abandon the traditional Roman morality for display and vice, to reject the laws of the magistrates for philosophical speculation. On the other hand, the main body of senators, with Cato and Scipio Aemilianus especially prominent in our tradition, strove to maintain the *mos maiorum* by accepting those imports which could be made to conform to it and rejecting those which did not" (*Moral and Political Tradition*, 36, cf. 41–43).

22. Livy 34.1–8 (LCL 9.412–38).

23. As Patrick Walsh comments: "The truth is surely that Livy, like all historians, can never completely dissociate the past from the present. In depicting historical occasions which have some parallel in his own day, his ears are subconsciously attuned to the echoes of the present" (*Livy: His Historical Aims and Methods* [Cambridge: Cambridge University Press, 1961], 17–18; cf. Edwards, *Politics of Immorality*, 176–77).

24. Livy 34.3 (LCL 9.420); trans. Page, LCL 9.421.

25. Livy's Cato even suggests that these matrons who are bent on attracting attention from male spectators are committing other sexual sins while on the streets. He asks: "Indeed, what else are they now doing in the streets and on the corners besides advising the plebs about the bill of the tributes and pushing for the repeal of the law?" (Livy 34.2 [LCL 9.416]).

26. Livy 34.3 (LCL 9.420).

27. Livy 34.4 (LCL 9.424).

28. Livy 34.2 (LCL 9.414); trans. Page, LCL 9.415, adapted.

29. Livy 34.3 (LCL 9.418); trans. Page, LCL 9.419, adapted.

30. Livy 34.4 (LCL 9.420).

31. Livy 34.6 (LCL 9.430; 9.432).

32. Livy 34.7 (LCL 9.436).

33. Livy 34.7 (LCL 9.436).

34. Livy 34.7 (LCL 9.436).

35. Livy 34.7 (LCL 9.436).

36. This is Veblen's derivative prestige of wards described on page 6 of the Introduction.

37. Note that both men vocalize their desire for Roman men to preserve their wealth and power in this moment of increased prosperity. Livy 34.7 (LCL 9.438).

38. As Catharine Edwards has shown, the most ardent moralizers of this period stood at the margins between social groups. Horace, the Senecas, and the

Plinys were "new men" who did not possess aristocratic lineages upon which to draw authority. They mobilized their authority, therefore, by aligning themselves with Roman virtuosity and the *mores maiorum* (Edwards, *Politics of Immorality*, 17; cf. Philip Hills, *Horace* [London: Bristol Classical Press, 2005], 9–14; William Dominik and William Wehrle, *Roman Verse Satire: Lucilius to Juvenal* [Wauconda: Bolchazy-Carducci Publishers, 1999], 6; Warren S. Smith, "Advice on Sex by the Self-Defeating Satirists," in *Satiric Advice on Women and Marriage*, ed. Warren S. Smith [Ann Arbor: University of Michigan Press, 2005], 114, 127–28).

39. Richard Hawley argues that such gender and sexual ideology was inculcated through Greek educational patterns and sources (" 'In a Different Guise': Roman Education and Greek Rhetorical Thought on Marriage," in *Satiric Advice on Women and Marriage*, ed. Warren S. Smith [Ann Arbor: University of Michigan Press, 2005], 26–38; cf. Alexander Dalzell, *The Criticism of Didactic Poetry: Essays on Lucretius, Virgil, and Ovid* [Toronto: University of Toronto Press, 1997], 136–37).

40. Prop. 3.13.3–8 (LCL 304); cf. Juv. 6.1–20, 6.286–91 (LCL 82–84, 106).

41. Women's naturally excessive temperament was further linked to (and characterized by) hyper-sexuality and lust, which were regarded as twin aspects of *incontinentia* (Edwards, *Politics of Immorality*, 5, 43–47, 63–97). Throughout these examples, effeminate men's dress and grooming practices are sometimes discussed alongside that of women, reinforcing the notion that a person's dress habits are a good indicator of his/her true gender.

42. Plin., *HN* 6.20.54; 11.26.76–27.77 (LCL 2.378; 3.478); cf. Petron., *Sat.* 55 (LCL 114); Sen., *Controv.* 2.5.7; 2.7.4 (LCL 1.324; 1.366); Sen., *Ben.* 7.9.5 (LCL 3.478).

43. Ov., *Medic.* 23, 31 (LCL 2, 4).

44. Ov., *Medic.* 31–32 (LCL 4). It is interesting that, although Ovid finds innate vanity in women, he, unlike other Roman writers, does not consider Roman women to be naturally adept at seduction. Rather, he purports to teach women what they do not instinctively know: "Become devoted to [my guidelines] so that you may learn to deceive" (*Ars am.* 3.616 [LCL 160]). To this end, Ovid offers his expert advice in the treatises *De medicamina faciei femineae* (*On Painting the Face*) and *Ars amatoria* (*Art of Love*).

45. Plin., *HN* 37.6 (LCL 10.172–76).

46. As Kelly Olson observes, the verb *fucare*—to paint, dye, or to use cosmetics—is linguistically related to terms meaning counterfeit, spurious, or falsified (*fucosus*) (*Dress and the Roman Woman*, 81).

47. Mart., *Epigram.* 9.37; cf. 6.12; 12.23 (LCL 2.264–65; 2.10; 3.108).

48. Lucr., *de rerum nat.* 4.1155–56, 60–63 (LCL 328–30).

49. Hor., *Sat.* 1.2.77–110 (LCL 24–26).

50. Ovid writes: "Let others delight in ancient times; I congratulate myself on having been born just now. This age suits my nature well" (*Ars am.* 3.121–22 [LCL 126]). He had to be careful, though, not to draw the ire of conservatives. In his didactic poems, in which Ovid advised women in the processes of beautification, he explicitly states that his recommendations were not directed at married women or unmarried noblewomen. As Karla Pollmann notes, however, Ovid's implicit audience is unclear, "primarily due to the ambiguity of terms like *vir*, *maritus*, *uxor*, and *coniunx*, which can mean 'husband' and 'wife,' respectively, but also 'lover' and 'beloved,' as the genre of love elegy adopted the terminology for its own purposes." Moreover, at times Ovid's advice seems particularly suited to illicit relationships. For instance, at one point Ovid offers advice on how a *puella* might elude her suspicious "partner." See Karla Pollmann, "Marriage and Gender in Ovid's

Erotodidactic Poetry," in *Satiric Advice on Women and Marriage*, ed. Warren S. Smith (Ann Arbor: University of Michigan Press, 2005), 94.

51. Ovid urges those women who possess natural beauty to use it while it lasts, for "there will be a time when you, who now shut out your lover, will lie alone and cold in the night. Nor will you find your door damaged by some nightly brawl. Nor will your threshold be sprinkled with roses in the morning. How quickly (ah me!) does the sagging flesh wrinkle, and the color vanishes from the bright cheeks! And the hairs that you will swear have been gray since your girlhood will suddenly spring up all over your head" (*Ars am.* 3.69–76 [LCL 122]; cf. Ov., *Medic.* 1–7 [LCL 2]).

52. Ov., *Ars am.* 3.105; 3.164 (LCL 124; 128); cf. *Ars am.* 3.199–202; 3.261–62; 3.771–86 (LCL 132; 136; 172).

53. Ov., *Ars am.* 3.199–202, 267, 269, 271, 274–76, 279–80 (LCL 132; 136). Similarly, in Lucan's *Pharsalia*, when the haggard witch Erictho struggles to revive the corpse of a fallen soldier, she threatens the gods in order to impel them to come to her aid. To Hecate, she warns: "You, Hecate, who are accustomed to putting on a deceptive appearance [cosmetics] before visiting the gods, I will expose your wasted and pale appearance to Erebes" (*Phars.* 6.736–738).

54. Ov., *Rem. am.* 343–44 (LCL 200).

55. Wyke, "Woman in the Mirror," 136–37, 147.

56. Juv. 6.458–59, 6.61–66; cf. 6.508–10 (LCL 120; 280–82).

57. Referencing Publilius, Petron., *Sat.* 55 (LCL 114).

58. Prop. 2.16.13–26 (LCL 168–70); cf. Mart., *Epigram.* 11.49 (LCL 3.44).

59. Sen., *Controv.* 2.7 (LCL 1.362–73).

60. Sen., *Controv.* 2.7.1 (LCL 1.364–65).

61. Sen., *Controv.* 2.7.5 (LCL 1.368).

62. Prop. 3.13 (LCL 304–10). Although in the first two books of his *elegies*, Propertius depicts his enslavement to "Cynthia," by Book Three, Propertius—the spurned lover—sets out to write against the sexual indulgences and female dominance of his time.

63. Ov., *Ars am.* 2.194–232 (LCL 78–82).

64. Juv. 6.486–510 (LCL 122–24).

65. Juv. 6.149–60; cf. 6.208–10; 6.347–65 (LCL 94–96; 96–98; 110).

66. Lucr., *de rerum nat.* 4.1123–30 (LCL 326).

67. Propertius bemoans his own expensive enslavement to Cynthia: "She's always sending me to the ocean to look for pearls, and ordering me to fetch gifts from Tyre itself . . . Oh, would that no man were rich at Rome . . . Never then would our girlfriends sell themselves for a gift, and a young girl would grow grey-haired in a single house" (Prop. 2.1616–22 [LCL 168–71]; cf. Hor., *Sat.* 1.2.47–61 [LCL 22]).

68. Lucr., *de rerum nat.* 4.1121 (LCL 326).

69. Tac., *Ann.* 3.53 (LCL 2.606); cf. Sen., *Ben.* 7.9.2–5 (LCL 3.476–78).

70. Tac., *Ann.* 3.52–55 (LCL 2.602–12).

71. Sall., *Cat.* 10–13 (LCL 16–22).

72. As Jennifer Knust writes: "The honor due a city, an emperor, or an individual man depended, in part, upon the chastity of the women they were expected to control. Conversely, corruption of city or empire was exemplified by the licentious behavior of these same women" (*Abandoned to Lust*, 39; cf. Edwards, *Politics of Immorality*, 42–47).

73. Juv. 6.1–20; 6.286–91 (LCL 82–84; 106); Livy 1 preface (LCL 1.6).

74. Prop. 3.13.25–38 (LCL 306–8).

75. Plin., *HN* 12.1.1–2; 2.63.157–58 (LCL 4.2; 1.292–94); cf. Sen., *Q. Nat.* 1.17.6; 3.15.3 (LCL 7.92; 7.234); Sen., *ep.* 94.56 (LCL 3.46).

76. Prop. 2.18D.23–26 (LCL 176).
77. Ovid writes: "Now Germany will send you some captives' hair; a vanquished nation will furnish your adornments" (*Am.* 1.14.45–46; cf. Ovid, *Ars am.* 3.163; Mart., *Epigram.* 14.26 and a discussion of both in Elizabeth Bartman, "Hair and the Artifice of Roman Female Adornment," *AJArch.* 105 [2001]: 14; Olson, *Dress and the Roman Woman*, 73–74; cf. Tert., *Virg.* 10.2 [CSEL 76.94]).
78. As Leslie Shumka puts it: a family's strong "financial situation afforded the leisure [for the matron] to engage in *cultus* and *ornatus* and to employ slaves or servants to assist her" ("Designing Women," 186).
79. Bartman, "Female Adornment," 7–12. We also know that some servants were charged with particular aspects of the matron's beautification regime by their titles. The *unctor* anointed the matron with perfumes and oils, the *ciniflo* or *cinerarius* curled the matron's hair, the *cosmeta* applied her makeup, and the *ornatrix* was in charge of her overall beautification (Olson, *Dress and the Roman Woman*, 99).
80. In a similar way, the *palla*—a bulky and heavy outer garment that required the woman to use one hand to hold it in place—additionally communicated the matron's life of leisure because she could hardly be productive in such an unwieldy garment. Lower-class and slave women who engaged in manual labor wore short tunics, whereas elite women wore longer tunics, voluminous *stola*, and the cumbersome *palla* (Olson, *Dress and the Roman Woman*, 25, 32, 36).
81. Clem. *paed.* 3.11.58 (PG 8.641). Clement encourages men to avoid such womanly practices and to wear their signet rings at the base of their fingers.
82. Economist Thorstein Veblen posited two means by which one's fiscal strength could be put on display: conspicuous leisure and conspicuous consumption. Just as a life of leisure illustrates one's pecuniary ability to "waste" time, the conspicuous display of rare and unnecessary possessions exhibits one's ability to "waste" money (*Leisure Class*, 35–67, 68–101). Here Veblen does not use the term "waste" to judge an expenditure as more or less legitimate than any other. Rather "these purchases are called 'waste' because they do not serve human life or human well-being on the whole," although they have the highest "utility" to their owners in terms of prestige rather than subsistence (*Leisure Class*, 97–98).
83. In Trier alone, Natalie Kampen has found this sort of stylized image "at least five times (excluding the many fragments of such scenes) with very little variation" (*Image and Status: Roman Working Women in Ostia* [Berlin: Mann, 1981], 92. For discussions of these images, see Kampen, *Image and Status*, 132–33; Suzanne Dixon, *Reading Roman Women: Sources, Genres and Real Life* (London: Duckworth, 2001), 19, 115, 125–29; Mary Harlow, "Female Dress, Third–Sixth Century: The Messages in the Media?" *AnTard* 12 (2004): 205; Eve D'Ambra, "Nudity and Adornment in Female Portrait Sculpture of the Second Century AD," in I, Claudia II: Women in Roman Art and Society, ed. Diana E. E. Kleiner and Susan B. Matheson (Austin: University of Texas Press, 2000), 111; Wyke, "Woman in the Mirror," 141–42. Leslie Shumka suggests that some of these monuments might memorialize the beautician rather than the adorned matron ("Designing Women," 185).
84. For example, see Prop. 1.15 (LCL 86) and Juv. 6.486–510 (LCL 122–24).
85. For a list of these sources, see Olson, *Dress and the Roman Woman*, 85–86; Ann Stout, "Jewelry as a Symbol of Status in the Roman Empire," in *Roman Costume*, 77–100.
86. Sen., *Ben.* 7.9.4–5 (LCL 3.478).

87. Ov., *Ars am.* 3.172 (LCL 130); Columella, *Rust.* 12.praef. 9 (LCL 3.178).
88. Plin., *HN* 12.41.84 (LCL 4.62). Elsewhere Pliny complains that "women spend a more enormous expense on their ears—in pearl earrings—than on any other part of their body" (*HN* 11.50.136 [LCL 3.516]).
89. In contradistinction to women, elite men exhibited the proper attachment to and use of their wealth, a stock motif of praise and blame in Greco-Roman literature as seen in Arist., *Eth. Nic.* 8.11; Cic., *Off.* 2.52–64; Aristoph., *Plut.* 559. For a discussion of the linguistic connection between maleness (*viris*) and virtue (*virtus*), see Edwards, *Politics of Immorality*, 20, 25 and Earl, *Moral and Political Tradition*, 20–21.
90. As Mary Harlow writes, "*Romanitas* and masculinity [were] terms [and concepts] that were synonymous to Roman men of the period" ("Female Dress," 204).
91. Knust, *Abandoned to Lust*, 27–28; Olson, *Dress and the Roman Woman*, 5; Smith, "Advice on Sex," 117–18. For a broader discussion of how the naturalization of gender characteristics can be used as a controlling device, see Elizabeth A. Clark, "Ideology, History, and the Construction of 'Woman' in Late Antique Christianity," *JECS* 2.2 (June 1994): 162.
92. For extended discussions on the dress that accompanied status changes in Roman society, see Edmondson, "Public Dress," and Kelly Olson, "The Appearance of the Young Roman Girl," in *Fabrics of Roman Culture*, 26–28, 139–50; Judith Lynn Sebesta, "Symbolism in the Costume of the Roman Woman," in *Roman Costume*, 46–53.
93. Laetitia La Follette, "The Costume of the Roman Bride," in *Roman Costume*, 54–64.
94. Recently Kelly Olson and Elaine Fantham have noted that headbands (*infulae*) and fillets (*vittae*) may have been worn only on special occasions—not at all times in public as the literary sources suggest—because they are rarely found in artistic representations (Olson, "Young Roman Girl," and Elaine Fantham, "Covering the Head at Rome: Ritual and Gender," both in *Fabrics of Roman Culture*, 145–47, 166–68).
95. Sebesta, "Symbolism," 48–50.
96. Physiognomists looked to permanent aspects of their appearance (such as hair, complexion, body type, and shape), as well as passing features of the body (such as an individual's voice, facial features, and movements), in moments of victory and distress in order to interpret their subjects' natural character and inclinations. Although there is only one extant technical handbook of physiognomy from this period—a third-century BCE text by Ps.-Aristotle, *Physiognomica*—several handbooks were written and circulated in Rome in subsequent generations: a second century CE text that is highly dependent on Ps.-Aristotle is Polemo of Laodicea's *de Physiognomia liber*; a fourth century CE handbook written by Adamantius the sophist, *Physiognomica*; and an anonymous (likely fourth-century CE) Latin handbook, *de Physiognomonia*, that relied heavily on Ps.-Aristotle and Polemo. The treatises can be found in Richard Foerster, *Scriptores physiognomonici graeci et latini*, 2 vols. (Lipsiae: B. G. Teubneri, 1893). For discussions of the science, see Elizabeth C. Evans, *Physiognomics in the Ancient World*, Transactions of the American Philosophical Society 59.5 (Philadelphia: American Philosophical Society, 1969); Georgia Frank, *The Memory of the Eyes: Pilgrims to Living Saints in Christian Late Antiquity* (Berkeley: University of California Press, 2000), 145–50; Tamsyn Barton, *Power and Knowledge: Astrology, Physiognomics, and Medicine under the Roman Empire* (Ann Arbor: University of Michigan Press, 1994). On the use of physiognomic principles by Roman historians,

biographers, and rhetoricians, see Elizabeth C. Evans, "Roman Descriptions of Personal Appearance in History and Biography." *HSPh* 46 (1935): 43–84.

97. Ps.-Arist., *Phgn.* 809b34–36 (LCL *Minor Works*, 112). The authors of the physiognomy handbooks, of course, neglect the fact that there are female lions and male panthers (Gleason, *Making Men*, 29). Elsewhere, Ps.-Aristotle concludes, one can discern that the female character is "petty and thievish, and in a word, deceitful" (*Phgn.* 810a8–9 [LCL Minor Works, 108–112]; cf. Polem., *Phgn.* [Foerster, *Scriptores Physiognomonici*, 194.4–14]).

98. Though still largely unrelated to differences in genitalia.

99. Gleason, *Making Men*, 35.

100. Judith Butler, *Undoing Gender* (New York: Routledge, 2004), 42.

101. As Maria Wyke summarizes: "The frivolity of the adorned wife is opposed to the dignity of her citizen husband, and her concern for luxury is opposed to the work ethic of the state . . . [the adorned woman symbolizes] all that is alien and pernicious to the traditionally-minded Roman male" ("Woman in the Mirror," 140, 141).

102. As Ria Berg has noted, men also used the beautification tools known as *mundus muliebris* (e.g., combs, mirrors, and certain adornments) even while they attempted to link such objects exclusively to the realm of women (Berg, "Wearing Wealth," 17–18).

103. For examples, see Valerie A. Tracy, "Roman Dandies and Transvestites," *EMC* 20 (1976): 60–63; Edwards, *Politics of Immorality*, 63–97; Knust, *Abandoned to Lust*, 30, 32–35. Of course, as Michael Koortbojian notes, men's dress could symbolize several different meanings and values at once: wearing Greek garments, such as the *pallium* and *crepidae*, could signal either one's affinity for foreign luxury or demarcate Roman victory over Greek culture ("Roman Portrait Statues," 82). Because the significance of dress was flexible, men needed to be careful to dress in ways that did not make them vulnerable to attacks from their opponents.

104. Suet., *Calig.* 52.1 (LCL vol. 1, 484).

105. *SHA, Elag.* 23.3–4 (LCL 2.150). Alexander Severus, on the contrary, was noted for casting aside purple dyes and gold, caring more about projecting *Romanitas* through virtue and valor than through his physical appearance: "He did away with the costly garments which Elagabalus had provided, and he dressed the soldiers who are called the Paraders, in bright uniforms, not costly, indeed, but elegant. Nor did he ever spend much for their standards or for the royal outfit of gold and silk, declaring that the imperial power was based, not on outward show, but on valour. For his own use he re-introduced the rough cloaks worn by Severus and tunics without the purple stripe and those with long sleeves and purple ones of small size" (*SHA, Alex. Sev.* 33.3–4 [LCL 2.242–243]).

106. For a discussion of this terminology, see Olson, *Dress and the Roman Woman*, 7–9.

107. Quint., *Inst.* 11.3.137 (LCL 4.316).

108. Edmondson, "Public Dress," 32–37.

109. Suet., *Aug.* 40.5, 44.2 (LCL 186–88, 194–96); *SHA, Hadr.* 22.2–4 (LCL 1.66). Romans were in fact the "*gens togata*." Although originally this phrase came from Vergil's *Aeneid* 1.282, it was famously revitalized by Augustus (Suet., *Aug.* 40).

110. Tac., *Ann.* 2.33 (LCL 3.430); cf. Dio 57.15.1 (LCL 7.148).

111. Of course, as Mary Harlow notes, by "the fifth and sixth centuries, elite dress"—both men's and women's—"became increasingly ornate." For a discussion of dress in this later period, see Harlow, "Female Dress," 210f.

NOTES TO CHAPTER 2

1. Jo. Chrys., *fem. reg.* 7 (PG 47.527); trans. Elizabeth A. Clark, *Jerome, Chrysostom, and Friends: Essays and Translations* (New York: E. Mellen Press, 1979), 237.
2. I borrow this phrase from Kate Cooper (*The Virgin and the Bride: Idealized Womanhood in Late Antiquity* [Cambridge: Harvard University Press, 1996], 44).
3. Of course, Romans could boast their virgins as well: the Vestals. Christians like Ambrose, however, argued that the Vestal virgins maintained their virginity for a shorter term than the Christian virgins, who made lifelong vows. Moreover, whereas the Vestals were compelled to become virgins (often selected from prominent families in childhood), Christian virgins made their vows voluntarily (*Virg.* 1.4 [PL 16.192–94]).
4. Knust, *Abandoned to Lust*, 89–112. Accusations of immorality were wielded against internal Christian opponents—particularly against those who held a less stringent view of Christian chastity—as well. For an analysis of the battles waged between pro- and anti-ascetic factions of early Christianity, see David G. Hunter, *Marriage, Celibacy, and Heresy in Ancient Christianity: The Jovinianist Controversy* (Oxford: Oxford University Press, 2007) and Knust, *Abandoned to Lust*, 143–63.
5. Peter Brown, "The Notion of Virginity in the Early Church," in *Christian Spirituality: Origins to the Twelfth Century*, ed. Bernard McGinn and John Meyendorff (New York: Crossroad, 1985), 427–43; Clark, *Ascetic Piety*, 176–77; idem, "Antifamilial Tendencies in Ancient Christianity" *JHSex* 5 (1995): 356–80. For a discussion of earlier critiques of non-Christian asceticism, see James A. Francis, *Subversive Virtue: Asceticism and Authority in the Second-Century Pagan World* (University Park: Pennsylvania State University Press, 1995).
6. As Hagith Sivan writes: "Asceticism provided an additional weapon in the arsenal" of aristocratic competition ("On Hymens and Holiness in Late Antiquity: Opposition to Aristocratic Female Asceticism at Rome," *JAC* 36 [1993]: 93; cf. Knust, *Abandoned to Lust*, 4–13). Speaking about Christian women more broadly, Alicia Batten writes: "Women's appearance would thereby be an important factor in deflecting social criticism and in maintaining whatever social status these early Christians had" ("Neither Gold nor Braided Hair [1 Timothy 2.9; 1 Peter 3.3]: Adornment, Gender, and Honour in Antiquity," *NTS* 55.4 [2009]: 500).
7. On Christians' adoption of familiar rhetorical tropes and practices, see Cameron, *Rhetoric of Empire*, 24–25.
8. These rhetorical tropes seem to have passed to Christians through the educational process. As Robert Kaster has noted, elites preserved the traditional *mores* that served to support social distinctions through grammatical training (*Guardians of Language: The Grammarian and Society in Late Antiquity* [Berkeley: University of California Press, 1988], 13–31). Maud Gleason adds that rhetorical training was the vehicle through which elite habits of thought transferred from one generation to the next: "the result was, for many generations, the smooth-flowing cultural reproduction of the patterns of speech, thought, and movement appropriate to a gentleman" (*Making Men*, xxiv; cf. Edwards, *Politics of Immorality*, 2–3).
9. Here I follow the lead of Patricia Cox Miller, who has brilliantly demonstrated how Christian writers' reports of desert ascetics shaped ways of perceiving the ascetic and especially his place in the earthly and cosmic realms ("Desert Asceticism and 'The Body from Nowhere' " *JECS* 2.2 [1994]: 137–53). More

recently, she has written more broadly about how texts "teach the reader how to see," bringing "sense and intellect together" ("Visceral Seeing: The Holy Body in Late Ancient Christianity," *JECS* 12.4 [2004]: 395, 409).

10. Cameron, *Rhetoric of Empire*, 222. So that Christians were both "showing and telling," as the title of her second chapter indicates. Later in the book, she concludes: "The issue of representation was central: if Christianity could not be adequately expressed . . . resort must be had to image, and where words failed, to the visual image" (*Rhetoric of Empire*, 226).

11. Brown, *Body and Society*, 34, 60, 64; Knust, *Abandoned to Lust*, 8–9.

12. Again, as Jaclyn Maxwell has recently shown, we ought not presume that Christian leaders were able to compel their congregants to think and act as they wished, but rather we ought to pay attention to the negotiations or exchanges between the two (*Christianization and Communication*, 56–58, 60–63, 94, 169–70).

13. Shaw, "*Askesis* and Appearance," 491, cf. 488–89, 493; cf. Rebecca Krawiec, "'Garments of Salvation': Representations of Monastic Clothing in Late Antiquity," *JECS* 17.1 (2009): 127, 131; Boulding, "Monastic Habit," 119. For example, Jerome connects Paula's vow to her change in appearance and distinction from other matrons when he asks her: "Is this the meaning of your vow to me that you would lead a religious life? Is it for this that you dress yourself differently from other matrons, and that you are perceived to be a religious?" (Jer., *ep*. 39.3 [CSEL 54.300]; trans. Fremantle, NPNF ser. 2, 6.51, adapted; cf. Jer., *epp*. 24.3, 130.5, 38.5 [CSEL 54.215–16, 56/1.180, 54.293]).

14. Kate Cooper writes: "The female figure of the virgin was the cultural icon by which [Christians] broadcast their message" (*Virgin and Bride*, x; cf. Leo Radista, "The Appearance of Women and Contact in Tertullian," *Athenaeum* 73 [1985]: 298).

15. In the words of Kenneth Burke: "To persuade men toward certain acts, religions would form the kinds of attitude which prepare men for such acts. And in order to plead for such attitudes as persuasively as possible, the religious always ground the exhortations (to themselves and others) in statements of the widest and deepest possible scope" (*The Rhetoric of Religion: Studies in Logology* [Boston: Beacon Press, 1961], v).

16. See Clem., *paed.* 2.12.127 (PG 8.552) in which Clement mistakenly attributes a paraphrase of 1 Tim. 2:9–10 to Peter. See also Tert., *Or.* 20 (PL 1.1183–84); Jo. Chrys., *hom. 28 in Heb.* 5 (PG 63.198–99); Or., *or.* 9 (PG 11.444); Cypr., *Hab. virg.* 8 (PL 4.447–48); Cypr., *Ad Quirin.* 3.1 (CCSL 3.75); and Comm., *Instr.* 60 (CCSL 128.54–55), who appeals to Paul and Isaiah together.

17. Jo. Chrys., *hom. 28 in Heb.* 11 (PG 63.198).

18. Tert., *Or.* 20 (PL 1.1183–84).

19. Clem., *paed.* 3.11.66 (PG 8.641).

20. The context of the 1 Tim. passage does clarify the meaning of γυνή and thus could be translated either as "wife" or "woman."

21. Cypr., *Hab. virg.* 8 (PL 4.447–48).

22. It is somewhat surprising that they do not cull the image of the richly adorned whore of Babylon from the Apocalypse of John. For a discussion of the potential meaning to be exploited in this text, see Frilingos, "Wearing It Well," 340–42.

23. Cypr., *Hab. virg.* 5 (PL 4.444–45). For Elizabeth A. Clark's discussion of this passage, see *Reading Renunciation: Asceticism and Scripture in Early Christianity* (Princeton: Princeton University Press, 1999), 140.

24. Clem., *paed.* 2.11.104 (PG 8.521); trans. Wood, FC 23.180.

25. 1 Cor. 10:23.
26. 1 Sam. 16.
27. Clem., *paed.* 3.2.12 (PG 8.572–73).
28. Referring to the Septuagint translation of Isa. 53:2, Clem., *paed.* 3.1.3 (PG 8.558–59); trans. Wood, FC 23.201.
29. Scholars have long debated which version of the scriptures Tertullian used: Did he translate the Greek himself or did he rely on an old Latin translation? For a discussion of the debate, see Geoffrey Dunn, *Tertullian* (London: Routledge, 2004), 20–21. Because a critical edition of the *Vetus Latina Mattaeum* is still in process, here I can not determine whether this translation is Tertullian's or not.
30. Tert., *Cult. fem.* 2.7.1–2 (CCSL 1.360–61); trans. Quain, FC 40.138, adapted.
31. Tert., *Cult. fem.* 2.6.3 (CCSL 1.359–60); trans. Quain, FC 40.137.
32. Cf. Cypr., *Hab. virg.* 16 (PL 4.455–56).
33. Clem., *paed.* 2.8.61 (PG 8.465); trans. Wood, FC 23.146.
34. Esth. 2:9, 2:12.
35. Clem., *paed.* 3.2.12–13 (PG 8.572–73).
36. Clem., *paed.* 2.12.119 (PG 8.540–41); trans. Wood, FC 23.191.
37. Clem., *paed.* 2.12.119 (PG 8.541); trans. Wood, FC 23.191–92.
38. Jo. Chrys., *hom.* 28 *in Heb.* 5 (PG 63.198).
39. *Const. apost.* 1.2 (SC 329.110–14); Tert., *Cult. fem.* 2.5 (CCSL 1.357–59); Clem., *paed.* 3.1–3 (PG 8.556–77); Ambr., *Virg.* 1.6.28 (PL 16.196–97).
40. Tert., *Cult. fem.* 2.5.5 (CCSL 1.358); trans. Quain, FC 40.136. Cf. Clem., *paed.* 2.12.127 (PG 8.551). It is for this reason that Tertullian also denounces actors who cross-dress on stage (Tert., *Spect.* 24 [CSEL 20.24]).
41. Cypr., *Hab. virg.* 16 (PL 4.455–56).
42. Clem., *paed.* 3.2.12 (PG 8.573); trans. Wood, FC 23.209.
43. *Const. apost.* 1.2 (SC 329.110–14); Clem., *paed.* 3.11.66 (PG 8.641); Ambr., *Virg.* 1.6.28–29 (PL 16.196–97).
44. Clem., *paed.* 3.2.6 (PG 8.561); trans. Wood, FC 23.204. Cf. Cypr., *Hab. virg.* 15 (PL 4.454–55); Tert., *Cult. fem.* 2.5.2 (CCSL 1.357–59).
45. Clem., *paed.* 2.12.127 (PG 8.552); trans. Wood, FC 23.197.
46. Clem., *paed.* 2.12.122 (PG 8.545).
47. Clem., *paed.* 3.2.11 (PG 8.572); cf. Jo. Chrys., *hom.* 4 *in* 1 Tim. (PG 62.523–24).
48. Clem., *paed.* 3.11.66 (PG 8.641); Cypr., *Hab. virg.* 15 (PL 4.454–55); Jo. Chrys., *catech.* 2.3 (PG 49.236).
49. Clem., *paed.* 2.12.129 (PG 8.553); Jo. Chrys., *hom. 30 in Mt.* (PG 57.368–69).
50. Tertullian writes: "Therefore, those things cannot be the best by nature which do not come from God, who is the Author of nature. Hence, they must be understood to be from the Devil, who is the corrupter of nature. Obviously, they cannot come from anyone else if they are not from God, because those things which are not of God must be of His rival" (*Cult. fem.* 1.8.2–3 [CCSL 1.350–51]; trans. Quain, FC 40, 126).
51. Clem., *paed.* 2.8.70 (PG 8.480). For a thorough analysis of Clement's opinions on fragrances, see Susan Ashbrook Harvey, *Scenting Salvation: Ancient Christianity and the Olfactory Imagination* (Berkeley: University of California Press, 2006), 40–44.
52. Tert., *Cult. fem.* 1.9 (CCSL 1.351–52).
53. Clem., *paed.* 2.12.119 (PG 8.541); trans. Wood, FC 23.191–92. Compare Pliny and Seneca's similar arguments in *HN* 2.63.157–58; 33.1.1–2 (LCL 1.292–94; 9.2); *Q. Nat.* 1.17.6, 3.15.3 (LCL 7.92; 7.234); and *ep.* 94.56 (LCL 3.46).

54. Tert., *Cult. fem.* 2.9 (CCSL 1.362–64); Jer., *ep.* 38.3 (CSEL 54.291).
55. Clem., *paed.* 2.8.73; 3.2.5 (PG 8.485; 8.560–61); Cypr., *Hab. virg.* 15 (PL 4.454–55).
56. Clem., *paed.* 2.10.106 (PG 8.572); trans. Wood, FC 23.181, emphasis added.
57. Clem., *paed.* 3.2.4 (PG 8.560); trans. Wood, FC 23.202.
58. Clem., *paed.* 3.2.5 (PG 8.560–61); trans. Wood, FC 23.203.
59. Referencing Exod. 32:1–20, Clement continues, "How fortunate the Hebrews of old would have been if they had taken hold of the ornaments of their women and thrown them away, or had simply put them in a melting pot! As it was, they fashioned them into a golden calf and made an idol of the calf, and so derived no benefit either from their art or from their plan" (*paed.* 2.12.126 [PG 8.549–52]; trans. Wood, FC 23.196–97; cf. Tert., *Cult. fem.* 2.13.6 [CCSL 1.369–70]).
60. Clem., *paed.* 2.8.72 (PG 8.484).
61. Tertullian writes, "People only wear fancy dress in public because of those gatherings and the desire to see and to be seen, either for the purpose of transacting the trade of wantonness or else of inflating their vanity. You, however, have no cause of appearing in public, except such as is serious" (*Cult. fem.* 2.11.1 [CCSL 1.366–67]; trans. Quain, FC 40.144–45).
62. Jo. Chrys., *catech.* 2.2 (PG 49.233).
63. Clem., *paed.* 3.11.63 (PG 8.637).
64. Jer., *ep.* 54.7 (CSEL 54.473). On the "mask" created by cosmetics, see also Clem., *paed.* 3.1.11 (PG 8.572).
65. Although we might expect early Christian writers to make copious use of the term *adultero*, which has connotations of both modification and adultery, in their arguments against adornments, it is surprisingly underutilized.
66. Cypr., *Hab. virg.* 17 (PL 4.456); trans. Deferrari, FC 36.46.
67. On Chrysostom's preaching on wealth and poverty, see Wendy Mayer and Pauline Allen, *John Chrysostom* (London: Routledge, 2000), 11–16, 28, 34–37; Maxwell, *Christianization and Communication*, 2–3, 69–72, 125–28.
68. Jo. Chrys., *stat.* 19 (PG 49.190). Here Chrysostom provokes a rivalry between different factions of his audience in order to shame the wealthy into heeding his advice on how to dress. For a discussion of the range of groups represented in Chrysostom's congregation and Chrysostom's attempts to play them against one another, see Maxwell, *Christianization and Communication*, 96–97.
69. Clem., *paed.* 2.12.120 (PG 8.541); trans. Wood, FC 23.192.
70. Clem., *paed.* 2.12.120; 3.7.39 (PG 8.544; 8.609); Jo. Chrys., *hom. 27 in Jo.* (PG 59.160–61).
71. Jo. Chrys., *Is. interp.* 6–7, 10 (PG 56.47–50, 56.53); trans. Duane A. Garrett, *An Analysis of the Hermeneutics of John Chrysostom's Commentary on Isaiah 1–8* (Lewiston: E. Mellen Press, 1992), 98–99.
72. Jo. Chrys., *hom. 27 in Jo.* (PG 59.161); trans. Goggin, FC 33.266, adapted.
73. Jo. Chrys., *Is. interp.* 9 (PG 56.52); trans. Garrett, *Commentary on Isaiah*, 97.
74. Jo. Chrys., *Is. interp.* 10 (PG 56.54). In fact, Chrysostom argues, Isaiah took pains to catalogue the items of ornamentation that led to the Jews' downfall so that future Christians might be thoroughly forewarned. Chrysostom quotes Isa. 3:16–24 at length to make his point clear: "[Isaiah] said, '[The Lord] will remove their glorious apparel; their ornament, the curls, the points.' By 'points' he means either some ornament on the head or the shape of the headband itself. 'The crescents.' This is a moon-shaped ornament for

the neck. 'The necklace.' This could refer to a veil. 'The facial cosmetics.' Here he seems to refer to makeup and eye shadow. 'The array of brilliant ornaments.' This refers to gold jewelry. 'The armlets.' This is gold worn about the arms. 'The bracelets.' This is jewelry worn on the wrist. 'The wreathed jewelry.' This is a golden ornament that goes about the head. 'The rings, the ornaments for the right hand.' These are wedding rings. 'The earrings, the clothing with scarlet borders and those with the purple band, the tapestries in their homes, the Laconian see-through apparel.' They were so eager for wantonness that they not only followed domestic fashions, but imported those of other peoples from far away, and traded with peoples overseas for them . . . He did not mention the country of origin for no reason when he mentions the clothing, but to indicate how lavishly wasteful they are. 'The garments of fine linen, purple, and scarlet, the linen with silver and gold woven in, and the precious summer garments of gold.' They neglected no type of ornamentation, either in clothing or any other kind of cosmetic, but the tyranny of wantonness had worked them into such frenzy that they went all the way down the road of extravagance" (*Is. interp.* 7–9 [PG 56.51]; trans. Garrett, *Commentary on Isaiah*, 95–96).

75. Referencing Mark 12:31, Matt. 22:39, and Luke 10:27, Jo. Chrys., *catech.* 2.2 (PG 49.233); Clem., *paed.* 2.12.120; 3.7.37 (PG 8.541–43; 8.608–9); Ambr., *Virg.* 1.6.28 (PL 16.196–97); Jo. Chrys., *hom. 27 in Jo.* (PG 59.160–62).

76. Clem., *paed.* 3.2.5–7 (PG 8.561–64).

77. Clem., *paed.* 2.10.115 (PG 8.536); trans. Wood, FC 23.188.

78. Elsewhere in the treatise, Clement makes the same point, asking: "Is it not absurd to advertise oneself as less comely and less valuable than Lydian scrapings?" (*paed.* 3.11.56 [PG 8.630]; trans. Wood, FC 23.244).

79. Clem., *paed.* 3.11.55 (PG 8.628); trans. Wood, FC 23.243.

80. Gen. 38:1–30.

81. Tert., *Cult. fem.* 2.12.3 (CCSL 1.368).

82. Clem., *paed.* 3.2.10 (PG 8.569–72); Jo. Chrys., *fem. reg.* 6 (PG 47.525); Gr. Naz., *Or.* 18.8 (PG 36.993).

83. Clem., *paed.* 3.2.10 (PG 8.569–72); trans. Wood, FC 23.207.

84. Clem., *paed.* 2.10.109; 3.2.10–11 (PG 8.528; 8.572); Jo. Chrys., *fem. reg.* 1 (PG 47.515); Jo. Chrys., *hom. 8 in I Tim.* (PG 62.541).

85. See Rom. 14:1–23; 1 Cor. 8:1–13; Lev. 19:14.

86. Tert., *Cult. fem.* 2.2.4 (CCSL 1.354–55); trans. Quain, FC 40.132.

87. Jo. Chrys., *fem. reg.* 1 (PG 47.515); trans. Clark, *Jerome, Chrysostom, and Friends*, 210. Blake Leyerle discusses how the blame shifts from the "roving eyes of men" to the "transgressive female gaze" in "John Chrysostom on the Gaze," *JECS* 1.2 (1993): 159–74.

88. Jo. Chrys., *fem. reg.* 1 (PG 47.515–16); trans. Clark, *Jerome, Chrysostom, and Friends*, 211, emphasis added. See also Cypr., *Hab. virg.* 9 (PL 4.448).

89. Tert., *Virg.* 14 (CSEL 76.100). For this reason, it was quite clear to Christian leaders that the appearance of Christian matrons and virgins was "dangerous" to the glances of men and thus leaders were forced to regulate their appearance in public (Tert., *Cult. fem.* 2.2.5; 2.3.1 [CCSL 1.355; 1.356–57]).

90. Clem., *paed.* 3.11.70 (PG 8.645); trans. Wood, FC 23.252. Clement and Tertullian here follow the notion of "copulation at a distance" found in Achilles Tatius's *Leukippe and Clitophon* 1.9 (B.P. Reardon, ed., *Collected Ancient Greek Novels* [Berkeley: University of California Press, 1989], 183).

91. Whether one followed the extramission theory of sight like Tertullian (as explained in Plato's *Timaeus* 45c–d and Galen's *De placitis Hippocratis et Platonis* 7.4–5) or the intromission theory of sight in which particles were believed to be emitted from visible objects and bounce off the eyes (a theory

advanced by Aristotle), for both sight fell under the species of "touch." For more detailed discussions of the material aspects of sight, see David C. Lindberg, *Theories of Vision from Al-Kindi to Kepler* (Chicago: University of Chicago Press, 1976), 1–17; Frank, *Memory of the Eyes*, 122–25.

92. Tert., *Cult. fem.* 1.6.1 (CCSL 1.348).
93. Tert., *Virg.* 2 (CSEL 76.82); Clem., *paed.* 3.2.10 (PG 8.569–72).
94. Jer., *ep.* 107.11 (CSEL 55.302).
95. Jer., *ep.* 54.16 (CSEL 54.483–84); trans. Fremantle, NPNF ser. 2, 6.108.
96. Jer., *ep.* 54.16 (CSEL 54.483–84); trans. Fremantle, NPNF ser. 2, 6.108, adapted. Jerome conveniently elides Judith's plot of seduction that leads to Holofernes's death in Jdt. 13:16.
97. Clem., *paed.* 3.11.68 (PG 8.644).
98. Further they argued that only Christians who employed the reasonable part (λογιστικός) of the soul would dress according to rational, godly utility. Because the other two parts of the soul—the irascible (θυμικός) and appetitive (ἐπιθυμητικός)—were always in flux, shifting one's focus from one object of desire to another, reason alone could lead one to make clothing choices based on life's necessities, rather than on the ever-changing whims of passion and desire (Clem., *paed.* 3.1.1 [PG 8.556–57]).
99. Clem., *paed.* 2.10.106–7 (PG 8.524–25); Tert., *Pall.* 3, 5 (CCSL 2.741; 2.748); Jo. Chrys., *hom.* 28 in Heb. 5–6 (PG 63.199–200); Bas., *ep.* 2.6 (LCL 1.20).
100. Clem., *paed.* 2.10.106–7 (PG 8.524).
101. Jo. Chrys., *hom.* 28 in Heb. 5 (PG 63.198).
102. Tert., *Pall.* 5–6 (CCSL 2.741–48).
103. Clement writes: "We must not completely turn away from such things, but take advantage of myrrh as an aid and remedy to stimulate our failing powers, for catarrh and chills and indispositions. The comic poet says somewhere, 'The nostrils are to be anointed with myrrh; the greatest secret of good health is to keep pleasant odors in the head.' There is even a practice of rubbing the feet with a salve made of either warming or of cooling oil, for its effects; when the head is congested, such a salve will draw the congestion off and away to a less important part of the body" (*paed.* 2.8.68 [PG 8.476]; trans. Wood, FC 23.151–52).
104. Clem., *paed.* 3.11.57 (PG 8.632); cf. Bas., *ep.* 2.6 (LCL 1.20–22).
105. A Roman wife's responsibility to please her husband was presumed in Roman society. Not only did matrons appeal to Juno *Viriplaca* ("Husband-Pleaser"), but also in *Fasti*, Ovid describes the April rituals performed in honor of "Virile Fortune" and Venus, in which the drinking of special potions, bathing, and wearing garlands made Roman matrons sexually attractive to their husbands. Suzanne Dixon notes that such behavior demonstrates "an institutionalized acknowledgment of women's responsibility for the sexual success of their marriage" (*Roman Women*, 43).
106. Augustine writes, "Husbands are the only men for whom women are allowed to deck themselves out, and that through concession, not command [of Scripture]" (*ep.* 245 1 [CSEL 57.582]; trans. Parsons, FC 32.229, adapted; cf. Clem., *paed.* 3.11.57 [PG 8.632]).
107. Aug., *Bon. coniug.* 14 (CSEL 41.206–7).
108. Aug., *Bon. coniug.* 13 (CSEL 41.204–5).
109. For example, see Jo. Chrys., *hom.* 28 *in Heb.* 5–6 (PG 63.199).
110. Tert., *Cult. fem.* 2.4 (CCSL 1.357); Ambr., *Virg.* 1.6.28 (PL 16.196–97); Jo. Chrys., *hom.* 4 in 1 Tim. (PG 62.524).
111. Jo. Chrys., *hom.* 61 *in Jo.* (PG 59.286); idem, *hom.* 4 in 1 Tim. (PG 62.524); Tert., *Cult. fem.* 2.4 (CCSL 1.357).

112. Jo. Chrys., *catech.* 2.4 (PG 49.238).
113. Jo. Chrys., *hom.* 30 *in Mt.* (PG 57.368–69); idem, *hom.* 4 in 1 Tim. (PG 62.526); idem, *hom.* 89 *in Mt.* (PG 58.788); cf. Clem., *paed.* 3.11.57 (PG 8.632); Ambr., *Virg.* 1.6.28 (PL 16.196–97); Tert., *Cult. fem.* 2.13 (CCSL 1.369–70).
114. Clem., *paed.* 2.12.118 (PG 8.540); trans. Wood, FC 23.191.
115. Clem., *paed.* 2.10.110 (PG 8.529).
116. Clem., *paed.* 3.1.1 (PG 8.556); trans. Wood, FC 23.199.
117. Jo. Chrys., *catech.* 2.4 (PG 49.238).
118. Jo. Chrys., *hom.* 61 *in Jo.* (PG 59.286–87).
119. Jo. Chrys., *hom.* 28 in Heb. 6 (PG 63.199).
120. Tert., *Cult. fem.* 2.13.3 (CCSL 1.369); trans. Quain, FC 40.148; cf. Ambr., *Virg.* 3.3 (PL 16.222–24).
121. Cypr., *Hab. virg.* 5 (PL 4.445); trans. Deferrari, FC 36.35.
122. Tert., *Cult. fem.* 2.13.3 (CCSL 1.369); trans. Quain, FC 40.148, emphasis added; cf. *Cult. fem.* 2.11.2; 2.13.1 (CCSL 1.366–67; 1.369).
123. Gr. Nyss., *virg.* 1 (PG 46.320).
124. Jer., *ep.* 45.3 (CSEL 54.325); cf. Tert., *Cult. fem.* 2.11 (CCSL 1.366–67).
125. Cypr., *Hab. virg.* 3 (PL 4.443); trans. Deferrari, FC 36.33.
126. Margaret Miles summarizes: "Christian, and especially ascetic, women must, according to prescriptive texts by male authors, give the same amount of attention to studied neglect of their physical appearance as secular women were thought to lavish on their dress, cosmetics, and hair. Advice given to consecrated virgins counseled constant attention to the body, while, ironically, denying care for the body and dress" (*Carnal Knowing*, 70).
127. Tert., *Cult. fem.* 2.1.2 (CCSL 1.352–53); trans. Quain, FC 40.130.
128. Here, Tertullian evokes Aristotelian divisions to strengthen his argument, though in fact he deviates from Aristotle's logic. Within broader discussions of change, Aristotle argued that a thing could undergo change while maintaining its essential identity. Observed changes to a thing's nonconstitutive, or *accidental*, attributes, Aristotle concludes, would not affect its *essential being*. Tertullian, on the other hand, hopes to persuade his readers that changes to their physical appearance are not merely accidental, but rather a crucial aspect or reflection of their *essential* identity. See Arist., *Met.* 1029b–1032a (LCL 17.320–36); idem, *Post. An.* 73a–73b, 75a (LCL 2.42–46, 2.58–60).
129. Tert., *Cult. fem.* 2.1 (CCSL 1.352–53), citing Matt. 5:48.
130. Most scholars now attribute this letter to Pelagius. See Robert F. Evans, *Four Letters of Pelagius* (New York: The Seabury Press, 1968), 13–31. For a recent dissenting opinion, see Sebastian Their, *Kirche bei Pelagius* (Berlin: Walter de Gruyter, 1999), 26–30.
131. Pelag., *ep. ad Claud.* 9–10 (CSEL 1.236–39).
132. Jo. Chrys., *hom.* 28 in Heb. 6 (PG 63.200); trans. NPNF 14.497, adapted, emphasis added; cf. Jo. Chrys., *hom.* 88 *in Mt.* (PG 58.786); idem, *hom.* 10 *in Col.* (PG 62.371).
133. Jo. Chrys., *hom.* 30 *in Rom.* (PG 60.665). Dressing produces an effect similar to fasting, as described by Patricia Cox Miller, because fasting "produces a body that looks different from conventional bodies" ("Desert Asceticism," 150).
134. Pall., *hist. Laus.* 46 (Butler, *Lausiac History*, 135); trans. Meyer, ACW 34.124, emphasis added.
135. On the potential for misunderstanding ascetics' ragged clothing as a sign of their lowly status rather than their exalted place within Christianity, see Krawiec, "Garments of Salvation," 132–33, 147–48.

136. Gr. Nyss., *v. Macr.* 7 [SC 178.164]; cf. Elm, *Virgins of God*, 84–88, 93–94.

137. Jer., *ep.* 22.27 (CSEL 54.183); trans. Fremantle, NPNF ser. 2, 6.33. In his letter to Nepotian, Jerome gives the same advice to a man: "Flee from both showiness and slovenliness in your dress; for the one projects vanity and the other pride" (*ep.* 52.9 [CSEL 54.430]).

138. Aug., *ep.* 211.10 (CSEL 57.363); trans. Parsons, FC 32.44, adapted; cf. Tert., *Cult. fem.* 2.11.2 (CCSL 1.366–67).

139. For descriptions of the *velatio*, see Jer., *ep.* 130.2 (CSEL 56/1.176–77); Ambr., *Virg.* 3.1.1 (PL 16.219–20); Bas. Anc., *virg.* 39 (PG 30.748–49); Siricius, *ep.* 10 (PL 13.1182–84). Additionally, Ambrose's homily, *De institutione virginis*, which was delivered at the consecration of Ambrosia, is an excellent window into these sorts of ceremonies (PL 16.305–34). For scholarly discussions of the ceremony, see Nathalie Henry, "A New Insight into the Growth of Ascetic Society in the Fourth Century AD: The Public Consecration of Virgins as a Means of Integration and Promotion of the Female Ascetic Movement," *SP* 35 (2001):102–9; idem, "The Song of Songs and the Liturgy of the *velatio* in the Fourth Century: From Literary Metaphor to Liturgical Reality," in *Continuity and Change in Christian Worship*, ed. R. N. Swanson (Woodbridge: Boydell Press, 1999), 18–28; cf. Hunter, *Jovinianist Controversy*, 32–33; Susanna Elm, *Virgins of God: The Making of Asceticism in Late Antiquity* (Oxford: Oxford University Press, 1994), 121; Boulding, "Monastic Habit," 120; F. J. Leroy, "La tradition manuscrite du 'de virginitate' de Basile d'Ancyre" *OCP* 38 (1972): 197.

140. Ambr., *Virg.* 3.1.1 (PL 16.219–20).

141. Hunter, *Jovinianist Controversy*, 227.

142. Tert., *Pall.* 4 (CCSL 2.742).

143. Clem., *paed.* 2.8.64 (PG 8.469).

144. Jo. Chrys., *subintr.* 9 (PG 47.508).

145. Ambr., *Virg.* 1.9.54 (PL 16.203–4); trans. Boniface Ramsey, *Ambrose* (London: Routledge, 1997), 88.

146. Clem., *paed.* 3.11.58; 3.2.10 (PG 8.632; 8.572).

147. Women, Tertullian asserts, define modesty as merely refusing men's advances no matter that such advances resulted from their beautification and seduction (*Cult. fem.* 2.1.3 [CCSL 1.352–53]; trans. Quain, FC 40.130).

148. Jer., *ep.* 128.2 (CSEL 56/1.157–58); trans. Fremantle, NPNF ser. 2, 6.258.

149. Jo. Chrys., *fem. reg.* 5 (PG 47.523).

150. Jer., *ep.* 130.6 (CSEL 56/1.182); trans. Fremantle, NPNF ser. 2, 6.263.

151. In fact, John Chrysostom hopes to further incentivize female ascetics by claiming that Jesus is a more "ardent lover" than any man (*fem. reg.* 9 [PG 47.532]; cf. Clark, "Celibate Bridegroom," 11).

152. Pelag., *ep. ad Claud.* 12 (CSEL 1.242). Here Pelagius mistakenly confuses the instructions found in 1 Pet. with 1 Tim.

153. Jer., *ep.* 22.38 (CSEL 54.203); Jo. Chrys., *fem. reg.* 7 (PG 47.528). Carrying the bridegroom metaphor even further, Jerome warns Eustochium that any female ascetic who fashions an attractive appearance will make her husband Christ jealous (*ep.* 22.25 [CSEL 54.180]).

154. Jo. Chrys., *fem. reg.* 7 (PG 47.528); trans. Clark, *Jerome, Chrysostom, and Friends*, 239. Cf. Jer., *ep.* 22.1 (CSEL 54.145); Jo. Chrys., *catech.* 2.4 (PG 49.237–39); idem, *hom. 30 in Mt.* (PG 57.369–70); idem, *hom. 28 in Heb.* (PG 63.201); idem, *hom. 8 in 1 Tim.* (PG 62.542).

155. References to the allure of chaste women can be found throughout Roman literature. Men are regularly cast as desiring virtuous women precisely because of their inaccessibility. In Livy's *History of Rome*, for instance, we read that Lucretia's chastity, as she "was engaged with her wool work, even though

late at night, with her maids around her," enflamed the voyeur Tarquinius
(Livy 1.57 [LCL 1.198]).

156. Ambr., *Virg.* 1.9.54 (PL 16.204).

157. Tert., *Virg.* 7 (CSEL 76.89).

158. Tert., *Cult. fem.* 2.1 (CCSL 1.352–53).

159. Jo. Chrys., *subintr.* 1 (PG 47.496); idem, *fem. reg.* 5 (PG 47.523); trans.
Clark, *Jerome, Chrysostom, and Friends*, 166, 229. Cf. *fem. reg.* 1, 4 (PG
47.515; 47.519–20) and *subintr.* 1, 12 (PG 47.495–97; 47.512). Chrysostom
offers an additional explanation for virgins' allure: neither childbirth nor
"childrearing dry up her flesh; to the contrary, these virgins stay in their
prime for a long time, since they remain untouched. After the birth and care
of children, the bodies of married women become feeble, but these women
[virgins] retain their beauty until they are forty, rivaling the virgins being led
to the nuptial chamber!" (Jo. Chrys., *subintr.* 1 [PG 47.496]; trans. Clark,
*Jerome, Chrysostom, and Friends*, 166.

160. For a thoughtful and lively discussion of the sublimation of sexuality and
desire in ascetic literature, see Virginia Burrus, *The Sex Lives of the Saints:
An Erotics of Ancient Hagiography* (Philadelphia: University of Pennsylvania Press, 2004).

161. Jer., *ep.* 117.7 (CSEL 55.430); cf. Jer., *ep.* 22.13 (CSEL 54.161).

162. Jer., *ep.* 130.18 (CSEL 56/1.199).

163. Jo. Chrys., *hom.* 8 in 1 Tim. (PG 62.541–42).

164. Jo. Chrys., *fem. reg.* 4 (PG 47.520); trans. Clark, *Jerome, Chrysostom, and
Friends*, 220.

165. Moreover, as Teresa Shaw notes, notions of women's deception are likewise
aligned with notions of impiety and even heresy. Shaw writes: "This anxiety
settles squarely on the image of the imposter, the false virgin and the heretic
masquerading as a pious and worthy claimant to the role, who is able to pull
off her deception by playing and looking the part" ("*Askesis* and Appearance," 496).

166. Tertullian claims that Christian women have few reasons to appear in public
because they should not attend the theater, games, or other "pagan" events
connected to "idolatry." He declares it even less appropriate for ascetics to be
found in such public places (*Cult. fem.* 2.11.1–2 [CCSL 1.366–67]; cf. Jer.,
*ep.* 22.23 [CSEL 54.175]; Jer., *ep.* 54.13 [CSEL 54.479]).

167. Bas. Anc., *virg.* 36 (PG 30.740–41); Elm, *Virgins of God*, 119, 121–22.

168. Offering advice to Gaudentius about how to best raise his virgin daughter,
Jerome writes, "She should not appear in public too freely or too frequently
attend crowded churches" (*ep.* 128.4 [CSEL 56/1.160]; trans. Fremantle,
NPNF ser. 2, 6.259). Moreover, in his letters to ascetic women, Jerome
copiously praised those who seldom appeared in public (*epp.* 107.9, 127.4,
130.19 [CSEL 55.300, 56/1.148, 56/1.199–200]; cf. Ambr., *Virg.* 3.3 [PL
16.222–24]).

169. Jer., *ep.* 22.23 (CSEL 54.175); trans. Mierow, ACW 33.156. Jerome writes
that ascetics should strive to be like Jesus's mother, Mary, who was terri-
fied by the angel's presence, not because of his heavenly nature, but because
she "had never been greeted by a man" (*ep.* 22.38 [CSEL 54.203]; trans.
Mierow, ACW 33.174; cf. Jer., *ep.* 107.7 [CSEL 55.298]).

170. See, for example, David Hunter's description of Demetrias's fame: "As Augustine noted, word of Demetrias' virginal consecration had spread throughout
the world at astonishing speed. Announcements of the event were accompanied by gifts to prominent churchmen. Several decades later the anonymous author of the *Epistula ad Demetriadem de vera humilitate* recalled
that the consecration of Demetrias had provoked 'many men who were then

prominent figures in the church' . . . to convey their congratulations and exhortations to the young virgin" (*Jovinianist Controversy*, 81).

171. Following this principle of conspicuous absence, Ovid counsels women to arrive late at a party, because this "delay stimulates desire; delay is the great seductress" (*Ars am.* 3.752 [LCL 170]).

172. Ambr., *Virg.* 2.4.22 (PL 16.212); trans. Ramsey, *Ambrose*, 96–97, emphasis added.

173. Kate Cooper is right to note that we must pay attention to the pleasure readers might derive from narratives in addition to pleasure described within narratives (Cooper, *Virgin and Bride*, 32). Here, I argue that the fantasy of the ascetic out of view is constructed through textual reports about her, especially reports pertaining to her virtue and inaccessibility.

174. Jer., *ep.* 45.3 (CSEL 54.325); trans. Fremantle, NPNF ser. 2, 6.59, emphasis added.

175. Jer., *vir. ill.* 54 (PL 23.701).

NOTES TO CHAPTER 3

1. See, for example, Jerome's praise of Lea, Asella, Blaesilla and Paula in *epp.* 23.2, 24.3, 38.4, 45.3 (CSEL 54.212–13, 54.215–16, 54.291–92, 54.325).

2. As we know, female asceticism took many forms in late antiquity. For a thorough discussion of these various forms, see Elm, *Virgins of God*, 25–59.

3. For a nice discussion on the overlaying of categories of difference, see Marjorie Garber, *Vested Interests: Cross-Dressing and Cultural Anxiety* (New York: Routledge, 1992), 17.

4. Amy Richlin, "Making up a Woman: The Face of Roman Gender," in *Off with Her Head! The Denial of Women's Identity in Myth, Religion, and Culture*, ed. Howard Eilberg-Schwartz and Wendy Doniger (Berkeley: University of California Press, 1995), 205–6.

5. Eilberg-Schwartz and Doniger, *Off with Her Head!*, 2.

6. Martin, *Corinthian Body*, 235–39.

7. Eilberg-Schwartz and Doniger, *Off with Her Head!*, 2.

8. They prove that dress could be a significant mode of ideology, a mode as significant as text. As Elizabeth Clark has asserted, "Although we have no body of literature by early Christian women which could be used to compare with that of the Fathers, we can infer even from the representations of these women by male writers that the gender ideology [the Fathers asserted] did not result in [women's] total silencing" ("Construction of 'Woman,'" 183).

9. It is unclear how much authority Tertullian had within his community. Although Jerome suggests that he was an ordained presbyter, Tertullian claims to be only a layperson (*vir. ill.* 53 [PL 23.698]; Tert., *Cast.* 7 [CCSL 2.1024–26]; Tert., *Mon.* 12 [CCSL 2.1247–48]). It is apparent from the sheer volume of his extant writings, however, that Tertullian was an influential figure in his North Africa community, both in the Catholic and New Prophecy stages of his career. For comprehensive studies on Tertullian, see Dunn, *Tertullian*; Eric Francis Osborn, *Tertullian, First Theologian of the West* (Cambridge: Cambridge University Press, 1997); Timothy D. Barnes, *Tertullian: A Historical and Literary Study* (Oxford: Oxford University Press, 1985).

10. Scholars have argued that Tertullian's theology can be best understood through the lens of his ethics; that is, that Tertullian's theology grew directly from his ethical concerns. See Gerald Lewis Bray, *Holiness and the Will of God: Perspectives on the Theology of Tertullian* (Atlanta: John Knox Press,

1979); Claude Rambaux, *Tertullien face aux morales des trois premiers siè-cles* (Paris: Les Belles Lettres, 1979).

11. The dating of Tertullian's treatises has proven to be difficult, complicating scholars' ability to decipher which works belonged to Tertullian's New Prophecy phase. Although some scholars posit that Tertullian's most ethically stringent treatises must have been written after his adoption of New Prophecy beliefs, others find this assumption problematic. We are thus left to textual clues, such as allusions to historical events, references to earlier writings, and clear and numerous references to New Prophecy ideas and terms, such as the Paraclete (Barnes, *Tertullian*, 30–56). *De virginibus velandis* offers contradictory evidence. On the one hand, there is no mention of the Spirit in the "rule of faith" that opens the treatise (Tert., *Virg.* 1 [CSEL 76.79]). Directly after the rule, however, Tertullian opposes those who think that "the work of God should either cease or should stop progressing" and who ignore the Paraclete, whom God sent to clarify Christian teaching and biblical interpretation (Tert., *Virg.* 1 [CSEL 76.80–81]; trans. Dunn, *Tertullian*, 143). This addendum to the "rule of faith," together with an underwhelming dependence on Spirit language and theology in the rest of the treatise, leads me to believe that this treatise was written early in Tertullian's New Prophecy phase.

12. Tert., *Virg.* 11 (CSEL 76.94).

13. 1 Cor. 11:4–10. For a nice discussion of the veiling controversy in Paul's time, see Richard Oster, "When Men Wore Veils to Worship: The Historical Context of 1 Corinthians 11:4," *NTS* 34.4 (1988): 481–505.

14. Dunn, *Tertullian*, 179 n.1. Conversely, Christoph Stücklin thinks this reference to an earlier Greek version refers to the brief mention of the incident in Tertullian's *De oratione* (*Tertullian, De virginibus velandis: Übersetzung, Einleitung, Kommentar. Ein Beitrag zur altkirchlichen Frauenfrage* [Bern: Herbert Lang, 1974], 108).

15. Moreover, if they immigrated from another region of the empire, they might have encountered an even broader range of veiling practices.

16. Tert., *Cor.* 4.2 (PL 2.80).

17. Tert., *Virg.* 17 (CSEL 76.102); trans. Dunn, *Tertullian*, 160.

18. Tert., *Virg.* 3 (CSEL 76.82); trans. Dunn, *Tertullian*, 145.

19. Tert., *Virg.* 17 (CSEL 76. 102); trans. Dunn, *Tertullian*, 160. For a detailed discussion of veiling practices in North Africa, see M. P. Monceaux, "Sur le voile des femmes en Afrique," *BSNAF* [1901]: 339–41). For a discussion of the way in which Tertullian attempted to limit the appeal to different customs, see Carly Daniel-Hughes, "'Wear the Armor of Your Shame!': Debating Veiling and the Salvation of the Flesh in Tertullian of Carthage," *SR* 39.2 (2010): 187–88.

20. Again, recall that Tertullian originally wrote this treatise in Greek, likely addressed to a Greek-reading audience, who would have understood the linguistic ambiguity of the term, γυνή. In the Latin treatise, Tertullian consistently uses the terms *uxor* and *mulier* to distinguish "wife" from "woman."

21. Tert., *Virg.* 11 (CSEL 76.96); trans. Dunn, *Tertullian*, 156, adapted. Earlier in the treatise Tertullian similarly reports, " . . . they use the name 'woman' in such a way that they do not consider that that [term] is suitable except for her alone who has submitted [to a man] . . ." (*Virg.* 5 [CSEL 76.85]; trans. Dunn, *Tertullian*, 147).

22. 1 Cor. 7:8–10, 25, emphasis added.

23. 1 Cor. 11:5: "But any woman who prays or prophesies with her head unveiled disgraces her head—it is one and the same thing as having her head shaved."

24. Tert., *Virg.* 4 (CSEL 76.83–84); trans. Dunn, *Tertullian*, 145–46, adapted; cf. Tert., *Or.* 20–22 (PL 1.1183–90).
25. Butler, *Bodies that Matter*, 4. Gillian Townsley suggests that a similar situation might have prompted the Corinthian veiling controversy in her article "*Gender Trouble* in Corinth: Que(e)rying Constructs of Gender in 1 Corinthians 11:12–16," *BCT* 2.2 (2006): 17.1–17.14.
26. Tertullian also mentions the incident in his treatise on prayer (*Or.* 21–22 [PL 1.1289–98]).
27. Tert., *Virg.* 3 (CCEL 76.82); cf. Tert., *Or.* 21 (CCSL 1.268).
28. Tert., *Virg.* 2 (CSEL 76.81). This is an intriguing argument because this treatise may have been written during Tertullian's New Prophecy phase. It confirms Joseph Moingt's argument that Tertullian could have separated from his own community without considering himself to be breaking with the Catholics, as well as Douglas Powell's claim that Tertullian's Montanist leanings were wholly acceptable within the Church because they did not challenge the church hierarchy, and especially the African bishops (Joseph Moingt, *Théologie trinitaire de Tertullien*, vol. 1 [Paris: Aubier, 1966], 57–59; Douglas Powell, "Tertullianists and Cataphrygians," *VC* 29.1 [1975]: 33–54).
29. See Tert., *Cult. fem.* 1.2 (CCSL 1.344–46); cf. Daniel Hoffman, "Tertullian on Women and Women's Ministry Roles in the Church," in *The Spirit and the Mind: Essays in Informed Pentecostalism*, ed. Terry L Cross and Emerson B. Powery (Lanham: University Press of America, 2000), 138–44.
30. These classes all fall under the umbrella category "woman" because "the particular is subject . . . to the general, because the general is prior, and the subsequent [is subject] to the antecedent, and the partial to the universal. It is understood in [the term] itself to which it is subject, and is signified in [the term] itself, because it is contained in [the term] itself" (Tert., *Virg.* 4 [CSEL 76.85]; trans. Dunn, *Tertullian*, 147).
31. Tert., *Virg.* 4 (CSEL 76.84).
32. Tert., *Virg.* 4 (CSEL 76.84); trans. Dunn, *Tertullian*, 146. Elsewhere, Tertullian writes: "For since he did not forget to make a distinction in another passage where the difference demands it—[there] he distinguishes both classes [woman and virgin] by designating each with its proper term—in a passage where he does not distinguish, since he does not name each, he does not intend any distinction" (*Or.* 22.2 [PL 1.1290–98]; trans. Daly, FC 40.177).
33. Tert., *Virg.* 4 (CSEL 76.84–85); trans. Dunn, *Tertullian*, 146–47.
34. Gen. 2.23. Tertullian also points to other parts of the biblical account in which Eve is again referred to as "woman" in her presumably virgin state: "the two were naked, Adam and his woman" (referencing Gen. 2:25, Tert., *Virg.* 5 [CSEL 76.86]; trans. Dunn, *Tertullian*, 148).
35. Referencing Gen. 2:24, Tert., *Virg.* 5 (CSEL 76.86); trans. Dunn, *Tertullian*, 148.
36. Tert., *Virg.* 5 (CSEL 76.87–88).
37. Tertullian writes, "Besides, Adam was not about to leave father and mother, whom he did not have, because of Eve. Therefore it does not apply to Eve because that which was said prophetically does not [apply] to Adam either. In fact, the prediction [is] about the situation of husbands who were about to leave their parents on account of a woman" (*Virg.* 5 [CSEL 76.87]; trans. Dunn, *Tertullian*, 149).
38. Tert., *Virg.* 6 (CSEL 76.88); trans. Dunn, *Tertullian*, 149.
39. Tert., *Virg.* 6 (CSEL 76.88); trans. Dunn, *Tertullian*, 150, adapted.
40. Tert., *Virg.* 6 (CSEL 76.88–89).
41. Tert., *Virg.* 1 (CSEL 76.79); cf. *Prot. Jas.* and Jer., *Helv.*

42. Tert., *Virg.* 5 (CSEL 76.87); trans. Dunn, *Tertullian*, 148–49. Tertullian might be pointing out the linguistic derivation of *'šh* from *'yš*, but it seems from his discussion of the Watcher myth that he is reading from a Greek translation of Genesis (*Virg.* 5, 7 [CSEL 76.87; 76.90]).
43. Cox Miller, "Desert Asceticism," 146.
44. Tert., *Virg.* 12 (CSEL 76.96).
45. Tert., *Virg.* 7 (CSEL 76.89). For a discussion of the way in which Paul—and by extension Tertullian—follows contemporary discussions about the symbolic value of hair in this passage, see Molly Myerowitz Levine, "The Gendered Grammar of Ancient Mediterranean Hair," in *Off with Her Head!*, 89.
46. 1 Cor. 11:14–15, emphasis added. As Dale Martin notes, the body here is understood to be an expression of one's identity that is both natural from birth and that must be trained to properly reflect an individual's social status (*Corinthian Body*, 25–29, 245–46). Paul may have recognized how weak his argument from nature was, because he immediately buttresses this claim with evidence from ecclesial custom, arguing that no church of God had provided precedence for unveiled women in church (1 Cor. 11:16).
47. Tert., *Virg.* 7–8 (CSEL 76.89–92); cf. Tert., *Or.* 22 (PL 1.1187–88). Here Tertullian follows a long line of tradition that understands hair to be a principal sign of gender difference. Aristotle, for instance, writes: "Women do not go bald because their nature is similar to that of children: both are incapable of producing seminal secretion. Eunuchs, too, do not go bald, because of their transition into the female state, and the hair that comes at a later stage they fail to grow at all, or if they already have it, they lose it, except for the pubic hair: similarly, women do not have the later hair, though they do grow the pubic hair. This deformity constitutes a change from the male state to the female" (Arist., *Gen. an.* 784a4–12 [LCL 524]). Looking to facial hair, Clement argues that the beard is the "mark of a man" and "is a token of his superior nature." Conversely, God created woman out of a hairless part of Adam. For Clement, therefore, gender is most evidently discernable according to one's hairiness (Clem., *paed.* 3.3; 3.11 [PG 8.580–81; 8.633–37]). See more detailed discussions of hair in David Satran, "Fingernails and Hair: Anatomy and Exegesis in Tertullian," *JTS* 40.1 (1989): 116–20; Myerowitz Levine, "Ancient Mediterranean Hair," 76–130, 85.
48. For example, Tert., *Cult. fem.* 2.5.2 (CCSL 1.358).
49. Tert., *Virg.* 12 (CSEL 76.97); trans. Dunn, *Tertullian*, 156.
50. Tert., *Virg.* 12 (CSEL 76.97); trans. Dunn, *Tertullian*, 156; cf. *Or.* 22 (PL 1.1187–89), in which Tertullian again appeals to appearances to support the "naturalness" of gender difference. In this chapter, Tertullian asserts that the custom of men wearing their hair short and women wearing their hair long (even before puberty) supports a stable, natural gender difference.
51. Tert., *Virg.* 12 (CSEL 76.97).
52. Elizabeth A. Clark explains why myths are so useful to the construction of gender and gendered subjects: it was "no accident that patristic writers turn largely to Biblical myths and historical narratives to create models of submission for female audiences" because these references to scripture and tradition intended to prove that certain aspects of femininity were natural through the retelling of history ("Construction of 'Woman,' " 162; cf. Butler, *Undoing Gender*, 9–10).
53. Here again Tertullian links his argument to Paul, specifically to Paul's phrase "because of the angels" in 1 Cor. 11. Although there has been much contemporary scholarship on how best to understand this vague reference, Tertullian reads the phrase to be an allusion to the Watcher myth of Gen. 6.

54. 1 En. 6.
55. *T. Reu.* 5; Cypr., *Hab. virg.* 14 (PL 4.452–54).
56. Tert., *Virg.* 7 (CSEL 76.90).
57. In fact, Tertullian claims to have witnessed the desire aroused by the "bloom" of virginity in his own community (*Virg.* 7 [CSEL 76.89]).
58. Tertullian makes similar arguments in his treatise, *Cult. fem.* 1.1–3 (CCSL 1.343–47) and Commodian also appealed to the Watcher myth as a way to historicize and naturalize femininity in *Instr.* 3 (CCSL 128.4).
59. Tert., *Cult. fem.* 1.1.1 (CCSL 1.343).
60. Tert., *Virg.* 10 (CSEL 76.93–94); cf. Tert., *Or.* 22.9 (PL 1.1189) in which Tertullian claims that the female ascetics remain unveiled in order to garner attention and honor. He chastises them, wondering why they ought to receive more public attention and esteem than male ascetics who have to quash even greater desire (presumably due to the women in their midst).
61. In Judith Butler's words, "The body posited as prior to the sign is always *posited or signified as prior*" (*Bodies That Matter*, 30, emphasis added).
62. Just as it is through reiterative practices that gender gains the impression of stability, so too is it through the failure to properly perform gender that the instability of the categories becomes immediately manifest. It is in this gap— this discontinuity—that the material *process* of gender construction is made visible. Judith Butler writes: "That this reiteration is necessary is a sign that materialization is never quite complete, that bodies never quite comply with the norms by which their materialization is impelled" (*Bodies That Matter*, 2, cf. 10, 94–95; idem, *Undoing Gender*, 215–16).
63. Tert., *Virg.* 3 (CSEL 76.83); trans. Dunn, *Tertullian*, 145, emphasis added.
64. See, for example, Tert., *Bapt.* 17 (PL 1.1328–29); idem, *Praescr.* 41 (PL 2.68–69). For a discussion of the "Pauline" source to which Tertullian's opponents appeal, see Stevan L. Davies, "Women, Tertullian and the Acts of Paul," *Semeia* 38 (1986): 139–43.
65. As Linda Coon has persuasively demonstrated, clerics, especially in the West, attempted to exhibit the authority vested in them through distinctive forms of dressing (Coon, *Sacred Fictions*, 63). Could the virgins' change in garb have been interpreted to be a similar claim of ecclesial status?
66. Tert., *Virg.* 9 (CSEL 76.92).
67. Tert., *Virg.* 9 (CSEL 76.92); trans. Dunn, *Tertullian*, 153.
68. Also, in Chapter 3 Tertullian reports that "those most chaste teachers" made their decisions about veiling without consulting custom. If, as *Sources Chré-tiennes* translator, Mattei, supposes, Tertullian is referring sarcastically to the unveiled virgins, this may signal his practical concern about this controversy (Tert., *Virg.* 3 [CSEL 76.82]).
69. Daniel Hoffman, on the contrary, understands Tertullian to have widened opportunities for women's roles in the church ("Tertullian on Women," 144–55). Hoffman, however, holds a minority position. Compare Émilien Lamirande, "Tertullien misogyne? Pour une relecture du *De cultu feminarum*," *ScEs* 39.1 (1987): 5–25; Elizabeth Carnelley, "Tertullian and Feminism," *Theology* 92.745 (1989): 31–35.
70. Much of the scholarship on Eustathius of Sebaste focuses on his supposed Arian tendencies, attempting to locate him within particular schools of Arians or Pneumatomachi. See especially the only full publication on Eustathius by Friedrich Loofs, *Eustathius von Sebaste und die Chronologie der Basilius-Briefe* (Halle: Niemeyer, 1898) and the abundant references to Eustathius in Philip Rousseau's *Basil of Caesarea* (Berkeley: University of California Press, 1994), 239–45. These treatments rely heavily on Basil's letters, in which Basil highlights his theological battles with Eustathius. Less work, however, has

been done on Eustathius's ascetic program and the profound influence it had on ascetic practices in Asia Minor. Susanna Elm and Anna Silvas's work are notable exceptions and significant contributions to understanding Eustathius's influence on ascetic practice in Asia Minor (Elm, *Virgins of God*, 106–11; Anna Silvas, *The Asketikon of St. Basil the Great* [Oxford: Oxford University Press, 2005], 53–60; cf. Jean Gribomont, "Eustathe le Philosophe et les voyages du jeune Basile de Césarée," *RHE* 54 [1959]: 115–24).

71. Anna Silvas notes that Canon 11 of the Council of Neocaesarea (315) set the minimum age for the ordination of a presbyter at thirty years old, which leads us to believe that Eustathius was at least this age when he returned from Alexandria (*Asketikon*, 53 n.10).

72. Sozom., *Hist. eccl.* 3.14 (Font. Chr. 73.2.390); cf. Silvas, *Asketikon*, 53; Wolf-Dieter Hauschild, "Eustathius von Sebaste," *TRE* 10 (1982): 549.

73. Sozom., *Hist. eccl.* 3.14 (Font. Chr. 73.2.390).

74. Bas., *ep.* 1 (LCL 1.2–6).

75. Bas., *epp.* 95, 98, 119, 223 (LCL 2.154–56, 2.164–70, 2.240–44, 3.302–4); Rousseau, *Basil of Caesarea*, 73–74; Loofs, *Eustathius von Sebaste*, 54; Gribomont, "Eustathe le Philosophe," 115; idem, "Eustathe de Sébaste," *Dictionnaire d'histoire et de géographie ecclésiastiques* 16 (1967): 28.

76. Sozom., *Hist. eccl.* 3.14 (Font. Chr. 73.2.390).

77. Bas., *ep.* 244 (LCL 3.456).

78. It is unclear if Eustathius forbade meat entirely, as Socrates writes, or if he merely limited which meats his followers could eat, as Sozomen explains (Socr., *Hist. eccl.* 2.43 [PG 67.353]; Sozom., *Hist. eccl.* 3.14 [Font. Chr. 73.2.390]).

79. Socr., *Hist. eccl.* 2.43 (PG 67.353).

80. Eustathius's opponents claimed that although his followers renounced marriage, they had not been trained in continence and therefore fell quite easily into adultery (Sozom., *Hist. eccl.* 3.14 [Font. Chr. 73.2.390–92]).

81. Socr., *Hist. eccl.* 2.43 (PG 67.353); Sozom., *Hist. eccl.* 3.14 (Font. Chr. 73.2.390–92). According to Sozomen, some of Eustathius's ardent defenders claimed that he did not institute these strict rules, especially those relating to marriage, but rather that they were the innovations of some of his more zealous disciples (*Hist. eccl.* 3.14 [Font. Chr. 73.2.390]). If this is the case, we might conclude that Eustathius held stricter views earlier in his life, but became more lax once he was ordained bishop of Sebesta, when it would have been nearly impossible for him to exclude the married members of his region.

82. Socr., *Hist. eccl.* 2.43 (PG 67.353); Sozom., *Hist. eccl.* 3.14 (Font. Chr. 73.2.390).

83. Basil, bishop of nearby Ancyra, purportedly advocated a similar ascetic ideal. It was, however, the transformation of the soul into an incorruptible condition—reflecting God's image—that freed female ascetics from their femininity. A female ascetic, therefore, was only allowed to live with her brothers and act like a man once she had achieved this advanced, masculine state, a state "achieved steadily and quietly not by leaps and bounds" (Elm, *Virgins of God*, 116).

84. Socr., *Hist. eccl.* 2.43 (PG 67.353); Sozom., *Hist. eccl.* 3.14 (Font. Chr. 73.2.390); Bas., *ep.* 223 (LCL 3.296); *Can. Syn. Gangr.* , canons 13, 17 (PG 137.1256; 137.1261); Elm, *Virgins of God*, 111, 125.

85. Socr., *Hist. eccl.* 2.43 (PG 67.353).

86. *Can. Syn. Gangr.* (PG 137.1240); trans. Silvas, *Asketikon*, 488. Of course Eustathius was not the only ascetic leader to institute distinctive dress. See, for example, Sozomen's descriptions of the attire of various Egyptian groups,

which relayed some "secret significance related to their philosophy" (*Hist. eccl.* [Font. Chr. 73.2.379–80]).

87. *Can. Syn. Gangr.* (PG 137.1240); trans. Yarbrough, "Council of Gangra," 450, adapted, emphasis added.

88. Jean Gribomont, "Eustathe de Sébaste," *Dictionnaire de spiritualité: ascétique et mystique, doctrine et histoire* 4.2 (1961): 1710; idem, "Le monachisme au IVᵉ siècle en Asie Mineure: de Gangres au Messalianisme" *SP* 2 (1957): 407; cf. Philip Beagon, "The Cappadocian Fathers, Women and Ecclesiastical Politics" *VC* 49.2 (1995): 174. Gribomont considers Eustathius's censure of riches to be an attack on the church's accumulation of wealth ("Eustathe de Sébaste," 1711).

89. The date of the council of Gangra is hotly disputed. Socrates places the council around 365, while Sozomen dates it more than twenty years earlier. The earlier date is favored by most scholars who look to the order of the most ancient collections of canon law, which place the Gangra canons before the canons of Antioch. Moreover, three participants of Gangra—Bithynicus, Philetus, and Proaeresius—are likely the same men who attended the Council of Sardica in 343 and the president of the Gangra council, Eusebius, could have been the bishop of Nicomedia, who died in 341. Others, including myself, prefer Socrates's later date. I agree with T. D. Barnes that the council president could have been Eusebius of Samosata and, thus, the council might have taken place as late as 379/380. Most importantly, though, a later date best explains why Basil (and his family) would have sought after Eustathius's mentorship in the 340s and 350s, because he had yet to be censured for his ascetic extremism. Also, because Sozomen reports that Eustathius was bishop at the time of the Gangra censure—he claims that Eustathius was "deprived of his episcopacy by those who were convened in Gangra" (*Hist. eccl.* 4.24)—a later date allows time for Eustathius to have climbed the ecclesial ranks. (It is unclear whether Eustathius was really deposed or not; the Gangra canons allowed for him and his followers to recant their position and remain in the church.) Finally, Anna Silvas has argued persuasively that Basil's *Rules* show evidence of responding to the warnings issued by the bishops at Gangra, thus becoming the *terminus ante quem* for dating purposes (although she dates the council to c. 340). It seems most plausible to me, therefore, to trust Socrates's date of around 365. In fact, I would even argue that this conciliar reprimand was the first phase of the fallout between Basil and Eustathius around this time. For full discussions of dating issues, see Gribomont, "Le monachisme," 401; Timothy D. Barnes, "The Date of the Council of Gangra," *JTS* 40.1 (1989): 121–24; Silvas, *Asketikon*, 25–28, 56–60, 486 n.1.

90. For a succinct summary of the council, see Silvas, *Asketikon*, 19–20.

91. See the following Gangra canons that address each of these issues—1: "If anyone finds fault with marriage . . . let such a one be anathema"; 3: "If anyone teaches a slave, under pretext of piety, to despise his master . . . let such a one be anathema"; 4: "If anyone discriminates against a married presbyter . . . let such a one be anathema"; 9: "If anyone practicing virginity or continence has withdrawn himself because he reviles the married state and not on account of the beauty and holiness of virginity, let such a one be anathema"; 10: "If anyone practicing virginity for the Lord's sake exalts himself over those who are married, let such a one be anathema"; 14: "If any woman forsakes her husband and would withdraw herself, because she reviles the married state, let such a one be anathema"; 15: "If anyone forsakes his or her own children . . . [and] on a pretext of asceticism, neglects them, let such a one be anathema"; 16: "If any child, specially of the faithful, withdraws from

142   *Notes*

his parents on a pretext of piety . . . let such a one be anathema" *Can. Syn. Gangr.* (PG 137.1241–69); trans. Silvas, *Asketikon*, 490–92, adapted.
92. Compare Aug., *Doct. chr.* 2.25.38–39 (CCSL 32.60).
93. *Can. Syn. Gangr.*, canon 17 (PG 137.1261); Silvas, *Asketikon*, 492, emphasis added.
94. *Can. Syn. Gangr.* (PG 137.1268); trans. Silvas, *Asketikon*, 493.
95. Matt. 19:21, Matt. 19:29, Mark 12:25, and Gal. 3:28.
96. Elm, *Virgins of God*, 130.
97. As punishment, he was banished from the communion of prayers (Socr., *Hist. eccl.* 2.43 [PG 67.352]; Sozom., *Hist. eccl.* 4.24 [Font. Chr. 73.2.537]; Elm, *Virgins of God*, 10, 107; Gribomont, "Eustathe de Sébaste," 27).
98. Although Gribomont is unsure of the date of the council of Neocaesarea, Elm fixes the council in 339 (Elm, *Virgins of God*, 107; Gribomont, "Eustathe de Sébaste," 28). At that time, he was forced to resign his office of presbyter (Hauschild, "Eustathius von Sebaste," 548; Loofs, *Eustathius von Sebaste*, 1–3, 54).
99. *Can. Syn. Gangr.* (PG 137.1268–69).
100. *Can. Syn. Gangr.*, canons 13, 17 (PG 137.1256; 137.1261). Again, it is interesting to note that the bishops do not ban short hair and cross-dressing altogether, but only that which purports to be an expression of unconventional gender identities.
101. *Cod. Theod.* 16.2.27; trans. Clyde Pharr, *Theodosian Code and Novels and the Sirmondian Constitutions* (Union, NJ: Lawbook Exchange, 2001), 444–45. For a list of later canons and conciliar statements on dress, see Coon, *Sacred Fictions*, 38–39.
102. Bas., *epp.* 130, 223, 263 (LCL 2.290–94; 3.286–312; 4.88–100).
103. Elm, *Virgins of God*, 74–77. It is interesting, though, that Basil never went so far as to censure the institution of slavery, which he described as part of God's natural order of human relationships (Elm, *Virgins of God*, 103).
104. Bas., *reg. br.* 210 (Silvas, *Asketikon*, 388–89); cf. *reg. fus.* 22.3 (Silvas, *Asketikon*, 220–23).
105. For a list of evidence that Basil's shorter *Rule* aimed to correct Eustathian excesses, see Silvas, *Asketikon*, 25–30.
106. On Eustathius's mixed monasteries and Basil's double monasteries, see Daniel Stramara, "Double Monasticism in the Greek East, Fourth through Eight Centuries," *JECS* 6.2 (1998): 271–80; Elm, *Virgins of God*, 68–75, 210–11; Gribomont, "Eustathe de Sébaste," 1711–12.
107. Stramara, "Double Monasticism," 288; Jean Gribomont, "Monasteries, Double," *New Catholic Encyclopedia*, vol. 9, ed. Berard Marthaler (Detroit: Gale, 2003), 784–85.
108. Although we know that Eustathius's monasteries welcomed men and women, there is no indication of how he arranged the living quarters. Although Silvas argues that Eustathius and Basil both operated double monasteries, her conclusions are based on a reading of Sozomen that is not convincing to me. Sozomen writes: "It is related that a certain man and woman, who, according to the custom of the Church, had devoted themselves to a life of virginity, were accused of coming together (ἄνδρα τινὰ καὶ γυναῖκα κατὰ Θεσμὸν Ἐκκλησίας παρθενίαν προσποιουμένους, καὶ εἰς ταὐτὸν συνιέναι διαβαλλομένους). He endeavoured to have them cease from their familiarity (σπουδάσαι τῆς πρὸς ἀλλήλους ὁμιλίας παῦσαι—*ut eos ab huiusmodi consuetudine revocaret*); but, failing to have any effect on them, he sighed deeply and said that a woman who had been lawfully cohabiting with her husband (ὡς κατὰ νόμον ἀνδρὶ συνοικοῦσα γυνὴ), having heard him discourse on the advantage of self-restraint (τοὺς περὶ σωφροσύνης λόγους ἀκούσασα αὐτοῦ), was so deeply

affected by it that she abstained from that intercourse it is right for wives to share with their own husbands (συνουσίας ἀπέσχετο ἧς γαμεταῖς θέμις πρὸς ἰδίους ἄνδρας κοινωνεῖν) and that the weakness of his powers of persuasion was, on the other hand, shown by the fact that the parties above mentioned persisted in their unlawful course" (Sozom., *Hist. eccl.* 3.14; trans. Silvas, *Asketikon*, 84–85). Silvas reads this passage as evidence that Eustathius opposed the cohabitation of male and female ascetics within monastic communities, whereas I interpret it to mean that he opposed individual "spiritual marriages," an arrangement that, in his view, was bound to fail.

109. As Philip Rousseau and Anna Silvas note, Basil was quite intent to rewrite history so as to minimize Eustathius's influence on him (Rousseau, *Basil of Caesarea*, 243; Silvas, *Asketikon*, 55). For a cogent summary of Eustathius and Basil's contentious falling out, which, according to my dating coincided with the Gangra censure, see Rousseau, *Basil of Caesarea*, 239–54.

110. Bas., *ep.* 263 (LCL 4.99–100); Gribomont, "Eustathe de Sébaste", 1710; Hauschild, "Eustathius von Sebaste," 549.

111. Philip Rousseau similarly suggests that Basil paired Eustathius (who was in fact an ardent opponent of Arianism) with Arians in order to undermine his authority and to silence Eustathius's accusations against Basil (Rousseau, *Basil of Caesarea*, 239).

112. Gr. Nyss., *v. Macr.* 11 (SC 178.174–76); trans. Woods Callahan, FC 58.170, adapted; cf. *v. Macr.* 7 (SC 178.164). For a discussion of the social repercussions of the flattened status distinctions in this household, see Elm, *Virgins of God*, 84–86, 92–94, 135.

113. Gr. Nyss., *v. Macr.* 32 (SC 178.246); cf. *v. Macr.* 29 (SC 178.236–38).

114. Bas., *ep.* 223 (LCL 3.302).

115. For excellent analyses of this letter, see Kate Cooper, "Insinuations of Womanly Influence: An Aspect of the Christianization of the Roman Aristocracy," *JRS* 82 (1992): 158–60; Claudia Kock, "Augustine's Letter to Ecdicia: A New Reading," *AugSt* 31.2 [2000]: 173–80; and Rebecca Krawiec, " 'From the Womb of the Church': Monastic Families," *JECS* 11.3 (2003): 292–95.

116. Aug., *ep.* 262.5 (CSEL 57.625). For detailed study of these transient monks who were not located in households or attached to monastic establishments, see Daniel Caner's study, *Wandering, Begging Monks: Spiritual Authority and the Promotion of Monasticism in Late Antiquity* (Berkeley: University of California Press, 2002).

117. Claudia Kock suggests that Ecdicia was not only writing to Augustine to be consoled, but also to curry his favor in what might be a legal battle for guardianship of the couple's son should they divorce over this issue. Although in situations of divorce legitimate children typically were raised by their fathers, there were instances in which notable men intervened in favor of the mother ("Letter to Ecdicia," 176–77).

118. Aug., *ep.* 262.3 (CSEL 57.623).

119. Aug., *ep.* 262.1 (CSEL 57.621).

120. Joyce E. Salisbury, *Church Fathers, Independent Virgins* (London; New York: Verso, 1991), 2.

121. Cooper, *Virgin and Bride*, 106–7; idem, "Womanly Influence," 158–60; Brown, *Body and Society*, 403–4.

122. Aug., *ep.* 262.4 (CSEL 57.624); trans. Elizabeth A. Clark, *St. Augustine on Marriage and Sexuality* (Washington DC: Catholic University of America Press, 1996), 26. This is consistent with Augustine's deliberations on the bonds of marriage between the holy parents of Jesus: Mary did not cease to be Joseph's wife even though the couple did not consummate their marriage

(Elizabeth A. Clark, " 'Adam's Only Companion': Augustine and the Early Christian Debate on Marriage," *RecAug* 21 [1986]: 151–52; Krawiec, "From the Womb," 293).

123. For example, see Elizabeth A. Clark, *Women in the Early Church* (Collegeville: Michael Glazier, 1983), 65; Elizabeth A. Clark, "Distinguishing 'Distinction': Considering Peter Brown's Reconsiderations," *AugSt* 36.1 (2005): 259–60.

124. Kim Power, *Veiled Desire: Augustine on Women* (New York: Continuum, 1996), 112; cf. Krawiec, "From the Womb," 292–94.

125. Brown, *Body and Society*, 404.

126. Rebecca Krawiec's recent *JECS* article is the notable exception. Here, Krawiec details the ways in which the clothing of male and female monks materialized the paradoxes and tensions of the ascetic life. For example, they represented both the humility of their renunciatory life, as well as their exalted spiritual identity and status within Christian communities. Krawiec ends the article with a brief analysis of Ecdicia, who illustrates the dangerous possibility of ascetic women who decide for themselves how they will dress ("Garments of Salvation," 148–49).

127. On women's dress and adornments as a repository for women's wealth, see Berg, "Wearing Wealth," 35, 50–62; Batten, "Adornment, Gender and Honour," 491–92. Sosiana is another example of a woman who gifted fine clothes—embroidered silk and garments encrusted with woven gold thread—and precious metals (possibly jewelry), although these gifts were given to the church to be altered into altar cloths and veils and melted down and recast as chalices and crosses (Jo. Eph., *vita* 55 [PO 19.191–96]).

128. Aug., *ep.* 262.9 (CSEL 57.628–29).

129. Aug., *ep.* 262.9 (CSEL 57.628–29); trans. Clark, *Marriage and Sexuality*, 29.

130. Alluding to Matt. 6:19–21, Aug., *ep.* 262.8 (CSEL 57.627–28); trans. Clark, *Marriage and Sexuality*, 28.

131. Although some scholars characterize Ecdicia's transgression as financial (Krawiec, "From the Womb," 292–93), Elizabeth Clark notes that nowhere does Augustine claim that Ecdicia overstepped her right to the property, leading readers to believe that there were no legal grounds on which to charge her ("Distinguishing 'Distinction,'" 260).

132. Aug., *ep.* 262.5–6 (CSEL 57.625–26).

133. Aug., *ep.* 262.9–10 (CSEL 57.628–30); cf. Cooper, "Womanly Influence," 159; Power, *Veiled Desire*, 125.

134. Augustine writes: "If in the matter of almsgiving and bestowing your property on the poor, a good and great work about which we have precise commandments from the Lord, you ought to have taken counsel with your husband, a believer, and one who was observing with you the holy vow of continence, and not to have scorned his will, how much more necessary was it for you not to change or adopt anything in your costume and garb against his will—a matter on which we read no divine commands!" (*ep.* 262.9 [CSEL 57.628]; trans. Clark, *Marriage and Sexuality*, 29.

135. Citing Esth. 14:16, Aug., *ep.* 262.10 (CSEL 57.629–30); trans. Clark, *Marriage and Sexuality*, 30.

136. See Kate Cooper's discussion of womanly influence in "Womanly Influence," 159.

137. Referencing 1 Pet. 3:1–6, Aug., *ep.* 262.7 (CSEL 57.627); trans. Clark, *Marriage and Sexuality*, 28.

138. Aug., *ep.* 262.7 (CSEL 57.627).

139. Aug., *ep.* 262.9 (CSEL 57.628).

140. Some scholars have attempted to identify these monks. On the one hand, G. Folliet argued that they were either the Messalians or Euchites to which Augustine refers nearly thirty years later in *De haeresibus* ("Des moines euchites à Carthage en 400–401," *SP* 2 [1957]: 386–99). Lope Cilleruelo and Juan-Manuel del Estal, on the other hand, argue that these "heretical" monasteries did not yet exist in Africa at this early date (Lope Cilleruelo, "Nota sobre el agustinismo de los monjes de Cartago," *La Ciudad de Dios* 172 [1959]: 365–69; Juan-Manuel del Estal, "Descertada opinión moderna sobre los monjes de Cartago," *La Ciudad de Dios* 172 [1959]: 596–616). Whatever their persuasion, Kenneth Steinhauser suggests that these Christian ascetics might have been influenced by Cynics' grooming practices ("The Cynic Monks of Carthage: Some Observations of *De opere monachorum*," in *Augustine: Presbyter Factus Sum*, ed. Joseph T. Lienhard, Earl C. Muller, and Roland J. Teskey [New York: Peter Lang, 1993], 457–60).
141. Aug., *Retract.* 2.21 (PL 32.638–39).
142. It is unclear if there were divisions between laypeople, clerics, and monks or between different groups of ascetics (Steinhauser, "Cynic Monks of Carthage," 456).
143. 1 Sam. 1:11; cf. Num. 6:2, 5; Judg. 13:5. Because it was not uncommon for ascetics to pattern their dress on that of biblical predecessors—namely, Elijah and Elisha for men—these monks were, at least in principle, not deviating from custom (Krawiec, "Garments of Salvation," 134–36).
144. Aug., *Mon.* 39–40 (CSEL 41.590–94). Although Augustine does not mention it as one of their rationale, the monks may additionally have been imitating the look of Greek philosophers whose long hair was a sign that their intellectual pursuits took precedence over even basic grooming. Approximately 200 years earlier Tertullian urged Christian men of Carthage to demonstrate their Christian piety by emulating the dress of philosophers. In particular, he asked them to cast aside the Roman toga in favor of the *pallium* (Tert., *Pall.*). It is plausible, therefore, that Augustine is battling the influence of his predecessor in the region. For a discussion of depictions of philosophers' hair, see Paul Zanker, *The Mask of Socrates: The Image of the Intellectual in Antiquity* (Berkeley: University of California Press, 1996), 259–64, 298–304.
145. On the latter point, Augustine follows Paul's interpretation in 2 Cor. 3:14.
146. Referencing Exod. 34:1–35, Aug., *Mon.* 39 (CSEL 41.591).
147. 2 Cor. 3:16, 18, emphasis added.
148. Aug., *Mon.* 39 (CSEL 41.591).
149. Most modern translators locate this phrase, τοῦτο δὲ παραγγελλων ουκ ἐπαινῶ (*hoc autem proecipio non laudans*), at the beginning of the next section rather than the end of the previous section like Augustine.
150. Referencing 1 Cor. 11:16–17, Augustine writes: "Now what is more unjust than that persons who do not wish to obey their superiors should wish to be obeyed by their inferiors? For, in so far as they give attention to their hair, they disobey, not us, but the Apostle, who in this regard would have no disputing at all, saying . . . 'Now this I command.' So that you are to submit to the authority of the one commanding you and not the mere oratorical skill of the one addressing you. For what is the reason, I wonder, why men wear their hair long contrary to the precept of the Apostle?" (*Mon.* 39 [CSEL 41.590]; trans. Muldowney, FC 16.388–89, adapted).
151. Aug., *Mon.* 40 (CSEL 41.593). Contrary to conventional judgments that located the male as the pinnacle of gender spectrum, the Carthaginian monks seem to have privileged the status of "un-men" as beyond the spectrum altogether (Stephen D. Moore, *God's Beauty Parlor: And Other*

*Queer Spaces in and around the Bible* [Stanford: Stanford University Press, 2001], 135–36).
152. Aug., *Mon.* 40 (CSEL 41.593).
153. Col. 3:9–10 and Eph. 4:22–24 as cited in Aug., *Mon.* 40 (CSEL 41.593–94); trans. Muldowney, FC 16.392–93, adapted.
154. Aug., *Mon.* 40 (CSEL 41.594); trans. Muldowney, FC 16.393, adapted.
155. Aug., *Mon.* 40 (CSEL 41.593–94).
156. Aug., *Mon.* 40 (CSEL 41.592); trans. Muldowney, FC 16.391.
157. Aug., *Mon.* 40 (CSEL 41.592); trans. Muldowney, FC 16.391. (The phrase "Perfect Man" is contested among the Greek manuscripts of Eph. 4.)
158. Kuefler, *Manly Eunuch*, 275.
159. Kuefler, *Manly Eunuch*, 277–78.

## NOTES TO CHAPTER 4

1. Although Evelyne Patlagean identifies twelve *Lives* of cross-dressing saints from this period, Stephen Davis counts eleven (Evelyne Patlagean, "L'histoire de la femme déguisée en moine et l'évolution de la sainteté feminine à Byzance," in *Structure sociale, famille, chrétienté à Byzance, IVᵉ-XIᵉ siècle* [London: Variorum Reprints, 1981], 600–2; Steven J. Davis, "Crossed Texts, Crossed Sex: Intertextuality and Gender in Early Christian Legends of Holy Women Disguised as Men," *JECS* 10.1 [2002]: 4, 8).
2. These stories were especially popular among monks—as is evidenced by the narratives' direct address to the "holy fathers and brothers"—and were an important part of the *apophthegmata* and the *vitae patrum*. See, for example, the introduction of the Syriac *Life of Saint Pelagia* (AMSS 6.616); trans. Sebastian P. Brock and Susan Ashbrook Harvey, *Holy Women of the Syrian Orient* (Berkeley: University of California Press, 1998), 41; Benedicta Ward, *Harlots of the Desert: A Study of Repentance in Early Monastic Sources* (Kalamazoo: Cistercian Publications, 1987), 57; Helen Waddell, *The Desert Fathers; Translations from the Latin with an Introduction* (New York: Henry Holt, 1936), 252.
3. Patlagean, "la femme déguisée," 605; Marie Delcourt, *Hermaphrodite: Myths and Rites of the Bisexual Figure in Classical Antiquity*, trans. Jennifer Nicholson (London: Studio Books, 1961), 84–102; Ward, *Harlots of the Desert*, 62; Bullough, "Transvestites," 1381; Castelli, "Pieties of the Body," 43–47; Alice-Marie Maffry Talbot, *Holy Women of Byzantium: Ten Saints' Lives in English Translation* (Washington DC: Dumbarton Oaks, 1996), 4–5; Valerie R. Hotchkiss, *Clothes Make the Man: Female Cross Dressing in Medieval Europe* (New York: Garland Publishing, 1996), 7–12. Laila Abdalla presents a notable exception to this position. She sees not a rejection of femininity in cross-dressing, but rather an embodied divestment of sexuality that enables the female saints to rescue and realize an idealized version of femininity ("Theology and Culture: Masculinizing the Woman," in *Varieties of Devotion in the Middle Ages and Renaissance*, ed. Susan C. Karant-Nunn [Turnhout: Brepols, 2003], 17–37).
4. Davis, "Crossed Texts," 31–36.
5. Davis, "Crossed Texts," 32; cf. Patricia Cox Miller, "Is There a Harlot in This Text? Hagiography and the Grotesque," *JMEMS* 33.3 (2003): 426–28.
6. Focusing particularly on devotional practice, Derek Krueger similarly attends to the confluence of writing and performance in *Writing and Holiness: The*

*Practice of Authorship in the Early Christian East* (Philadelphia: University of Pennsylvania Press, 2004).

7. I agree with Judith Butler that drag that forces a radical "reconsideration of the *place* and stability of the masculine and feminine" subverts the gender binary (*Gender Trouble*, 177). I disagree, however, that conspicuous drag is effective in this regard (Butler, *Bodies that Matter*, 121–40; idem, *Gender Trouble*, vii–xxvi).

8. See, for example, Davis, "Crossed Texts," 4, 14; Talbot, *Holy Women of Byzantium*, vii–xv; Cyril Mango's introduction to the *Life of Saint Matrona* (Talbot, *Holy Women of Byzantium*, 13).

9. For example, when summarizing the *Life of Mary, Called Marinos*, Stephen Davis writes: " . . . it is not until after [Mary's] death that her *true* identity is *revealed*" ("Crossed Texts," 3, emphasis added).

10. *Vit. Euphr.* (Agnes Smith Lewis, ed., *Select Narratives of Holy Women from the Syro-Antiochene or Sinai Palimpsest vol. I* [London: C. J. Clay and Sons, 1900], 81a); trans. Lewis, *Select Narratives vol. II*, 52.

11. For an excellent overview of the recent scholarship on these texts, see Davis, "Crossed Texts," 4–10.

12. Burrus, *Sex Lives of the Saints*, 128.

13. Davis, "Crossed Texts," 4, 8; Patlagean, "la femme déguisée," 600–2; A. C. Dionisotti, "Translated Saints: Wisdom and Her Daughters" *JECS* 16.2 (2008): 165–80.

14. For an overview of the cross-dressing activities of Thecla, Charitine, and Mariamne, see Hotchkiss, *Clothes Make the Man*, 20–21. For theories on the origins of the cross-dressing motif in classical literature, see Hermann Usener, *Legenden der heiligen Pelagia* (Bonn: A. Marcus, 1879); Ludwig Radermacher, *Hippolytos und Thekla: Studien zur Geschichte von Legende und Kultus* (Vienna: Alfred Hölder, 1916); Rosa Söder, *Die apokryphen Apostelgeschichten und die romanhafte Literatur der Antike* (Stuttgart: W. Kohlhammer, 1932).

15. Although these saints are regularly cast as "holy harlots," only two protagonists fit such a characterization: Pelagia converted from a life of prostitution and Theodora fled from a marriage in which she committed adultery.

16. For example, see *Vit. Sus.* (AASS Sept. 6. 154F); Greek *Vit. Apoll.* (James Drescher, *Three Coptic Legends: Hilaria, Archellites, the Seven Sleepers* [Cairo: Institut Français d'archéologie orientale, 1947], 156); *Vit. Hil.* (Drescher, *Three Coptic Legends*, 3); Latin *Vit. Pelag.* 12 (PL 73.669); Syriac *Vit. Pelag.* 41 (AAMS 6.643–44); *Vit. Mar.* (Lewis, *Select Narratives, vol. I*, 71b; Lewis, *Select Narratives, vol. II*, 38); *Act. Eugen.* (Lewis, *Select Narratives, vol. I*, 23b–24b); *Vit. Euphr.* (Lewis, *Select Narratives, vol. I*, 78b–80b).

17. As Marjorie Garber writes: "Womanliness *is* mimicry, *is* masquerade" (*Vested Interests*, 355, emphasis original).

18. There are multiple extant versions of this popular *vita*. Several scholars believe the freestanding *vita* was an expansion of a story related by John Chrysostom in *Hom. 67 in Mt.* 3 (PG 58.636–37). The Greek text can be found in Usener, *heiligen Pelagia*, 1–16. The Syriac text (thought to be a translation of the Greek) can be found in *Acta Martyrum et Sanctorum Syriace* 6.616–49. The Latin text can be found in PL 73.663–72. For a full discussion of the manuscripts, see Pierre Petitmengin, *Pélagie la Pénitente: Métamorphoses d'une légende* (Paris: Études augustiniennes, 1981), 13–18.

19. In both versions of the *vita*, Bishop Nonnus is in on the secret. In fact, in the Syriac *Life* Nonnus gave Pelagia his own clothing to wear (*Vit. Pelag.* 41 [AMSS 6.643]). Although the Latin *Life* less clearly implicates Nonnus in

Pelagia's initial cross-dressing, when Nonnus sends his disciple to visit "Pelagius" in the desert it becomes clear that he was aware of her new life "as a man" (*Vit. Pelag.* 12–13 [PL 73.669–70]).

20. Likewise, when Abba Daniel's disciple discovers that Anastasios has "women's breasts" while preparing "him" for burial, the narrative observes that "he kept silent and said nothing." Again, the readers are fully aware of the secret. See *Vit. Dan.* 7 (M. F. Nau, "Texte syriaque," *ROC* 5 [1900]: 398); trans. Brock and Harvey, *Holy Women*, 147.

21. The other is the *Life of Bishop Paul and Priest John*. In Chapter 9 the bishop confesses to having admitted an orphaned girl into the male monastery sixteen years prior. Again, this is a scene within the larger story of two male monks. (There exists one Greek manuscript of this *Life* available in the *Patriarchik Vivliotheke* series [Bruxelles: Culture et civilisation, 1963]. Several Syriac editions exist, but have yet to be published (M. F. Nau, "Hagiographie syriaque" *ROC* 15 [1910]: 56–60).

22. The Syriac text can be found in Nau, "Texte syriaque," 391–401. The Greek text, edited by L. Clugnet, can be found in the same volume, *ROC* 5 (1900): 370–91 and BHG 79–80. For discussions on the dating of the narrative cycle, see Patlagean, "la femme déguisée," 600 and Hans Georg Beck, *Kirche und theologische Literatur im Byzantinischen Reich* (München: C. H. Beck, 1959), 396–97.

23. *Vit. Dan.* 6 (Nau, "Texte syriaque," 398); trans. Brock and Harvey, *Holy Women*, 147.

24. *Vit. Dan.* 8 (Nau, "Texte syriaque," 398); trans. Brock and Harvey, *Holy Women*, 147. The disciple repeats this description of Anastasia's dried-up nipples in the next chapter of the narrative. See my discussion on page 96.

25. By casting Justinian in a particularly negative light—accusing him of lacking sexual moderation and control—this narrative might be participating in the Christological debates of the sixth century. Because Justinian wrote several treatises against the "Monophysites," it is plausible that this narrative was composed within a Miaphysite community hoping to slander one of their chief opponents. For a description of Justinian's Christological position and a collection of his Christological writings, see Kenneth Paul Wesche, *On the Person of Christ: The Christology of Emperor Justinian* (Crestwood: St. Vladimir's Seminary Press, 1991).

26. Many scholars have argued that the legends of cross-dressing saints follow patterns set by the Greek Romances. In the Romance genre, the constant threats to the protagonists' safety and chastity function to heighten readers' anxiety. Here, I argue that the threats to the cross-dressers' disguise works to cements readers' understanding of the saints' gender through a similar anxiety. For discussions of these classical antecedents and devices, see Radermacher, *Hippolytos und Thekla*; Söder, *Die apokryphen Apostelgeschichten*, 127–28; Delcourt, *Hermaphrodite*, 99; Zoja Pavlovskis, "The Life of St. Pelagia the Harlot: Hagiographic Adaptation of Pagan Romance," *CF* 30 (1976): 142.

27. The Greek texts can be found in AASS Nov. 3.790–813 (*Vita prima*); AASS Nov 3.813–22 and PG 116.919–54 (*Vita altera*); and AASS Nov. 3.822–23 (*Vita tertia*).

28. *Vit. Matron.* 4 (AASS Nov. 3.792E); trans. Talbot, *Holy Women of Byzantium*, 23. *Vit. Matron.* 7 similarly stresses Matrona's secretive activities (AASS Nov. 3.794A).

29. For the Greek text, see Marcel Richard, "La vie ancienne de Sainte Marie surnommée Marinos," in *Corona Gratiarum: Miscellanea Patristica, Historica et Liturgica* (Brugge: Sint Pietersabdij, 1975), 87–94. For the Syriac text,

see Lewis, *Select Narratives vol. I*, 70a–76b. The Latin text can be found in *ROC* 6 (1901): 357–78. For a discussion on the dating of the text, see Richard, "Sainte Marie," 83–87 and Patlagean, "la femme déguisée," 601.

30. *Vit. Mar.* 5 (Richard, "Sainte Marie," 88; Lewis, *Select Narratives, vol. I*, 71b–72a).

31. The Coptic text and an English translation can be found in Drescher, *Three Coptic Legends*, 1–13 (Coptic) and 69–82 (English). For the Syriac version, see A. J. Wensinck, *Legends of Eastern Saints: Chiefly from Syriac Sources*, vol. II (Leyden: E. J. Brill, 1911), 1–30 (Syriac) and 37–57 (English). For discussions on dating, see Wensinck, *Eastern Saints*, 9–16; Drescher, *Three Coptic Legends*, 121–31; Patlagean, "la femme déguisée," 601.

32. The narrator reports that her femininity was further obscured because she ceased to menstruate and lost her breasts as a result of strict ascetic practice (*Vit. Hil.* [Drescher, *Three Coptic Legends*, 6]; cf. *Vit. Apoll.* 216v–217r [Drescher, *Three Coptic Legends*, 157]; Latin *Vit. Pelag.* 14 [PL 73.670]; Syriac *Vit. Pelag.* 45 [AMSS 6.645–46]; *Vit. Mar.* 5 [Richard, "Sainte Marie," 88; Lewis, *Select Narratives, vol. I*, 72a]). For a broader discussion of how fasting and ascetic practice altered bodily processes, see Teresa Shaw, *The Burden of the Flesh: Fasting and Sexuality in Early Christianity* (Minneapolis: Fortress Press, 1998), 240–46.

33. See, in particular, Cox Miller, "Hagiography and the Grotesque" 427; Burrus, *Sex Lives of the Saints*, 144; Davis, "Crossed Texts," 20–24. For full discussions of the liminality of eunuchs in antiquity, see Kuefler, *Manly Eunuch*, 273–82; Kathryn M. Ringrose, "Living in the Shadows: Eunuchs and Gender in Byzantium," in *Third Sex, Third Gender: Beyond Sexual Dimorphism in Culture and History*, ed. Gilbert Herdt (New York: Zone Books, 1994), 85–109.

34. Lactantius, for example, brands the eunuch a "half-man" (*semivir*), elsewhere claiming that castration makes eunuchs "neither men nor women" (Lact., *Inst.* 1.17, 1.21 [CSEL 19.65, 19.81; trans. Kuefler, *Manly Eunuch*, 249). Augustine too annuls eunuchs' masculinity, arguing that the castrated man is "neither changed into a woman nor allowed to remain a man" (Aug., *Civ.* 7.24 [CCSL 47.207]; trans. Kuefler, *Manly Eunuch*, 249). On the extreme ambivalence Christians felt toward the figure of the eunuch, see Kuefler, *Manly Eunuch*, 245–82.

35. Lucian, *Syr. D.* 51 (J. L. Lightfoot, *Lucian: On the Syrian Goddess* [Oxford: Oxford University Press, 2003], 276–78); cf. Kuefler, *Manly Eunuch*, 251–52; Maarten Vermaseren, *Cybele and Attis: the Myth and the Cult*, trans. A. M. H. Lemmers (London: Thames and Hudson, 1977), 97.

36. Firm. Mat., *Err. prof. rel.* 4.2 (PL 12.990A-B); trans. Forbes, ACW 37.50–51.

37. *Vit. Matron.* 5 (AASS Nov. 3.792A–793B); trans. Talbot, *Holy Women of Byzantium*, 24.

38. She then offers an explanation that she hopes will satisfy her brother: "The woman to whom I formerly belonged was lovingly disposed toward me, maintaining me with all generosity and luxury, and she shrank not from putting old about my ears, so that many of those who saw me said that I was a girl" (*Vit. Matron.* 5 [AASS Nov. 3.792A–793B]; trans. Talbot, *Holy Women of Byzantium*, 24). Her explanation keeps jewelry firmly rooted in the realm of women.

39. *Vit. Matron.* 5 (AASS Nov. 3.793A); trans. Talbot, *Holy Women of Byzantium*, 25.

40. *Vit. Hil.* (Drescher, *Three Coptic Legends*, 6); trans. Drescher, *Three Coptic Legends*, 75.

41. *Act. Eugen.* 9 (F. C. Conybeare, *The Armenian Apology and Acts of Apollonius and Other Monuments of Early Christianity* [London: Swan Sonnenschein & Co., 1896], 168; Lewis, *Select Narratives, vol. I*, 31b).
42. The Latin text can be found in PL 73.643–52 and AASS Feb 2.537–40. An alternate Latin version can be found in AASS Feb 2.540–44. For the Syriac text, see Lewis, *Select Narratives, vol. I*, 76b–85a.
43. *Vit. Euphr.* (Lewis, *Select Narratives, vol. I*, 83a); trans. Lewis, *Select Narratives, vol. II*, 56.
44. *Vit. Hil.* (Drescher, *Three Coptic Legends*, 8); trans. Drescher, *Three Coptic Legends*, 77.
45. Syriac *Vit. Pelag.* 44–45 (AMSS 6.645–46); trans. Brock and Harvey, *Holy Women*, 59–60, emphasis added.
46. This theme is clearly patterned after the false accusations of Potiphar's wife of Gen. 39. For a discussion of the intertextuality of these stories, see Davis, "Crossed Texts," 25–28.
47. As Gillian Cloke argues: "Women were essentially sinful because essentially sexual" (*Female Man of God*, 33).
48. *Vit. Mar.* 3 (Richard, "Sainte Marie," 88). There is a lacuna at this point in the Syriac text.
49. *Vit. Mar.* 9–10 (Richard, "Sainte Marie," 89–90; Lewis, *Select Narratives, vol. I*, 72b–73b).
50. *Vit. Hil.* (Drescher, *Three Coptic Legends*, 6); trans. Drescher, *Three Coptic Legends*, 75.
51. *Vit. Hil.* (Drescher, *Three Coptic Legends*, 6, 10–11). In addition to the above examples, see also *Vit. Apoll.* for a similar accusation from a monk's sister (Drescher, *Three Coptic Legends*, 152–61; BHG 3.148). Also, when Susanna/John refuses to comply with the sexual advances of a female ascetic, the spurned woman accuses him of rape in *Vit. Sus.* 5–9 (AASS Sept 6.155A–157B). Finally, when Eugenia/Eugenios rejected the temptations of Melania, a woman he had healed, she likewise accused the monk of rape (*Act. Eugen.* 11–12 [Conybeare, *Monuments*, 171–74; Lewis, *Select Narratives, vol. I*, 34b–37b]).
52. Derek Krueger reminds us that saints' *Lives* materialized the bodies of the saints through narration even after they departed: "The textual body was never fully disembodied, and writers participated in the creation of matter" (*Writing and Holiness*, 133, cf. 148–49).
53. *Vit. Mar.* 9–11, 20 (Richard, "Sainte Marie," 89–90, 93–94; cf. Lewis, *Select Narratives, vol. I*, 72b–73b, 75b–76a).
54. The Latin text can be found in PL 73.606–24 and the Syriac text can be found in Lewis, *Select Narratives, vol. I*, 21a–52b. For an English translation of the Armenian version, see Conybeare, *Monuments*, 157–89. Because the Syriac text does not have numbered section breaks, I use the Armenian section numbers throughout.
55. *Act. Eugen.* 12; trans. Conybeare, *Monuments*, 172, emphasis added. This passage is absent from the Syriac version.
56. *Act. Eugen.* 14 (Conybeare, *Monuments*, 175; Lewis, *Select Narratives, vol. I*, 38a).
57. *Vit. Mar.* 11 (Richard, "Sainte Marie," 90; cf. Lewis, *Select Narratives, vol. I*, 73b); trans. Talbot, *Holy Women of Byzantium*, 9; cf. Lewis, *Select Narratives, vol. II*, 41.
58. *Vit. Mar.* 14 (Richard, "Sainte Marie," 91; cf. Lewis, *Select Narratives, vol. I*, 74a); trans. Talbot, *Holy Women of Byzantium*, 10; cf. Lewis, *Select Narratives, vol. II*, 44.
59. Cox Miller, "Visceral Seeing," 400–1.

60. *Act. Eugen.* 15; trans. Conybeare, *Monuments*, 77.
61. *Act. Eugen.* (Lewis, *Select Narratives, vol. I*, 39b); trans. Lewis, *Select Narratives, vol. II*, 21, emphasis added.
62. The Greek text and Latin translation can be found in AASS Sept. 6.153–60.
63. *Vit. Sus.* 9 (AASS Sept. 6.157A).
64. *Vit. Sus.* 12–13 (AASS Sept. 6.158E–F).
65. *Vit. Mar.* (Lewis, *Select Narratives, vol. I*, 75a); trans. Lewis, *Select Narratives, vol. II*, 44. The Latin is less dramatic: "But as they were preparing to wash him, they discovered that he was a woman, and shrieking, they all began to cry out in a single voice, 'Lord have mercy' " (*Vit. Mar.* 18 [Richard, "Sainte Marie," 93]; trans. Talbot, *Holy Women of Byzantium*, 11).
66. *Vit. Mar.* 18–20 (Lewis, *Select Narratives, vol. I*, 75b; cf. Richard, "Sainte Marie," 93).
67. *Vit. Mar.* 20 (Richard, "Sainte Marie," 94); trans. Talbot, *Holy Women of Byzantium*, 11. The Syriac reads: "Then the abbot led him by the hand and showed him his unbelief" *(Vit. Mar.* [Lewis, *Select Narratives, vol. I*, 76a]; trans. Lewis, *Select Narratives, vol. II*, 45).
68. *Vit. Mar.* 21 (Lewis, *Select Narratives, vol. I*, 75b–76a); trans. Lewis, *Select Narratives, vol. II*, 45. Unfortunately, the text does not specify whether the monk was dressed in men's or women's clothes for burial.
69. Syriac *Vit. Pelag.* 50 (AMSS 6.648); trans. Brock and Harvey, *Holy Women*, 61.
70. Latin *Vit. Pelag.* 15 (PL 73.670); trans. Ward, *Harlots of the Desert*, 74. For a fascinating discussion of the monks' attempt to keep this secret, see Cox Miller, "Hagiography and the Grotesque" 423–24.
71. *Vit. Euphr.* (Lewis, *Select Narratives, vol. I*, 84b–85a); trans. Lewis, *Select Narratives, vol. II*, 58–59.
72. *Vit. Dan.* 8 (Nau, "Texte syriaque," 399); trans. Brock and Harvey, *Holy Women*, 147, emphasis added.
73. Hilaria seems to be the only monk whose request "do not let my habit be taken off me but let me be buried with it" is obliged. Only after s/he is buried does Abba Pambo declare her true gender identity (*Vit. Hil.* [Drescher, *Three Coptic Legends*, 12]).
74. *Vit. Euphr.* (Lewis, *Select Narratives vol. I*, 80b–81a; Lewis, *Select Narratives vol. II*, 52). The Syriac reads:

ܘܡܠܠܬ ܥܡ ܬܪܥܐ ܘܐܡܪܬ ܠܗ̇: ܐܚܝ ܐܢ ܛܒܬ ܥܘܠ ܘܐܡܪ ܠܗ ܠܪܝܫ ܕܝܪܐ ܕܡܗܝܡܢܐ
ܚܕ ܡܢ ܦܠܛܝܢ ܐܬܐ ܩܐܡ ܠܬܪܥܐ ܠܒܪ ܘܨܒܐ ܕܢܡܠܠ ܥܡܟ ܘܗܘ ܥܠ ܬܪܥܐ ܘܐܫܬܛܚܬ
ܠܪܝܫ ܕܝܪܐ ܒܪܟܗ̇. ܦܩܕ ܠܗ ܕܢܨܠܐ ܘܗܘ ܥܠ ܥܙܐ ܢܦܫܗ ܘܐܘܕܝ ܬܫܒܘܚܬܐ ܘܟܕ ܗܘܬ
ܨܠܘܬܐ ܝܬܒܘ: ܐܡܪ ܠܗ̇ ܪܝܫ ܕܝܪܐ: ܠܡܢܐ ܐܫܬܘܬܦܬ ܠܘܬܢ ܝܢܫܬ ܐܠܗܐ ܕܟܝ:
ܐܡܪܐ ܠܗ ܗܝ: ܐܢܐ ܐܒܝ ܡܢ ܦܠܛܝܢ ܐܬܝܬ، ܘܪܚܡܬ ܐܗܘܐ ܒܐܣܟܝܡܐ ܕܐܝܚܝܕܝܐ...
ܫܡܥܬ ܓܝܪ ܡܛܠ ܡܕܒܪܢܘܬܟ ܘܡܛܠ ܕܝܪܐ ܗܢܐ ܘܐܬܝܬ ܐܦ ܐܢܐ ܕܐܗܘܐ ܒܝܢܬܟܘܢ ܐܦ ܡܢ
ܐܬܘܢ ܠܡܫܠܡܘܬܝ،... ܐܡܪ ܠܗ ܪܝܫ ܕܝܪܐ ܠܛܒܬܐ ܐܬܝܬ ܒܪܝ:... ܐܡܪ ܠܗ ܬܘܒ ܪܝܫ ܕܝܪܐ
ܒܪܝ، ܗܢܘ ܐܬܘܬܗ، ܥܡܟܝ. ܐܡܪ ܠܗ ܘܡܢ ܕܩܘܡ ܡܢܝ:

The Latin reads: *[Euphrosyne] nuntiavit per ostiarium abbati, dicens: Eunuchus quidam de palatio veniens, ante ostium stat, cupiens loqui tecum. Egresso autem abbate, projecit se Euphrosyna in terra, et facta oratione sederunt. Dicit ei senex: Quid est quod huc venisti, fili? Dicit ei Euphrosyna: Ego quidem de palatio fui eunuchus, et desiderium habui semper conversationem monachorum, et civitas nostra nunc valde habet hoc stadium conversationis. Notum autem factum est mihi de bona vestra conversatione, et cupio habitare vobiscum. Habeo enim et possessiones multas, et si dominus dederit requiem, adduco eas huc. Dicit ei senex: Bene venisti, fili: ecce monasterium; si placet, habita nobiscum. Et dicit ei senex ille: Quod est nomen tuum? Dicit ei: Smaragdus* (*Vita S. Euphrosynae, virginis* [PL 73:646]).

75. *Vit. Euphr.* (Lewis, *Select Narratives vol. I*, 81a); trans. Lewis, *Select Narratives vol. II*, 52.
76. *Vit. Euphr.* (Lewis, *Select Narratives vol. I*, 81a); trans. Lewis, *Select Narratives vol. II*, 53.
77. This curiosity might be explained by a psychological reading of the narratives. John Anson has provocatively argued that the cross-dressing figures within these narratives worked to satiate monks' longing for a female presence within their unisex communities, while their guilt for such longings could be displaced onto the cross-dresser herself, "making her appear guilty of the very temptation to which the monks are most subject; finally, after she has been punished for their desires, their guilt is compensated by turning her into a saint with universal remorse and sanctimonious worship" ("The Female Transvestite in Early Monasticism: The Origin and Development of a Motif," *Viator* 5 [1974]: 30). This passage, however, seems to indicate not a longing for a female presence but a reflection of homoerotic desire that is already present within the communities. (Compare also the numerous passages in ascetic literature regarding the temptation of beautiful young boys in the monastery.) From this perspective, these legends might work to absolve male monks of homoerotic desires first by translating them into heterosexual desire and then projecting the guilt and shame onto the imaginary cross-dressing women.
78. *Vit. Euphr.* (Lewis, *Select Narratives vol. I*, 82a–82b).
79. This narrative, as well, should perhaps be read in the context of the Origenist controversy. In this scene the protagonist imparts wisdom that appears to promote an Origenist position of the preexistence of rational minds, which "fell" into corporeal bodies and hoped one day to return to their original state. See Elizabeth A. Clark, *The Origenist Controversy: The Cultural Construction of an Early Christian Debate* (Princeton: Princeton University Press, 1992).
80. *Vit. Euphr.* (Lewis, *Select Narratives vol. I*, 83a). The Syriac text reads:

ܘܟܕ ܐܬܐ ܕܝܢ ܐܒܘܗ̇ ܠܘܬ ܐܒܐ ܘܐܡܪ ܠܗ ܕܒܪ ܠܟܝ، ܦܦܢܘܛܝܣ ܘܐܘܒܠܝܗܝ ܠܘܬ
ܐܝܟ ܐܡܪܗ ܠܓܘܣ. ܐܙܠ ܕܢܐܬܪ ܬܡܢ: ܘܩܡܠܗ ܘܐܘܒܠܗ ܠܘܬܗ: ܟܕ ܕܝܢ ܚܙܬܗ
ܐܘܦܪܘܣܘܢܐ ܠܐܒܘܗ̇: ܟܠܗ̇ ܐܬܡܠܝܬ ܗܘܬ ܡܢ ܕܡܥܝ̈ܗ̇. ܐܒܘܗ̇ ܕܝܢ ܣܒܪ ܗܘܐ ܠܗ̇ ܕܟܠ
ܐܦ ܡܬܬܥܝܩܘܬܐ ܐܬܬܥܝܩ ܗܘ، ܕܡܕܡܥܢ ܟܠ ܟܠܗ ܠܐ ܐܬܒܪܗܡ ܐܒܘܗ̇. ...ܟܕ ܕܝܢ
ܗܘܬ ܠܗ̇ ܠܒܟ: ܘܚܪܝܬ ܡܡܠܠܐ ܠܗ ܥܠ ܡܪܢܚܡܢܘܬܐ ܘܕܚܠܬܐ ܘܣܡܟܐ ܘܢܚܡܬܐ.
ܘܡܛܠ ܣܘܪ̈ܬܐ ܕܢܦܩܬܐ: ܟܕ ܕܝܢ ܡܠܠ ܗܘܐ ܥܠܝܗ ܐܡܪ ܠܓܘܣ ܠܗܘ ܕܦܦܢܘܛܝܣ ܠܒܝܫ
ܗܘܐ ܘܟܠܗ ܡܠܐ ܗܘܐ ܕܡܥܐ

81. *Vit. Euphr.* (Lewis, *Select Narratives vol. I*, 85a); trans. Lewis, *Select Narratives vol. II*, 59.
82. Susan Ashbrook Harvey, "Women in Early Byzantine Hagiography: Reversing the Story," in *That Gentle Strength: Historical Perspectives on Women in Christianity*, ed. Lynda L. Coon, Katherine J. Haldane, and Elisabeth W. Sommer (Charlottesville: University Press of Virginia, 1990), 48.
83. Greek *Vit. Mar.* 14 (Richard, "Sainte Marie," 91; cf. Lewis, *Select Narratives, vol. I*, 74a); trans. Talbot, *Holy Women of Byzantium*, 10, emphasis added; cf. Lewis, *Select Narratives, vol. II*, 44.
84. *Vit. Mar.* 19 (Richard, "Sainte Marie," 93; Lewis, *Select Narratives vol. I*, 75a).
85. Greek *Vit. Mar.* 19 (Richard, "Sainte Marie," 93).

86. *Vit. Matron.* 4 (AASS Nov. 3.792E); trans. Talbot, *Holy Women of Byzantium*, 23, adapted.
87. Matrona is also referred to with masculine pronouns and as "Babylos" when the abbot Basianos is talking about "him" with a deacon who understands him to be a eunuch. Again, the language of the narrative reflects the degree of successful "passing" within the narrative (*Vit. Matron.* 29 [AASS Nov. 3.803e]).
88. "But know thou this, that God has already revealed to me concerning thee, Eugenia, whence thou are and whose daughter thou art and who are come with thee; all this the Lord showed to me" (*Act. Eugen.* 7–8 [Conybeare, *Monuments*, 166–67; Lewis, *Select Narratives, vol. I*, 30a–30b]).
89. *Act. Eugen.* 9 (Lewis, *Select Narratives, vol. I*, 32a); trans. Lewis, *Select Narratives, vol. II*, 13; cf. Conybeare, *Monuments*, 169.
90. Harvey, "Byzantine Hagiography," 50. Patricia Cox Miller agrees that we should read these cross-dressing figures "as a realization of a contradiction central to the late ancient Christian (male) imagination, a contradiction expressed by the seemingly simple phrase 'holy woman' . . . a not-quite coherent construct—and as such brings to its most acute expression the problematic quality of early Christian attempts to construct a representation of female holiness" ("Hagiography and the Grotesque," 423–26, 429–30; cf. Cloke, *Female Man of God*, 219–21).
91. Hotchkiss, *Clothes Make the Man*, 19. See also Vern Bullough's article, which argues for a reading of transvestism strictly in terms of status gain and loss ("Transvestites," 1381–94).
92. Voragine, *Legenda aurea* as cited in Hotchkiss, *Clothes Make the Man*, 20.
93. *Vit. Euphr.* 15 (PL 73.651; AASS Feb. 2.541). As Valerie Hotchkiss concludes, "The moral valence of maleness provides the premise for praising disguised women" (*Clothes Make the Man*, 20).
94. Garber, *Vested Interests*, 29; Charlotte Suthrell, *Unzipping Gender: Sex, Cross-Dressing and Culture* (New York: Berg, 2004), 17.
95. For example, Pelagia adopts Bishop Nonnus's clothing (Syriac *Vit. Pelag.* 41 [AMSS 6.643]; Latin *Vit. Pelag.* 12 [PL 73.669]).
96. There is no erasure or confusion of gender. If the hope was to confound gender distinctions and boundaries altogether, we should expect to find corollary narratives of men dressing as women. Why does the blurring of gender not work in reverse? It is simply because a move in this direction would be a "dressing down," rather than a "dressing up"; it would convey a demotion in virtue. See Bullough, "Transvestites," 1382–83, 1392; cf. Garber, *Vested Interests*, 60. Of course one can find exceptions to this rule. For instance, when Sergius and Bacchus refused to engage in battle, they were ridiculed by being stripped of their (male) military garb, re-dressed in women's clothes, and paraded through the city. In this case, the men reinterpreted the significance of the transvestism as evidence that they had been clothed in "garments of salvation" and that they were the "brides" of Christ. See John Boswell's discussion and translation of this text in *Same-Sex Unions in Premodern Europe* (New York: Villard Books, 1994), 146–56, 375–90.
97. Readers must use their imagination also because ascetics' breasts diminished from excessive fasting and bodily discipline; several legends remark on the "dried-up" or "shriveled" nature of the ascetics' breasts. For a discussion of ascetics' bodies, see Shaw, *Burden of the Flesh*, 244–47.
98. Like Barthes's written clothing, the narrative "freezes an endless number of possibilities" for interpreting the significance of cross-dressing (Barthes, *Fashion System*, 13).

99. On other rationalizations of cross-dressing, see Garber, *Vested Interests,* 165–85.

100. For a discussion of "narrative closure," which, White argues, structures the moral meaning of narratives, see Hayden White, *The Content of the Form: Narrative Discourse and Historical Representation* (Baltimore: Johns Hopkins University Press, 1987), 5–8, 21–25.

101. The narrative theories of Hayden White and Hans Kellner provide a helpful lens through which to understand how the *Lives* limit the meaning of cross-dressing. These historiographers help us see how narratives impose a singular and coherent structure on a multivalent and "chaotic" reality, selectively choosing singular interpretive frames that obscure other possibilities. For White's discussion of "explanatory structures," see *Content of the Form,* 11 and his earlier work, *Metahistory: The Historical Imagination in Nineteenth-Century Europe* (Baltimore: Johns Hopkins University Press, 1975). Hans Kellner cleverly terms the imposition of narrative structure "getting the story crooked" in *Language and Historical Representation: Getting the Story Crooked* (Madison: University of Wisconsin Press, 1989).

102. This convention is also present in *Lives* of saintly men. As David Brakke has demonstrated, for instance, Athanasius's *Life of Antony* self-consciously framed the holy man as obedient to ecclesial structures and as a defender of the orthodox beliefs held by Alexandrian clerics (*Athanasius and the Politics of Asceticism* [New York: Clarendon Press, 1995], 201–65).

103. Syriac *Vit. Pelag.* 36 (AMSS 6.639–43; Brock and Harvey, *Holy Women,* 55–58).

104. *Vit. Euphr.* (Lewis, *Select Narratives* vol. I, 79a–80b).

105. *Vit. Dan.* 8 (Nau, "Texte syriaque," 399–400). This convention is also found in the Ethiopic *Acts of Thekla,* which depicts Paul himself cutting Thecla's hair and dressing her in men's garments (Goodspeed, *Ethiopic Martyrdoms,* 8).

106. See, for example, *Vit. Sus.* 10 (AASS Sept. 6.157B–C); *Act. Eugen.* 7 (Conybeare, *Monuments,* 167; Lewis, *Select Narratives,* vol. I, 30a–30b; Lewis, *Select Narratives,* vol. II, 11).

107. The notable exception, of course, is the story of Anastasia from the *Life of Abba Daniel*; although Anastasia is shown to be obedient to the famous monk, she is running from the emperor, who pursues her as a love interest. So, in this story, political leaders, ascetic leaders, and the cross-dresser are not aligned on a single hierarchy. For a discussion of other means by which clerics attempted to corral and absorb the authority of female ascetics, see Hunter, *Jovinianist Controversy,* 224–30; idem, "Clerical Celibacy and the Veiling of Virgins: New Boundaries in Late Ancient Christianity," in *The Limits of Ancient Christianity: Essays on Late Antique Thought and Culture in Honor of R. A. Markus,* eds. William E. Klingshirn and Mark Vessey (Ann Arbor: University of Michigan Press, 1999), 139–52.

# Bibliography

Abdalla, Laila. "Theology and Culture: Masculinizing the Woman." In *Varieties of Devotion in the Middle Ages and Renaissance*, edited by Susan C. Karant-Nunn, 17–37. Turnhout: Brepols, 2003.

Anson, John. "The Female Transvestite in Early Monasticism: The Origin and Development of a Motif." *Viator* 5 (1974): 1–32.

Armour, Ellen T., and Susan M. St. Ville, eds. *Bodily Citations: Religion and Judith Butler*. New York: Columbia University Press, 2006.

Arthur, Linda, ed. *Religion, Dress and the Body*. Oxford: Berg, 1999.

Aspegren, Kerstin. *The Male Woman: A Feminine Ideal in the Early Church*. Stockholm: Almqvist and Wiksell, 1990.

Balsdon, J. P. V. D. "Women's Daily Life: Dress, Coiffure, Make-up and Jewels." In *Roman Women: Their History and Habits*, 252–65. London: Bodley Head, 1962.

Barnes, Ruth, and Joanne Eicher. *Dress and Gender: Making and Meaning in Cultural Contexts*. Oxford: Berg, 1993.

Barnes, Timothy D. "The Date of the Council of Gangra." *Journal of Theoretical Studies* 40.1 (1989): 121–24.

———. *Tertullian: A Historical and Literary Study*. Oxford: Oxford University Press, 1985.

Barthes, Roland. *The Fashion System*. Translated by Matthew Ward and Richard Howard. New York: Hill and Wang, 1983.

Bartman, Elizabeth. "Hair and Artifice of Roman Female Adornment." *American Journal of Archaeology* 105 (2001): 1–25.

Barton, Carlin. *The Sorrows of the Ancient Romans: The Gladiator and the Monster*. Princeton: Princeton University Press, 1993.

Barton, Tamsyn. *Power and Knowledge: Astrology, Physiognomics, and Medicine under the Roman Empire*. Ann Arbor: University of Michigan Press, 1994.

Batten, Alicia. "Clothing and Adornment." *Biblical Theology Bulletin* 40.3 (2010): 148–59.

———. "Neither Gold nor Braided Hair (1 Timothy 2:9; 1 Peter 3:3): Adornment, Gender and Honour in Antiquity." *New Testament Studies* 55 (2009): 484–501.

Beagon, Philip. "The Cappadocian Fathers, Women and Ecclesiastical Politics" *Vigiliae christianae* 49.2 (1995): 165–79.

Beck, Hans Georg. *Kirche und theologische Literatur im Byzantinischen Reich*. München: C. H. Beck, 1959.

Bennett, Tony. *The Birth of the Museum: History, Theory, Politics*. London: Routledge, 1995.

Berg, Ria. "Wearing Wealth: *Mundus Muliebris* and *Ornatus* as Status Markers for Women in Imperial Rome." In *Women, Wealth and Power in the Roman Empire*, edited by Pävi Setälä, Ria Berg, Riikka Hälikkä, Minerva Keltanen,

Janne Pölönen, and Ville Vuolanto, 15–73. Rome: Institutum Romanum Finlandiae: 2002.

Bergmann, Bettina, and Christine Kondoleon, eds. *The Art of Ancient Spectacle.* New Haven: Yale University Press, 1999.

Bieber, Margarete. "Stola." *Paulys Realencyclopädie der classischen Altertumswissenschaft* (1931): 56–62.

Bonfante, Larissa. *Etruscan Dress.* Baltimore: Johns Hopkins University Press, 1975.

Børrensen, Kari Elisabeth. "Male-Female, a Critique of Traditional Christian Theology." *Temenos* 13 (1977): 31–42.

Boswell, John. *Same-Sex Unions in Premodern Europe.* New York: Villard Books, 1994.

Boulding, Maria. "Background to a Theology of the Monastic Habit." *The Downside Review* 98.331 (1980): 110–23.

Bourdieu, Pierre. *La distinction. Critique sociale du jugement.* Paris: Éditions de Minuit, 1979.

Boyarin, Daniel. "Gender." In *Critical Terms for Religious Studies,* edited by Mark C. Taylor, 117–35. Chicago: University of Chicago Press, 1998.

———. "Paul and the Genealogy of Gender." *Representations* 41 (1993): 1–33.

Brakke, David. *Athanasius and the Politics of Asceticism.* New York: Clarendon Press, 1995.

Bray, Gerald Lewis. *Holiness and the Will of God: Perspectives on the Theology of Tertullian.* Atlanta: John Knox Press, 1979.

Brock, Sebastian P., and Susan Ashbrook Harvey. *Holy Women of the Syrian Orient.* Berkeley: University of California Press, 1998.

Brown, Peter. *Power and Persuasion in Late Antiquity: Towards a Christian Empire.* Madison: University of Wisconsin Press, 1992.

———. "Bodies and Minds: Sexuality and Renunciation in Early Christianity." In *Before Sexuality: The Construction of Erotic Experience in the Ancient Greek World,* edited by David Halperin, John Winkler, and Froma Zeitlin, 479–94. Princeton: Princeton University Press, 1990.

———. *The Body and Society: Men, Women, and Sexual Renunciation in Early Christianity.* New York: Columbia University Press, 1988.

———. "The Notion of Virginity in the Early Church." In *Christian Spirituality: Origins to the Twelfth Century,* edited by Bernard McGinn and John Meyendorff, 427–43. New York: Crossroad, 1985.

Bullough, Vern L. "Transvestites in the Middle Ages." *American Journal of Sociology* 79.6 (1974): 1381–94.

Burke, Kenneth. *The Rhetoric of Religion: Studies in Logology.* Boston: Beacon Press, 1961.

Burrus, Virginia. "Mapping as Metamorphosis: Initial Reflections on Gender and Ancient Religious Discourse." In *Mapping Gender in Ancient Religious Discourses,* edited by Todd Penner and Caroline Vander Stichele, 1–10. Leiden: Brill, 2007.

———. *The Sex Lives of the Saints: An Erotics of Ancient Hagiography.* Philadelphia: University of Pennsylvania Press, 2004.

———. *"Begotten, Not Made": Conceiving Manhood in Late Antiquity.* Stanford: Stanford University Press, 2000.

———. "Word and Flesh: The Bodies and Sexuality of Ascetic Women in Christian Antiquity." *Journal of Feminist Studies in Religion* 10.1 (1994): 27–51.

———. "Chastity as Autonomy: Women in the Stories of the Apocryphal Acts." *Semeia* 38 (1986): 101–17.

Butler, Judith. *Undoing Gender.* New York: Routledge, 2004.

———. *Gender Trouble: Feminism and the Subversion of Identity.* New York: Routledge, 1999.

———. *Bodies That Matter: On the Discursive Limits Of "Sex."* New York: Routledge, 1993.

———. "Performative Acts and Gender Constitution: An Essay in Phenomenology and Feminist Theory." In *Performing Feminisms: Feminist Critical Theory and Theatre*, edited by Sue-Ellen Case, 270–82. Baltimore: Johns Hopkins University Press, 1990.

———. "Variations on Sex and Gender: Beauvoir, Wittig and Foucault." In *Feminism as Critique: On the Politics of Gender*, edited by Seyla Benhabib and Drucilla Cornell, 128–42. Minneapolis: University of Minnesota Press, 1987.

Calef, Susan. "Rhetorical Strategies in Tertullian's *De Cultu Feminarum*." PhD diss., University of Notre Dame, 1996.

Cameron, Averil. *Christianity and the Rhetoric of Empire: The Development of Christian Discourse.* Berkeley: University of California Press, 1991.

———. "Redrawing the Map: Early Christian Territory after Foucault." *Journal of Roman Studies* 76 (1986): 266–71.

Caner, Daniel. *Wandering, Begging Monks: Spiritual Authority and the Promotion of Monasticism in Late Antiquity.* Berkeley: University of California Press, 2002.

Carnelley, Elizabeth. "Tertullian and Feminism." *Theology* 92.745 (1989): 31–35.

Carter, Michael. *Fashion Classics from Carlyle to Barthes.* Oxford: Berg, 2003.

Carter, Michael J. "(Un)dressed to Kill: Viewing the *Retiarius*." In *Roman Dress and the Fabrics of Roman Culture*, edited by Jonathan Edmondson and Alison Keith, 113–35. Toronto: University of Toronto Press, 2008.

Castelli, Elizabeth. " 'I Will Make Mary Male': Pieties of the Body and Gender Transformation of Christian Women in Late Antiquity." In *Body Guards: The Cultural Politics of Gender Ambiguity*, edited by Julia Epstein and Kristina Straub, 29–49. New York: Routledge, 1991.

———. "Virginity and Its Meaning for Women's Sexuality in Early Christianity." *Journal for Feminist Studies in Religion* 2.1 (1982): 61–88.

Cilleruelo, Lope. "Nota sobre el agustinismo de los monjes de Cartago." *La Ciudad de Dios* 172 (1959): 365–69.

Clark, Elizabeth A. "The Celibate Bridegroom and His Virginal Brides." *Church History* 77:1 (2008): 1–25.

———. "Distinguishing 'Distinction': Considering Peter Brown's Reconsiderations," *Augustinian Studies* 36.1 (2005): 259–60.

———. *History, Theory, Text: Historians and the Linguistic Turn.* Cambridge: Harvard University Press, 2004.

———. *Reading Renunciation: Asceticism and Scripture in Early Christianity.* Princeton: Princeton University Press, 1999.

———. "The Lady Vanishes: Dilemmas of a Feminist Historian after the 'Linguistic Turn.' " *Church History* 67.1 (1998): 1–31.

———. "Holy Women, Holy Words: Early Christian Women, Social History, and the 'Linguistic Turn.' " *Journal of Early Christian Studies* 6.3 (1998): 413–30.

———. *St. Augustine on Marriage and Sexuality.* Washington, DC: Catholic University of America Press, 1996.

———. "Antifamilial Tendencies in Ancient Christianity." *Journal of the History of Sexuality* 5 (1995): 356–80.

———. "Ideology, History, and the Construction of 'Woman' in Late Ancient Christianity." *Journal of Early Christian Studies* 2.2 (1994): 155–84.

———. *The Origenist Controversy: The Cultural Construction of an Early Christian Debate.* Princeton: Princeton University Press, 1992.

———. "Sex, Shame, and Rhetoric: En-gendering Early Christian Ethics." *Journal of the American Academy of Religion* 49 (1991): 221–45.

————. *Ascetic Piety and Women's Faith: Essays on Late Ancient Christianity,* *Studies in Women and Religion.* Lewiston: E. Mellen Press, 1986.

————. *Women in the Early Church.* Collegeville: Michael Glazier, 1983.

————. *Jerome, Chrysostom, and Friends: Essays and Translations.* New York: E. Mellen Press, 1979.

Clark, Gillian. "Women and Asceticism in Late Antiquity: The Refusal of Status and Gender." In *Asceticism,* edited by Vincent Wimbush and Richard Valantasis, 33–48. New York: Oxford University Press, 1995.

————. *Women in Late Antiquity: Pagan and Christian Lifestyles.* Oxford: Clarendon Press, 1993.

Cleland, Liza, Mary Harlow, and Lloyd Llewellyn-Jones, eds. *The Clothed Body in the Ancient World.* Oxford: Oxbow, 2005.

Cloke, Gillian. *This Female Man of God: Women and Spiritual Power in the Patristic Age 350–450.* New York: Routledge, 1994.

Cobb, L. Stephanie. *Dying to Be Men: Gender and Language in Early Christian Martyr Texts.* New York: Columbia University Press, 2008.

Colburn, Cynthia, and Maura Heyn, eds. *Reading a Dynamic Canvas: Adornment in the Ancient Mediterranean World.* Newcastle: Cambridge Scholars Publishing, 2008.

Consolino, Franca Ela. "Female Asceticism and Monasticism in Italy from the Fourth to the Eighth Centuries." In *Women and Faith: Catholic Religious Life in Italy from Late Antiquity to the Present,* edited by Lucetta Scaraffia and Gabriella Zarri, 8–30. Cambridge: Harvard University Press, 1999.

Coon, Lynda. *Sacred Fictions: Holy Women and Hagiography in Late Antiquity.* Philadelphia: University of Pennsylvania Press, 1997.

Cooper, Kate. *The Fall of the Roman Household.* Cambridge: Cambridge University Press, 2007.

————. *The Virgin and the Bride: Idealized Womanhood in Late Antiquity.* Cambridge: Harvard University Press, 1996.

————. "Insinuations of Womanly Influence: An Aspect of the Christianization of the Roman Aristocracy." *Journal of Roman Studies* 82 (1992): 150–64.

Cordwell, Justine M., and Ronald A. Schwarz, eds. *The Fabrics of Culture: The Anthropology of Clothing and Adornment.* The Hague: Mouton Publishers, 1979.

Cox Miller, Patricia. "Visceral Seeing: The Holy Body in Late Ancient Christianity." *Journal of Early Christian Studies* 12.4 (2004): 391–411.

————. "Is There a Harlot in This Text? Hagiography and the Grotesque." *Journal of Medieval and Early Modern Studies* 33.3 (2003): 419–35.

————. "Desert Asceticism and 'The Body from Nowhere.' " *Journal of Early Christian Studies* 2.2 (1994): 137–53.

Craik, Jennifer. *The Face of Fashion: Cultural Studies in Fashion.* New York: Routledge, 1994.

Croom, Alexandra T. *Roman Clothing and Fashion.* Gloucester: Tempus, 2002.

Cunnington, Cecil Willett. *Why Women Wear Clothes.* London: Faber and Faber, 1941.

D'Ambra, Eve. "Nudity and Adornment in Female Portrait Sculpture of the Second Century AD." In *I, Claudia II: Women in Roman Art and Society,* edited by Diana E. E. Kleiner and Susan B. Matheson, 101–14. Austin: University of Texas Press, 2000.

D'Angelo, Mary Rose. "Veils, Virgins, and the Tongues of Men and Angels." In *Off with Her Head: The Denial of Women's Identity in Myth, Religion, and Culture,* edited by Howard Eilberg-Schwartz and Wendy Doniger, 131–64. Berkeley: University of California Press, 1995.

Dalby, Andrew. *Empire of Pleasures: Luxury and Indulgence in the Roman World.* New York: Routledge, 2000.

Dalzell, Alexander. *The Criticism of Didactic Poetry: Essays on Lucretius, Virgil, and Ovid.* Toronto: University of Toronto Press, 1997.

Dangel, Jacqueline. "L'Asie des poètes latins de l'époque républicaine." *Ktèma* 10 (1985):175–92.

Daniel-Hughes, Carly. " 'Wear the Armor of Your Shame!': Debating Veiling and the Salvation of the Flesh in Tertullian of Carthage," *Sciences Religieuses* 39.2 (2010): 179–201.

Davies, Stevan L. "Women, Tertullian and the Acts of Paul." *Semeia* 38 (1986): 139–43.

Davis, Fred. *Fashion, Culture, and Identity.* Chicago: University of Chicago Press, 1992.

Davis, Stephen J. "Crossed Texts, Crossed Sex: Intertextuality and Gender in Early Christian Legends of Holy Women Disguised as Men." *Journal of Early Christian Studies* 10.1 (2002): 1–36.

Dean-Jones, Lesley. *Women's Bodies in Classical Greek Science.* Oxford: Clarendon Press, 1994.

Del Estal, Juan-Manuel. "Descertada opinión moderna sobre los monjes de Cartago." *La Ciudad de Dios* 172 (1959): 596–616.

Delcourt, Marie. *Hermaphrodite: Myths and Rites of the Bisexual Figure in Classical Antiquity.* Translated by Jennifer Nicholson. London: Studio Books, 1961.

Dionisotti, A. C. "Translated Saints: Wisdom and Her Daughters." *Journal of Early Christian Studies* 16.2 (2008): 165–80.

Dixon, Suzanne. *Reading Roman Women: Sources, Genres and Real Life.* London: Duckworth, 2001.

Dominik, William, and William Wehrle. *Roman Verse Satire: Lucilius to Juvenal.* Wauconda: Bolchazy-Carducci Publishers, 1999.

Drescher, James. *Three Coptic Legends: Hilaria, Archellites, the Seven Sleepers.* Cairo: Institut Français d'archéologie orientale, 1947.

Dunn, Geoffrey. "Rhetoric and Tertullian's *De virginibus velandis*." *VC* 59.1 (2005): 1–30.

———. *Tertullian.* London: Routledge, 2004.

Earl, Donald C. *The Moral and Political Tradition of Rome.* Ithaca: Cornell University Press, 1967.

Edmondson, Jonathan. "Public Dress and Social Control in Late Republican and Early Imperial Rome." In *Roman Dress and the Fabrics of Roman Culture*, edited by Jonathan Edmondson and Alison Keith, 21–46. Toronto: University of Toronto Press, 2008.

Edmondson, Jonathan, and Alison Keith, eds. *Roman Dress and the Fabrics of Roman Culture.* Toronto: University of Toronto Press, 2008.

Edwards, Catharine. *The Politics of Immorality in Ancient Rome.* Cambridge: Cambridge University Press, 2002.

———. "Unspeakable Professions: Public Performance and Prostitution in Ancient Rome." In *Roman Sexualities*, edited by Judith P. Hallett and Marilyn B. Skinner, 66–95. Princeton: Princeton University Press, 1997.

Eicher, Joanne. *Dress and Ethnicity: Change Across Space and Time.* Oxford: Berg, 1995.

Eilberg-Schwartz, Howard, and Wendy Doniger. *Off with Her Head! The Denial of Women's Identity in Myth, Religion, and Culture.* Berkeley: University of California Press, 1995.

Elm, Susanna. *Virgins of God: The Making of Asceticism in Late Antiquity.* Oxford: Oxford University Press, 1994.

Entwistle, Joanne. *The Fashioned Body: Fashion, Dress and Modern Social Theory.* Cambridge: Polity Press, 2000.

Evans, Elizabeth C. *Physiognomics in the Ancient World.* Transactions of the American Philosophical Society 59.5. Philadelphia: American Philosophical Society, 1969.

———. "Roman Descriptions of Personal Appearance in History and Biography." *Harvard Studies in Classical Philology* 46 (1935): 43–84.

Evans, Mary. *Costume Throughout the Ages.* Philadelphia: J. B. Lippincott, 1930.

Evans, Robert F. *Four Letters of Pelagius.* New York: The Seabury Press, 1968.

Fantham, Elaine. "Covering the Head at Rome: Ritual and Gender." In *Roman Dress and the Fabrics of Roman Culture,* edited by Jonathan Edmondson and Alison Keith, 158–71. Toronto: University of Toronto Press, 2008.

Feest, Christian. "European Collecting of American Indian Artefacts and Art." *Journal of the History of Collections* 5.1 (1993).

Finn, Thomas M. *Early Christian Baptism and the Catechumenate: Italy, North Africa, and Egypt.* Collegeville: Liturgical Press, 1992.

———. *Early Christian Baptism and the Catechumenate: West and East Syria.* Collegeville: Liturgical Press, 1992.

Flügel, John Carl. *The Psychology of Clothes.* London: Hogarth Press, 1930.

Foerster, Richard. *Scriptores physiognomonici graeci et latini,* 2 vols. Lipsiae: B. G. Teubneri, 1893.

Folliet, G. "Des moines euchites à Carthage en 400–401." *Studia Patristica* 2 (1957): 386–99.

Francis, James A. *Subversive Virtue: Asceticism and Authority in the Second-Century Pagan World.* University Park: Pennsylvania State University Press, 1995.

Frank, Georgia. *The Memory of the Eyes: Pilgrims to Living Saints in Christian Late Antiquity.* Berkeley: University of California Press, 2000.

Frilingos, Chris. "Wearing It Well: Gender at Work in the Shadow of Empire." In *Mapping Gender in Ancient Religious Discourses,* edited by Todd Penner and Caroline Vander Stichele, 333–49. Leiden: Brill, 2007.

Gaines, Jane, and Charlotte Herzog, eds. *Fabrications: Costume and the Female Body.* New York: Routledge, 1990.

Garber, Marjorie B. *Vested Interests: Cross-Dressing and Cultural Anxiety.* New York: Routledge, 1992.

Garrett, Duane A. *An Analysis of the Hermeneutics of John Chrysostom's Commentary on Isaiah 1–8.* Lewiston: E. Mellen Press, 1992.

Gasparro, Giulia Sfameni. "Asceticism and Anthropology: *Enkrateia* and 'Double Creation' in Early Christianity." In *Asceticism,* edited by Vincent L. Wimbush and Richard Valantasis, 127–46. New York: Oxford University Press, 1995.

———. "Image of God and Sexual Differentiation in the Tradition of *Enkrateia.*" In *The Image of God: Gender Models in Judaeo-Christian Tradition,* edited by Kari Elisabeth Børrensen, 134–69. Minneapolis: Fortress Press, 1995.

Gilhus, Ingvild Sælid. "Male and Female Symbolism in the Gnostic *Apocryphon of John.*" *Temenos* 19 (1983): 33–43.

Gleason, Maud. *Making Men: Sophists and Self-Presentation in Ancient Rome.* Princeton: Princeton University Press, 1995.

———. "The Semiotics of Gender: Physiognomy and Self-Fashioning in the Second Century C.E." In *Before Sexuality: The Construction of Erotic Experience in the Ancient Greek World,* edited by David Halperin, John Winkler, and Froma Zeitlin, 389–415. Princeton: Princeton University Press, 1990.

Gould, Graham. "Women in the Writings of the Fathers: Language, Belief and Reality." In *Women and the Church,* edited by W. J. Sheils and D. Woods, 1–13. Oxford: Blackwell, 1990.

Gribomont, Jean. "Monasteries, Double." In *New Catholic Encyclopedia,* vol. 9, edited by Berard Marthaler, 784–85. Detroit: Gale, 2003.

———. "Eustathe de Sébaste." *Dictionnaire d'histoire et de géographie ecclésiastiques* 16 (1967): 26–33.

———. "Eustathe de Sébaste." *Dictionnaire de spiritualité: ascétique et mystique, doctrine et histoire* 4.2 (1961): 1708–12.

———. "Eustathe le Philosophe et les voyages du jeune Basile de Césarée." *Revue d'Histoire Ecclésiastique* 54 (1959): 115–24.

———. "Le monachisme au IVᵉ siècle en Asie Mineure: de Gangres au Messalianisme." *Studia Patristica* 2 (1957): 400–15.

Harlow, Mary. "Dress in the *Historia Augusta*: The Role of Dress in Historical Narrative." In *Clothed Body in the Ancient World*, edited by Liza Cleland, Mary Harlow, and Lloyd Llewellyn-Jones, 143–53. Oxford: Oxbow Books, 2005.

———. "Female Dress, Third–Sixth Century: The Messages in the Media?" *Antiquité tardive* 12 (2004): 203–15.

Harrison, Verna. "Male and Female in Cappadocian Theology," *Journal of Theological Studies* 41.2 (1990): 441–71

Harvey, Susan Ashbrook. *Scenting Salvation: Ancient Christianity and the Olfactory Imagination*. Berkeley: University of California Press, 2006.

———. "Women in Early Byzantine Hagiography: Reversing the Story." In *That Gentle Strength: Historical Perspectives on Women in Christianity*, edited by Lynda L. Coon, Katherine J. Haldane, and Elisabeth W. Sommer, 36–59. Charlottesville: University Press of Virginia, 1990.

Hauschild, Wolf-Dieter. "Eustathius von Sebaste." *Theologische Realenzyklopädie* 10 (1982): 547–50.

Hawley, Richard. " 'In a Different Guise': Roman Education and Greek Rhetorical Thought on Marriage." In *Satiric Advice on Women and Marriage*, edited by Warren S. Smith, 26–38. Ann Arbor: University of Michigan Press, 2005.

Henry, Nathalie. "A New Insight into the Growth of Ascetic Society in the Fourth Century AD: The Public Consecration of Virgins as a Means of Integration and Promotion of the Female Ascetic Movement." *Studia Patristica* 35 (2001): 102–9.

———. "The Song of Songs and the Liturgy of the *velatio* in the Fourth Century: From Literary Metaphor to Liturgical Reality." In *Continuity and Change in Christian Worship* , edited by R. N. Swanson, 18–28. Woodbridge: Boydell Press, 1999.

Heuzey, Léon Alexandre. *Histoire du costume antique d'après des études sur le modèle vivant*. Paris: É. Champion, 1922.

Hills, Philip. *Horace*. London: Bristol Classical Press, 2005.

Hoffman, Daniel. "Tertullian on Women and Women's Ministry Roles in the Church." In *The Spirit and the Mind: Essays in Informed Pentecostalism*, edited by Terry L Cross and Emerson B. Powery, 133–55. Lanham: University Press of America, 2000.

Hogan, Pauline Nigh. *No Longer Male and Female: Interpreting Galatians 3:28 in Early Christianity*. London: T & T Clark, 2008.

Hope, Thomas. *Costumes of the Greeks and Romans*. New York: Dover Publications, 1962.

Hotchkiss, Valerie R. *Clothes Make the Man: Female Cross Dressing in Medieval Europe*. New York: Garland Publishing, 1996.

Houston, Mary G. *Ancient Greek, Roman and Byzantine Costume and Decoration*. London: Adam & Charles Black, 1947.

Hunter, David G. . *Marriage, Celibacy, and Heresy in Ancient Christianity: The Jovinianist Controversy*. Oxford: Oxford University Press, 2007.

———. "Clerical Celibacy and the Veiling of Virgins: New Boundaries in Late Ancient Christianity." In *The Limits of Ancient Christianity: Essays on Late*

Antique Thought and Culture in Honor of R. A. Markus, eds. William E. Klingshirn and Mark Vessey, 139–52. Ann Arbor: University of Michigan Press, 1999.

Jacobs, Andrew. Remains of the Jews: The Holy Land and Christian Empire in Late Antiquity. Stanford: Stanford University Press, 2004.

Kahlos, Maijastina. Debate and Dialogue: Christian and Pagan Cultures, c. 360–430. Aldershot: Ashgate, 2007.

Kampen, Natalie. Image and Status: Roman Working Women in Ostia. Berlin: Mann, 1981.

Kaster, Robert A. Guardians of Language: The Grammarian and Society in Late Antiquity. Berkeley: University of California Press, 1988.

Kellner, Hans. Language and Historical Representation: Getting the Story Crooked. Madison: University of Wisconsin Press, 1989.

Knust, Jennifer Wright. Abandoned to Lust: Sexual Slander and Ancient Christianity. New York: Columbia University Press, 2006.

Kock, Claudia. "Augustine's Letter to Ecdicia: A New Reading." Augustinian Studies 31.2 (2000): 173–80.

Köhler, Karl, and Emma von Sichart. Praktische Kostümkunde. London: G. G. Harrap, 1928.

Koortbojian, Michael. "The Double Identity of Roman Portrait Statues: Costumes and Their Symbolism at Rome." In Roman Dress and the Fabrics of Roman Culture, edited by Jonathan Edmondson and Alison Keith, 71–93. Toronto: University of Toronto Press, 2008.

Kraemer, Ross. "The Conversion of Women to Ascetic Forms of Christianity." Signs 6 (1980/81): 298–307.

Krawiec, Rebecca. " 'Garments of Salvation': Representations of Monastic Clothing in Late Antiquity," Journal of Early Christian Studies 17.1 (2009).

———. " 'From the Womb of the Church': Monastic Families." JECS 11.3 (2003): 283–307.

Krueger, Derek. Writing and Holiness: The Practice of Authorship in the Early Christian East. Philadelphia: University of Pennsylvania Press, 2004.

Kuefler, Mathew. The Manly Eunuch: Masculinity, Gender Ambiguity, and Christian Ideology in Late Antiquity. Chicago: University of Chicago Press, 2001.

Kunst, Christiane. "Ornamenta Uxoria. Badges of Rank or Jewellery of Roman Wives?" The Medieval History Journal 8.1 (2005): 127–42.

La Follette, Laetitia. "The Costume of the Roman Bride." In The World of Roman Costume, edited by Judith Lynn Sebesta and Larissa Bonfante, 54–64. Madison: University of Wisconsin Press, 2001.

Lamirande, Émilien. "Tertullien misogyne? Pour une relecture du De cultu feminarum." Science et Esprit 39.1 (1987): 5–25.

Laqueur, Thomas. Making Sex: Body and Gender from the Greeks to Freud. Cambridge: Harvard University Press, 1990.

Laver, James. Costume in Antiquity; 480 Illustrations. London: Thames and Hudson, 1964.

Leroy, F. J. "La tradition manuscrite du 'de virginitate' de Basile d'Ancyre." Orientalia Christiania Periodica 38 (1972): 195–208.

Leyerle, Blake. "John Chrysostom on the Gaze." Journal of Early Christian Studies 1.2 (1993): 159–74.

Lightfoot, J. L. Lucian: On the Syrian Goddess. Oxford: Oxford University Press, 2003.

Lindberg, David C. Theories of Vision from Al-Kindi to Kepler. Chicago: University of Chicago Press, 1976.

Llewellyn-Jones, Lloyd, and Sue Blundell. Women's Dress in the Ancient Greek World. London: Duckworth, 2002.

Lloyd, Genevieve. *Man of Reason: "Male" and "Female" in Western Philosophy.* Minneapolis: University of Minnesota Press, 1993.

Loofs, Friedrich. *Eustathius von Sebaste und die Chronologie der Basilius-Briefe.* Halle: Niemeyer, 1898.

Marshall, F.H. "Dress." In *A Companion to Latin Studies,* edited by John Edwin Sandys, 190–200. Cambridge: Cambridge University press, 1929.

Martin, Dale B. *The Corinthian Body.* New Haven: Yale University Press, 1995.

Maxwell, Jaclyn L. *Christianization and Communication in Late Antiquity: John Chrysostom and His Congregation in Antioch.* Cambridge: Cambridge University Press, 2006.

Mayer, Wendy, and Pauline Allen. *John Chrysostom.* London: Routledge, 2000.

McNamara, Jo Ann. "Sexual Equality and the Cult of Virginity in Early Christian Thought." *Feminist Studies* 3.314 (1976): 145–58.

Meeks, Wayne A. "The Image of the Androgyne: Some Uses of a Symbol in Earliest Christianity." *History of Religion* 13.3 (1974): 165–208.

Miles, Margaret R. *Carnal Knowing: Female Nakedness and Religious Meaning in the Christian West.* New York: Vintage Books, 1989.

Moingt, Joseph. *Théologie trinitaire de Tertullien, vol. 1.* Paris: Aubier, 1966.

Monceaux, M. P. "Sur le voile des femmes en Afrique." *Bulletin de la Société Nationale des Antiquaires de France* (1901): 339–41.

Moore, Stephen D. *God's Beauty Parlor: And Other Queer Spaces in and around the Bible.* Stanford: Stanford University Press, 2001.

Myerowitz Levine, Molly. "The Gendered Grammar of Ancient Mediterranean Hair." In *Off with Her Head! The Denial of Women's Identity in Myth, Religion, and Culture,* edited by Howard Eilberg-Schwartz and Wendy Doniger, 76–130. Berkeley: University of California Press, 1995.

Olson, Kelly. "Cosmetics in Roman Antiquity: Substance, Remedy, Poison." *Classical World* 102.3 (2009): 291–310.

———. "The Appearance of the Young Roman Girl." In *Roman Dress and the Fabrics of Roman Culture,* edited by Jonathan Edmondson and Alison Keith, 139–57. Toronto: University of Toronto Press, 2008

———. *Dress and the Roman Woman: Self-Presentation and Society.* London/ New York: Routledge, 2008.

Ortner, Sherry B., and Harriet Whitehead. *Sexual Meanings: The Cultural Construction of Gender and Sexuality.* Cambridge: Cambridge University Press, 1981.

Osborn, Eric Francis. *Tertullian, First Theologian of the West.* Cambridge: Cambridge University Press, 1997.

Oster, Richard. "When Men Wore Veils to Worship: The Historical Context of 1 Corinthians 11:4." *New Testament Studies* 34.4 (1988): 481–505.

Patlagean, Evelyne. "L'histoire de la femme déguisée en moine et l'évolution de la sainteté feminine à Byzance." In *Structure sociale, famille, chrétienté à Byzance, IVᵉ–XIᵉ siècle,* 597–623. London: Variorum Reprints, 1981.

Pavlovskis, Zoja. "The Life of St. Pelagia the Harlot: Hagiographic Adaptation of Pagan Romance." *Classical Folio* 30 (1976): 138–49.

Pearce, Susan. "Objects as Meaning; or Narrating the Past." In *Objects of Knowledge,* edited by Susan Pearce, 125–40. London: Athlone Press, 1990.

Penner, Todd, and Caroline Vander Stichele, eds. *Mapping Gender in Ancient Religious Discourses.* Leiden: Brill, 2007.

Petitmengin, Pierre. *Pélagie la Pénitente: Métamorphoses d'une légende.* Paris: Études augustiniennes, 1981.

Pollmann, Karla. "Marriage and Gender in Ovid's Erotodidactic Poetry." In *Satiric Advice on Women and Marriage,* edited by Warren S. Smith, 92–110. Ann Arbor: University of Michigan Press, 2005.

Pölönen, Janne. "The Division of Wealth between Men and Women in Roman Succession (ca. 50 BC–AD 250)." In *Women, Wealth and Power in the Roman Empire*, edited by Pävi Setälä, Ria Berg, Riikka Hälikkä, Minerva Keltanen, Janne Pölönen, and Ville Vuolanto, 147–79. Rome: Institutum Romanum Finlandiae: 2002.

Powell, Douglas. "Tertullianists and Cataphrygians." *Vigiliae christianae* 29.1 (1975): 33–54.

Power, Kim. *Veiled Desire: Augustine on Women*. New York: Continuum, 1996.

Radermacher, Ludwig. *Hippolytos und Thekla: Studien zur Geschichte von Legende und Kultus*. Vienna: Alfred Hölder, 1916.

Radista, Leo. "The Appearance of Women and Contact in Tertullian." *Athenaeum* 73 (1985): 297–326.

Rambaux, Claude. *Tertullien face aux morales des trois premiers siècles*. Paris: Les Belles Lettres, 1979.

Reardon, B. P., ed. *Collected Ancient Greek Novels*. Berkeley: University of California Press, 1989.

Ribeiro, Aileen. *The Art of Dress: Fashion in England and France 1750 to 1820*. New Haven: Yale University Press, 1995.

Richlin, Amy. "Making Up a Woman: The Face of Roman Gender." In *Off with Her Head! The Denial of Women's Identity in Myth, Religion, and Culture*, edited by Howard Eilberg-Schwartz and Wendy Doniger, 185–213. Berkeley: University of California Press, 1995.

Ringrose, Kathryn M. "Living in the Shadows: Eunuchs and Gender in Byzantium." In *Third Sex, Third Gender: Beyond Sexual Dimorphism in Culture and History*, edited by Gilbert Herdt, 85–109. New York: Zone Books, 1994.

Roach, Mary Ellen, and Joanne Bubolz Eicher, eds. *Dress, Adornment, and the Social Order*. New York: John Wiley & Sons, 1965.

Rousseau, Philip. *Basil of Caesarea*. Berkeley: University of California Press, 1994.

Salisbury, Joyce E. *Church Fathers, Independent Virgins*. London/New York: Verso, 1991.

Salzman, Michele R. "Pagans and Christians." In *The Oxford Handbook of Early Christian Studies*, edited by Susan Ashbrook Harvey and David G. Hunter, 186–202. Oxford: Oxford University Press, 2008.

Satran, David. "Fingernails and Hair: Anatomy and Exegesis in Tertullian." *Journal of Theological Studies* 40.1 (1989): 116–20.

Schneider, Jane, and Annette B. Weiner. *Cloth and Human Experience*. Washington, DC: Smithsonian Institution Press, 1989.

Schroer, Silvia, ed. *Images and Gender: Contributions to the Hermeneutics of Reading Ancient Art*. Göttingen: Vandenhoeck & Ruprecht, 2006.

Schulenburg, Jane Tibbetts. *Forgetful of Their Sex: Female Sanctity and Society, Ca. 500–1100*. Chicago: University of Chicago Press, 1998.

Sebesta, Judith Lynn. "Symbolism in the Costume of the Roman Woman." In *The World of Roman Costume*, edited by Judith Lynn Sebesta and Larissa Bonfante, 46–53. Madison: University of Wisconsin Press, 2001.

———. "Women's Costume and Feminine Civic Morality in Augustan Rome." *Gender & History* 9.3 (1997): 529–41.

Sebesta, Judith Lynn, and Larissa Bonfante. *The World of Roman Costume*. Madison: University of Wisconsin Press, 1994.

Shaw, Teresa. "*Askesis* and the Appearance of Holiness." *Journal Early Christian Studies* 6.3 (1998): 485–99.

———. *The Burden of the Flesh: Fasting and Sexuality in Early Christianity*. Minneapolis: Fortress Press, 1998.

Shumka, Leslie. "Designing Women: The Representation of Women's Toiletries on Funerary Monuments in Roman Italy." In *Roman Dress and the Fabrics of Roman Culture*, edited by Jonathan Edmondson and Alison Keith, 172–91. Toronto: University of Toronto Press, 2008.

Silvas, Anna. *The Asketikon of St. Basil the Great.* Oxford: Oxford University Press, 2005.

Simmel, Georg. "Fashion." *International Quarterly* 10.1 (1904): 130–55.

Sivan, Hagith. "On Hymens and Holiness in Late Antiquity: Opposition to Aristocratic Female Asceticism at Rome." *Jahrbuch für Antike und Christentum* 36 (1993): 81–93.

Smith, Warren S. "Advice on Sex by the Self-Defeating Satirists." In *Satiric Advice on Women and Marriage*, edited by Warren S. Smith, 111–28. Ann Arbor: University of Michigan Press, 2005.

Söder, Rosa. *Die apokryphen Apostelgeschichten und die romanhafte Literatur der Antike.* Stuttgart: W. Kohlhammer, 1932.

Spelman, Elizabeth V. "Woman as Body: Ancient and Contemporary Views." *Feminist Studies* 8.1 (1982): 108–31.

Steinhauser, Kenneth B. "The Cynic Monks of Carthage: Some Observations of *De opere monachorum.*" In *Augustine: Presbyter Factus Sum*, edited by Joseph T. Lienhard, Earl C. Muller, and Roland J. Teskey, 455–62. New York: Peter Lang, 1993.

Stout, Ann. "Jewelry as a Symbol of Status in the Roman Empire." In *The World of Roman Costume*, edited by Judith Lynn Sebesta and Larissa Bonfante, 77–100. Madison: University of Wisconsin Press, 2001.

Stramara, Daniel. "Double Monasticism in the Greek East, Fourth through Eight Centuries." *Journal of Early Christian Studies* 6.2 (1998): 269–312.

Stücklin, Christoph. *Tertullian, De virginibus velandis: Übersetzung, Einleitung, Kommentar. Ein Beitrag zur altkirchlichen Frauenfrage.* Bern: Herbert Lang, 1974.

Suthrell, Charlotte. *Unzipping Gender: Sex, Cross-Dressing and Culture.* New York: Berg, 2004.

Swancutt, Diana M. "*Still* before Sexuality: 'Greek' Androgyny, the Roman Imperial Politics of Masculinity and the Roman Invention of the *Tribas.*" In *Mapping Gender in Ancient Religious Discourses*, edited by Todd Penner and Caroline Vander Stichele, 11–61. Leiden: Brill, 2007.

Swift, Ellen. *Roman Dress Accessories.* Buckinghamshire: Shire Publications, 2003.

Taborsky, Edwina. "The Discursive Object." In *Objects of Knowledge*, edited by Susan Pearce, 50–77. London: Athlone Press, 1990.

Talbot, Alice-Mary Maffry. *Holy Women of Byzantium: Ten Saints' Lives in English Translation.* Washington, DC: Dumbarton Oaks, 1996.

Taylor, Lou. *Establishing Dress History.* Manchester: Manchester University Press, 2004.

Their, Sebastian. *Kirche bei Pelagius.* Berlin: Walter de Gruyter, 1999.

Thill, Gérard. *Les époques gallo-romaine et mérovingienne au Musée d'histoire et d'art.* Luxembourg: Musée d'histoire et d'art, 1972.

Townsley, Gillian. "*Gender Trouble* in Corinth: Que(e)rying Constructs of Gender in 1 Corinthians 11:12–16." *Bible & Critical Theory* 2.2 (2006): 17.1–17.14.

Tracy, Valerie A. "Roman Dandies and Transvestites," *Echos de monde classique* 20 (1976): 60–63.

Upson-Saia, Kristi. "Gender and Narrative Performance in Early Christian Cross-Dressing Saints' *Lives.*" *Studia Patristica* XLV (2010): 43–48.

Usener, Hermann. *Legenden der heiligen Pelagia.* Bonn: A. Marcus, 1879.

Veblen, Thorstein. *The Theory of the Leisure Class: An Economic Study in the Evolution of Institutions.* New York: The Macmillan Company, 1899.

Vermaseren, Maarten. *Cybele and Attis: The Myth and the Cult.* Translated by A. M. H. Lemmers. London: Thames and Hudson, 1977.

Vogt, Kari. " 'Becoming Male': A Gnostic and Early Christian Metaphor." In *The Image of God: Gender Models in Judaeo-Christian Tradition*, edited by Kari Elisabeth Børrensen, 170–86. Minneapolis: Fortress Press, 1995.

Waddell, Helen. *The Desert Fathers: Translations from the Latin with an Introduction*. New York: Henry Holt, 1936.

Walsh, Patrick Gerard. *Livy: His Historical Aims and Methods*. Cambridge: Cambridge University Press, 1961.

Ward, Benedicta. *Harlots of the Desert: A Study of Repentance in Early Monastic Sources*. Kalamazoo: Cistercian Publications, 1987.

Warwick, Alexandra, and Dani Cavallaro, eds. *Fashioning the Frame: Boundaries, Dress, and the Body*. Oxford: Berg, 1998.

Wesche, Kenneth Paul. *On the Person of Christ: The Christology of Emperor Justinian*. Crestwood: St. Vladimir's Seminary Press, 1991.

White, Hayden. *The Content of the Form: Narrative Discourse and Historical Representation*. Baltimore: Johns Hopkins University Press, 1987.

———. *Metahistory: The Historical Imagination in Nineteenth-Century Europe*. Baltimore: Johns Hopkins University Press, 1975.

Williams, Craig. *Roman Homosexuality: Ideologies of Masculinity in Classical Antiquity*. New York: Oxford University Press, 1999.

Wilson, Lillian May. *The Clothing of the Ancient Romans*. Baltimore: Johns Hopkins University Press, 1938.

Wyke, Maria. "Woman in the Mirror: The Rhetoric of Adornment in the Roman World." In *Women in Ancient Societies: An Illusion of the Night*, edited by Léonie J. Archer, Susan Fischler, and Maria Wyke, 134–51. New York: Routledge, 1994.

Zanker, Paul. *The Mask of Socrates: The Image of the Intellectual in Antiquity*. Berkeley: University of California Press, 1996.

# Index

**A**

adornment: as aesthetic deception,
22–24, 38, 41–43, 67, 88, 92,
118n2; cosmetics, 2–3, 7, 14,
22–24, 27, 34, 38, 40–44, 47,
50–52, 56–57, 60, 66–68, 75,
121n46; *cultus*, 20, 31; expense
of, 24–25, 27–29, 44–46, 50;
and frivolity, 1, 15, 125n101;
imported from abroad, 7, 16–17,
20, 22–25, 27, 41–42, 106–107;
jewelry, 1–2, 7, 14, 16, 22–27,
31, 38, 40–43, 45, 47, 49, 50,
52, 56–57, 60, 77, 90, 118n2;
*ornatus*, 20, 23, 31; pearls, 1,
16, 22, 26, 27, 37, 40, 42, 50,
52, 122n67, 124n88; purchased
for lovers and wives, 24–25;
renunciation of, 1, 14, 34–35,
36–48, 51–53, 70, 76–78, 83; as
a sign of femininity, 17, 29–31,
67; as a sign of honor, 20–21,
31; as a sign of status, 1–2, 5–7,
16, 19–21, 26–30, 33–35, 48,
51–53
adultery, 22–24, 47, 76
alms, 44–46, 76–79, 80, 144n134
Ambrose of Milan, 45, 50, 53–57, 126n3
Anastasia/Anastasios, 89, 96, 102
Aristides, Aelius, 16
Aristotle, 10, 130n91, 132n128,
138n47
artificial beauty, 22–24, 38, 41–43, 67,
88, 92, 118n2; 121n46
asceticism, Christian, 1–3, 33–35,
51–58, 59–83, 84–103
Augustine of Hippo, 49, 53, 75–79,
80–83, 116n36, 131n106,
134n170, 149n34

Augustus, emperor, 31, 115n33,
125n109
authority: based on distinction, 2–3,
4–7; of Christian councils, 59,
73, 75, 106; of elite Roman men,
6–7, 18–19, 21, 26–29, 30–32,
107; of husbands, 6, 20–21,
76–79; and social rivalries, 2–3,
9, 31, 33–36, 48, 58, 61, 83,
104, 106–107, 126n6; within
Christian hierarchies, 3, 7, 14,
60, 69–71, 76–79, 102, 104,
106–107. *See also* superiority

**B**

baptism, 11, 82, 116n37
Barthes, Roland, 8, 153n98
Basil of Ancyra, 53, 140n83
Basil of Caesarea, 2, 70, 74–75, 118n55
beautification: regimens, 23, 27, 45, 67;
represented on funerary monuments, 27–28
beauty: artificial, 22–24, 38, 41–43, 67,
88, 92, 118n2; 121n46; of Jesus,
38; lost with age, 23, 37, 42–43,
50; of pious Christians, 43, 47,
50–51, 55–58, 91–92, 98
Bourdieu, Pierre, 5
Boyarin, Daniel, 12
breasts, female, 14, 23, 61, 89, 94–96,
100–101, 106, 148n20, 148n24,
149n32, 153n97
Brown, Peter, 76–77
Butler, Judith, 8–9, 30, 111nn21–24,
125n100, 137n25, 138n52,
139nn61–62, 147n7

**C**

Cameron, Averil, 34

Carthaginian monks, 80–83
Carthaginian virgins, 61–69, 71, 75, 80
Castelli, Elizabeth, 13, 117n54
Chrysostom, John, 33, 36, 37, 40, 42,
   44–45, 47–50, 52, 54–56
Clark, Elizabeth, 12
Clark, Gillian, 2
Clement of Alexandria, 12–13, 37–50,
   54
clothing. *See* dress
conquest, Roman, 6–7, 15–16, 27
cosmetics, 2–3, 7, 14, 22–24, 27, 34,
   38, 40–44, 47, 50–52, 56–57,
   60, 66–68, 75, 121n46
costume. *See* dress
cross-dressing, 9, 14, 70–72, 84–103,
   106
crowns, 29, 39, 42–43
Cyprian of Carthage, 37–39, 41, 44, 51

**D**

Davis, Stephen, 84–85
Dio, 31
disguises, adopting, 44, 86, 88–92, 93,
   94, 96–100, 102
Doniger, Wendy, 60
dress: advice and prescriptions, 1–3, 14,
   34–58; of brides, 29; of Christians, 1–3, 33–58; and deception,
   23, 38, 88, 91, 100, 118n2; and
   discourse, 7–10, 14, 61, 66,
   68, 72, 75, 79, 83, 104–106; as
   disguise, 44, 86, 88–92, 93, 94,
   96–100, 102; and distinction,
   2–3, 4–7, 16, 20, 31, 33–36, 48,
   51–53, 56, 58, 62, 69–70, 77,
   79, 107; of elite Roman matrons,
   18–29; fabrics, 2, 16, 22, 25,
   27, 29, 31, 38, 40, 42, 52, 57,
   62, 102, 130n74; and gender,
   3–4, 6–8, 13–14, 18, 19–32,
   54–58; humble dress, 1–3, 5–6,
   34–35, 48, 51–52, 54, 56, 79;
   interpretation of, 1, 5, 8–10, 14,
   18–29, 31, 33–58, 85, 102–103,
   105–107; manner of dressing, 6,
   11, 15, 68, 73, 75, 78–79, 101,
   105; mourning garments, 2, 29,
   34, 52; narrating dress, 85–96,
   102–103; of the poor, 2, 30, 52,
   56; public displays of, 3, 4, 7, 35,
   48, 50, 51–53, 55–58, 61–83,
   104; purposes of, 48–50; and
   scripture, 37–40; and seduction,

20, 22–23, 26, 46–50, 55–58,
   67–68, 118n2; and status, 1–2,
   5–7, 19–21, 26–30, 33–35, 46,
   48, 50, 51–53, 59; signification
   of, 6–8, 15, 18–29, 31, 33–58,
   85, 102–103, 105–106; transgressive dress, 3, 61–83, 84–85;
   and wastefulness, 5–6, 15,
   24–25, 27–29, 45, 50, 77, 118n1,
   123n82, 130n74; of widows, 29,
   34, 36, 47, 63–64, 75–79

**E**

Ecdicia, 75–79
Edwards, Catharine, 16–17
effeminacy, 11, 31, 73, 83, 90, 104
Eilberg-Schwartz, Howard, 60
Elm, Susanna, 72
Emmelia, 53, 74–75
Eugenia/Eugenios, 91, 93–95, 99–101
eunuchs, 59, 81, 86, 89–91, 97, 99
Euphrosyne/Esmeraldus, 91, 95–98,
   101–102
Eustathius of Sebaste, 69–75

**F**

fabrics, 2, 16, 22, 25, 27, 29, 31, 38,
   40, 42, 52, 57, 62, 102, 130n74.
   *See also* silk
fasting, 57, 70, 92, 99, 103, 132n133,
   149n32, 153n97
femininity: characteristics associated
   with, 6, 15, 17–18, 19–26, 29,
   54–58, 67–68, 79, 92, 94–96,
   98, 105, 107; of cross-dressing
   saints, 73, 88–96; performance
   of, 3, 8–9, 29–32, 54–58. *See
   also* gender *and* masculinity
Flügel, John Carl, 4
funerary monuments, 27–28

**G**

Galen, 10, 130n91
*galli*, 90
Gangra, council of, 71–73, 106,
   141nn89–91
garb. *See* dress
gender: ancient definitions of, 10–14,
   61, 63–69, 70–73, 75, 81–82,
   85, 94, 104–106; and the body,
   10, 13–14, 61, 66–67, 82, 89–90,
   93–96, 98, 100–103, 105–106; as
   explained by Christian theology,
   11–13, 63–68, 70–73, 105–106;

crises, 59–83; and cross-dressing, 70–72, 75, 84–103, 106; difference, 3, 8, 12–14, 29–32, 55, 61, 63–65, 68–69, 73–74, 81, 83, 87, 103, 105–107; performance of, 3, 8, 10–11, 13–14, 17–18, 29–32, 35, 54–58, 59–83, 104–105; registers of, 10–13, 100–101, 105; terms, 96–101; transformation of, 3, 13–14, 63–64, 69–72, 81–82, 84–86, 90, 96, 99, 102, 106–107; of virgins in scripture, 65, 82. *See also* femininity *and* masculinity

Gleason, Maud, 30, 113nn30–32, 126n8
gold, 1, 19–20, 22–23, 25, 27, 31, 37–38, 40, 42–43, 45, 47, 50, 52, 56–57, 76–77. *See also* jewelry
Gregory of Nazianzus, 118n55
Gregory of Nyssa, 51, 53, 112n27, 116n41, 118n55
Gribomont, Jean, 71, 74

**H**
hair: association of long hair with women, 14, 59–61, 66–68, 72–73, 75, 80–81, 106; dyes, 27, 38–39, 41, 44, 68; facial hair, 89–90; of foreigners, 27; hairnet (*reticulum luteum*), 29, 43; hairpieces, 22, 52, 67; hairstyles, 2, 24, 27, 29, 37–39, 50, 52–53, 60, 67; headbands and fillets (*infulae*; *vittae*), 25, 29, 124n94; long-haired men, 80–83; of prophets in scripture, 80–81; short-haired women, 59–60, 70–73, 75, 87–88, 92, 97, 99, 102; wigs, 22, 27, 38–39, 44
Harvey, Susan Ashbrook, 98, 100–101
head coverings, 2, 29, 43, 53, 56–57, 60–69, 75, 80–82, 106, 118n2
hierarchy, Christian, 3, 7, 14, 60, 69–71, 76–79, 102, 104, 106–107
Hilaria/Hilarion, 90–91, 93
Horace, 22–23, 25

**I**
identity: ascetic, 1–3, 11–14, 33–35, 51–58, 59, 68, 70–71, 76–77, 79, 105; Christian, 2–3, 33–36, 48, 50–51, 58, 59, 70–72; as

constructed and communicated through appearance, 1–3, 4–9; gender, 4, 10–14, 29–32, 54–58, 85–88, 94–96, 96–100, 103, 107
immorality: false accusations of cross-dressing saints', 92–94; foreign, 7, 16–17, 25, 29–31, 34; pagan, 33–34, 41, 44, 46, 48, 107; women's, 7, 17–18, 19–26, 29–31, 34–35, 54–55, 104–105, 107. *See also* sins *and* vice
*incontinentia*, 16, 21–22, 29

**J**
Jerome, 1–2, 13, 42, 44, 47–48, 51, 53–58
jewelry, 1–2, 7, 14, 16, 22–27, 31, 38, 40–43, 45, 47, 49, 50, 52, 56–57, 60, 77, 90, 118n2. *See also* gold *and* silver
John of Ephesus, 13
Juvenal, 23–24

**K**
Keufler, Matthew, 83
Knust, Jennifer Wright, 17, 119nn11–13, 122n72, 124n91, 126n4

**L**
Laqueur, Thomas, 10
*Lex Oppia*, 19–21
Livy, 19–21
Lucretius, 22, 24–25
*luxuria*, 1, 15–19, 21–22, 25, 29

**M**
Macrina, 53, 74–75, 112n27, 118n55
make-up. *See* cosmetics
Martial, 22, 27
Mary/Marinos, 89–90, 92–95, 98
masculinity: characteristics associated with, 3, 6, 12–13, 89–90, 101; perceived, 85–91, 97, 99–100; performance of, 10–11, 14, 30–31, 91, 99–100, 104; secondary, 85–86 88, 90–91, 96, 103; virile women, 3, 11–13, 54, 58, 84, 105–106. *See also* gender *and* femininity
Matrona/Babylas, 89–91, 99
Miller, Patricia Cox, 66, 126n9, 132n133, 153n90
monastery, double, 74

moral decline, Roman, 16–17, 19, 25
moralists, Roman, 16–26, 30–31, 33
morality. *See* immorality *and* sins *and* superiority, moral

**N**
naked bodies, 22, 45, 49, 94–96, 98, 100
nipples. *See* breasts, female

**O**
Olson, Kelly, 18, 110n18, 115nn33–34, 120n19, 121n46, 123nn79–80, 123n85, 124n92
Oppian laws, 19–21
ornamentation. *See* adornment
Ovid, 23, 27

**P**
*palla*, 25, 123n80
Palladius, 52–53, 115n35
Paul, 37–38, 40, 49, 62–67, 80–82, 115n36, 127n16, 136n13, 138nn45–46, 138n53, 139n64, 145n145, 154n105
Paula, 57–58, 127n13, 135n1
Pelagia/Pelagius, 88–92, 95, 102
Pelagius, 52, 55
performativity studies, 4–9
perfume, 7, 16, 22, 27, 39–40, 45, 47, 49, 54, 128n51
physiognomy, 30
Pliny the elder, 16, 26, 121n38
power. *See* authority
Power, Kim, 76
Propertius, 22, 24–26
prostitutes, 45–46, 47, 49–50, 64

**Q**
Quintilian, 31

**R**
renunciation: of lavish dress and adornments, 1, 14, 34–48, 51–53, 70, 76–78, 83, 105; of marriage and/or sexual activity, 1–2, 12–13, 34–35, 46–48, 63, 70–71, 75–76, 79, 81, 92, 96, 105; of status, 1–2, 51–53, 55, 70; of vice, 3, 14, 51–53, 54, 105, 107
*Romanitas*, 5–7, 17, 25–26, 29, 124n90, 125n105

**S**
Salisbury, Joyce, 76

scriptural directives regarding dress, interpreting, 37–40
self-indulgence, 5; characteristic of foreigners, 17, 25; characteristic of women, 22, 40, 106
self-mastery, 5–6; of Christians, 33–34, 48, 50, 63, 83; of Roman men, 7, 17, 24–25, 106; thwarted by women's beauty, 20, 24, 56–57, 67–68, 122n62, 122n67
Seneca, 26, 120n38
servants, 6, 24, 27–29, 45, 48, 53, 55, 70–72, 82, 99, 110n18, 123nn78–80
Shaw, Teresa, 35, 134n165, 149n32, 153n97
shows, 43–44, 46
silk, 22, 25, 31, 40, 52, 57, 125n105, 144n127. *See also* fabric
Silvas, Anna, 74, 140n70, 141n89
silver, 16, 22, 27, 42, 76–77. *See also* jewelry
sins: against Creation, 41–43, 73; greed, 3, 6, 17, 20, 22, 26, 29, 40; idolatry, 43–44; lying, 41; pride, 23, 41, 53, 55, 72, 78–79, 105; sexual sins, 46–48, 92–94; vanity, 3, 6, 14, 17, 19–20, 22–23, 29, 40, 54–55, 68, 73, 78, 105, 107. *See also* immorality *and* vice
Siricius, 53
slaves. *See* servants
Socrates, historian, 70
*sophrosyne*, 33, 54
Soranus, 10
Sozomen, historian, 70
*stola*, 18, 29
"stumbling block" passages, use of, 46–47, 53, 67–68, 100
superiority: cultural superiority, 5–6, 16–17, 26, 55, 58, 107; moral superiority, 5–6, 9, 17, 29, 33–34, 36, 55, 58, 59, 104, 107; natural superiority, 5–6, 9, 20, 25, 30–32, 68, 73; pecuniary superiority, 5–6, 27–29. *See also* authority

**T**
Tacitus, 25, 31
Tertullian of Carthage, 36–37, 39, 41–43, 46–47, 49–51, 53–54, 56, 61–69, 73, 75, 79, 80, 82, 105–106
theater, 43, 46, 54, 71, 114n33

Theodosian Code, 59, 73
trade, 6–7, 15–16

**V**

Veblen, Thorstein, 5–6, 110n13–15,
  120n36, 123n82
veiling ceremony (*velatio*), 53, 57
veils. *See* head coverings
vice: gendered, 6–7, 14–15, 17, 19–22,
  25–26, 29–31, 34–35, 54–56,
  68, 78, 104, 107; foreign, 6–7,
  16–17, 22, 25, 29–31, 34;
  pagan, 33–34, 41, 43–44, 46,
  48, 107; renunciation of, 3, 14,
  51–53, 54, 105, 107. *See also*
  immorality *and* sins
virginity, Christian, 33–34, 51–52, 65
virtue: Christian, 2–3, 6–7, 9, 14,
  33–35, 41, 50–53, 57–58, 79,

99; gendered, 3, 5–6, 12–13, 18,
  29–32, 54, 58, 60–61, 68, 83,
  89, 100–101, 104–105, 124n89;
  Roman, 6, 17, 25

**W**

wealth: display of, 5–7, 19–21, 27,
  48, 50, 52; renunciation of, 2,
  44–46, 55, 76–77, 79; wasted on
  expensive clothing and adornments, 7, 24–25, 27–29, 44–46,
  50, 77; of women, 18, 26, 29,
  107
widows, 29, 34, 47, 63–64, 74–79
women: *gune*, 63, 98, 127n20, 136n20;
  virile women, 3, 11–13, 54, 58,
  84, 105–106; wealth of, 18, 26,
  29, 107
Wyke, Maria, 18, 125n101